The Jazz Revolution

The Jazz Revolution

Twenties America & the Meaning of Jazz

Kathy J. Ogren

OXFORD UNIVERSITY PRESS
New York   Oxford

For my mother Kathleen Joanne Ogren
and to the memory of my father Robert A. Ogren

Oxford University Press

Oxford   New York   Toronto
Delhi   Bombay   Calcutta   Madras   Karachi
Kuala Lumpur   Singapore   Hong Kong   Tokyo
Nairobi   Dar es Salaam   Cape Town
Melbourne   Auckland

and associated companies in
Berlin   Ibadan

First published in 1989 by Oxford University Press, Inc.,
200 Madison Avenue, New York, New York 10016

First issued as an Oxford University Press paperback, 1992

Oxford is a registered trademark of Oxford University Press

Library of Congress Cataloging-in-Publication Data
Ogren, Kathy J.
The Jazz Revolution: Twenties America and the meaning of jazz / Kathy J. Ogren.
p.   cm.   Bibliography: p.   Includes index.
1. Jazz music—United States. 2. Music and society. 3. United
States—Popular culture—History—20th century. I. Title.
ML3508.O37 1987
781´.57´0973—dc19   88-22596   CIP   MN

"Jazzonia" and "The Cat and the Saxophone" are Copyright 1926
by Alfred A. Knopf, Inc. and renewed 1954 by Langston Hughes.
Reprinted from *The Weary Blues*; by Langston Hughes, by permis-
sion of the publisher.

ISBN 0-19-505153-X
ISBN 0-19-507479-3 (PBK.)

10 9 8 7 6 5 4 3 2 1

Printed in the United States of America

Acknowledgments

Like most jazz performances, this book is not a solo act. I have depended on contributions from others.

Most of my primary materials came from two outstanding jazz archives that contain valuable oral histories as well as other research materials. Curtis Jerde and the staff of the William Ransom Hogan Jazz Archive at Tulane University, New Orleans, helped me find oral histories and photographs. Dan Morgenstern and the staff of the Rutgers University Institute for Jazz Studies, Newark, likewise guided me through the riches of their collection. The Special Collections staff of the University of California Library, Los Angeles, provided useful information about West Coast entertainment, particularly in the George P. Johnson Negro Film Collection. Robert Brubaker and the Prints and Photographs staff at the Chicago Historical Society gave me useful pointers about jazz photographs. Summer research grants from the University of Redlands made possible my trips to the archives. The inter-Library Loan, Special Collections, and Periodicals staff of the Milton S. Eisenhower Library at The Johns Hopkins University, and the staff of the George Armacost Library at The University of Redlands also helped me track down sources.

The Jazz Revolution: Twenties America and the Meaning of Jazz began as my Ph.D. thesis. I received many helpful comments from members of my dissertation committee, although I was unable to incorporate all of their suggestions. Consequently, I'd like to thank my supervisors Ronald G. Walters and Vernon Lidtke, and committee members Yves-Alain Bois, Toby Ditz, Gillian Feeley-Harnick, and Daniel O. Naiman. Donald Brenneis, Robert A. Hill, Tyrus Miller, Daniel Wilson, and Deanna Shemek read all or parts of the dissertation and I appreciate their encouragement.

Several people proofread and offered critiques of the manuscript. Ronald G. Walters and Curt Jerde provided insightful comments on the introduction and Chapter One, Pat Wasielewski noted several important misconceptions in Chapter Two, and Sidney J. Lemelle read the entire text and gave generously of his time and counsel. In this, as in many projects, I owe special thanks to Ronald G. Walters, Daniel Horowitz, and Helen Lefkowitz Horowitz. While tolerating my eccentricities, they nevertheless continued to give sound advice and solid support. This acknowledgment is but a small measure of my appreciation for their patience and confidence in my efforts.

Sharon Widomski and Marilynn Lawrence somehow managed to make clean copy out of my writing and typing. Neva Makgetla rescued me from a serious jam on the word-processor. Tyrico Z. Tyler checked references for me, and, with Mark Ankcorn, helped prepare the final draft. Roland Marchand sent me the perfect magazine illustration and Zeph Makgetla helped me with photographic tasks.

I am grateful for the sensible recommendations and advice of my editor, Sheldon Meyer. The Oxford University Press staff, especially, Rachel Toor and Leona Capeless, gave careful and much-appreciated attention to preparing the manuscript. Celia Petty prepared the index.

Although I cannot properly acknowledge all of them, many friends, family members, colleagues, and students cheered my progress and ensured the completion of this project. In particular, I thank James Sandos and Patricia Wasielewski of The University of Redlands, who regularly reminded me to make this book a priority. Ida Altman, Allyson Smith, Nancy Langer,

Karen Holden, Tyrus Miller, Deanna Shemek, Bill Roberts, Debra Roberts, Ahmed Sehrawy, Sharon Smith, Lance Selfa, and Dan Shelton made sure I had a place to stay, the appropriate coordinates for negotiating new cities, and peace and quiet in which to work. Roxanne Wilson and Dan Shelton shared both the exhilaration and frustration of this adventure—their optimism often served me well.

My mother, Kathleen Joanne Ogren, never hesitated to give me material and emotional support for writing *The Jazz Revolution: Twenties America and the Meaning of Jazz*. With gratitude, I dedicate this book to her and to the memory of my father, both of whom first taught me the gift of song.

Contents

The Jazz Revolution

Introduction: The Significance of the Jazz Controversy for Twenties America

> The Salvation Army of Cincinnati obtained a temporary injunction today to prevent the erection of a moving picture theatre adjoining the Catherine Booth Home for Girls, on the grounds that music emanating from the theatre would implant "jazz emotions" in the babies born at the home. The plaintiffs realize that they live in a jazz age declared the suit, . . . "But we are loathe to believe that babies born in the maternity hospital are to be legally subjected to the implanting of jazz emotions by such enforced proximity to a theater and a jazz palace."
>
> New York Times, 1926

Nineteen twenties readers of the *New York Times* would not have been surprised by the above item from Cincinnati, Ohio. Throughout the decade, the *Times* as well as other newspapers, recorded a growing controversy concerning the influence of jazz. Reports came not only from American cities, but also from Europe. Most of the articles documented fears about the spread of this new form of popular music. As suggested in the Cincinnati Salvation Army complaint, jazz was both a popular craze and a music used to describe the ambience or mood of the decade.

One can plausibly argue that the debate over jazz was just one of many that characterized American social discourse in the 1920s. Dualistic descriptive schemes seem to characterize best the major economic and social changes of the post-war era, and histories of the decade typically characterize it as a battle of opposites. On the one hand it was a "return to normalcy" after World War I, and on the other hand, youthful, exuberant, and "roaring."[1]

Certainly the end of the Great War marked the beginning of a troubled peace. The acrimonious fight over ratification of the League of Nations Treaty concluded with defeat for Woodrow Wilson's plan, and the nation wearily drifted towards increased isolation. American class and ethnic tensions had already been unleashed by wartime jingoism, which culminated in the Palmer Raids and Red Scare of 1917–20. America's civil liberties record was permanently scarred when nonconformists were harassed, and in some cases deported, on the bases of ethnic background or political conviction.[2]

American leftists and radicals found their organizations on the defensive following the political repression at home, despite the fact that 900,000 Americans voted for Socialist party candidate Eugene Debs in 1920. Similarly, American labor began the decade with a wave of strike activity—including the Seattle General Strike in support of the Russian Revolution in 1918—but by the end of the 1920s, labor union membership fell from about 5 million in 1921 to less than 3.5 million in 1929. Returning veterans joined the ranks of the unemployed as demobilization slowed down the economy immediately following the war.

American race relations exploded in a series of urban riots stretching from East St. Louis in July 1917 through Charleston, S.C., Longview, Texas, Washington, D.C., and Chicago, in the "Red Summer" of 1919. In all cases, racial violence was fueled by the competition for jobs between returning war veterans and black workers who had replaced them during the war. A number of factors contributed to the Great Migration of 500,000 blacks out of the South before and after World War I, although most were looking for relief from rural poverty and political repression. Black migrants were often optimistic about starting new lives in rapidly growing northern cities like New York and Chicago, but they resented the appalling overcrowding that was the result of residential segregation. When white vigilantes invaded black neighborhoods in the 1919 race riots, blacks held their ground to defend their hard-fought gains in the new urban "meccas."[3]

Jazz histories have typically portrayed the 1917 closing of New Orleans's Storyville red light district by military officials as the main impetus behind the movement of jazz musicians to new jobs and audiences in northern cities. In fact, musicians were part of the general migration and several of them witnessed the race riots since they made their living in the entertainment districts located in segregated black neighborhoods. The war itself most directly affected those musicians who were drafted or had enlisted in the army and performed in military bands.

For many Americans, these political, racial, and social conflicts appeared to wane with the growth of a strong economy—prompting some to point to the elections of Republicans Warren G. Harding and Calvin Coolidge as cause for celebration. Presumably, American voters who supported Coolidge also endorsed his philosophy: "brains are wealth and wealth is the chief end of man" and the "business of America is business," when they gave the Republicans landslide victories in 1920 and 1924.[4]

Many economic indicators did point to unprecedented prosperity. Industrial production boomed and the gross national product rose 40%. The expanded availability of consumer products like automobiles, electrical appliances, radios, and telephones indicated the importance of consumer spending in this "second industrial revolution," with affluent Americans receiving the greatest benefits. This revolution in consumption patterns directly affected blues and jazz musicians because their music was disseminated to a larger audience as a result of the expanded availability of their music on radio and phonograph recordings.

The audience for jazz was inadvertently stimulated when Congress passed the Volstead Act, which banned the manufacture and sale of alcoholic beverages, in 1919. Nightclub and entertainment venues that provided an escape from Prohibition were common locations for jazz performance. Clubs like Chicago's Club Alabam or Harlem's famed Cotton Club flourished when sophisticated urbanites consumed good music, food, and drink and danced to the latest musical fad. These establishments were often tied to bootlegging rings, like Al Capone's, and as a consequence many performers found themselves on a gangster's payroll. Jazz was immediately associated with the carnal pleasures of the cabaret.

Prohibition advocates often justified their campaign on the grounds that they were preserving "traditional" American values. Religious fundamentalists joined the anti-saloon agitators in denouncing modernism, the growth of science, immigration, and urbanization as symbols of moral decay. The 1925 legal battle between William Jennings Bryan and Clarence Darrow, over John Scopes's right to teach evolution in a Tennessee school, turned the modernist versus fundamentalist clash into a national spectacle. The argument over jazz split down similar lines.[5]

Exhortations of fundamentalists fell on ears supposedly deafened by the exciting sounds and sights of the jazz band. The attractiveness of urban nightlife was embraced by American youth in revolt against what they saw as stuffy prewar society, and their critique joined that of young intellectual dissenters who published an alternative set of beliefs that they hoped would challenge the general confidence in commercial values. Writers and critics like Malcolm Cowley and Ernest Hemingway chose to exile themselves from America and eschew its materialism, gentility, and parochialism. Labeled the "lost generation" by Gertrude Stein, these and other non-conformists registered their resistance to American society through artistic experimentation and the hedonistic pursuit of dancing, drinking, fast cars, and sexual freedom. For them, the newest musical sensation—jazz—became the specific symbol of rebellion and of what was new about the decade.[6]

The centrality of jazz in our historical memory is neither an accident nor a facile convention derived from the "roaring twenties" stereotype. Jazz and its practitioners were directly affected by or participated themselves in major changes taking place in the teens and 1920s. Although the partisans in the jazz controversy sometimes drew on the other arguments that raged in the 1920s, the music itself and the circumstances under which it was performed embodied social change. The Cincinnati Salvation Army's injunction sounds comical today, but the debate over jazz should not be dismissed as trivial argument. Americans shared a common perception that jazz had transforming qualities that could last beyond the time of a song and the space of a cabaret act. For many Americans, to argue about jazz was to argue about the nature of change itself.

Jazz was indeed a powerful new music, characterized by syncopation, polyrhythms, improvisation, blue tonalities, and a strong beat. It rose to popularity amidst strident criticism and extravagant praise. Detractors criticized jazz's musical characteristics—unless they dismissed it as noise—and its origins in lower-class black culture. Jazz lovers hailed the same sounds as everything from exciting entertainment to an antidote for repressive industrial society.

Americans on all sides of the jazz debate found the music symbolic of fundamental—and provocative—changes they were experiencing in the maturing post-World War I urban and industrial society. The music represented the end of an earlier era and the transition to a modern one. The renowned conductor Leopold Stokowski predicted:

> Jazz has come to stay because it is an expression of the times, of the breathless, energetic, superactive times in which we are living, it is useless to fight against it . . . America's contribution to the music of the past will have the same revivifying effect as the injection of new, and in the larger sense, vulgar blood into dying aristocracy . . . The Negro musicians of America are playing a great part in this change. The jazz players make their instruments do entirely new things, things finished musicians are taught to avoid. They are pathfinders into new realms.[7]

Stokowski was joined by hundreds of thousands of other participants in jazz performance—all of whom found in the music a voice with which they acknowledged, celebrated, and coped with change.

What is striking about the jazz controversy is that jazz communicated change across vast racial and cultural dividing lines, despite its development from a participatory and distinct black musical culture. Jazz performance in the twenties may well have played a role in what anthropologist Victor Turner describes as "public reflexivity" in which a group "communicates itself to itself."[8] In the case of jazz, this process is particularly interesting since it was a music most closely identified with blacks and entertainers—two social groups often labeled marginal—yet it helped white Americans with diverse social backgrounds explain their world. "Jazz emotions" did indeed seem to penetrate physical—and social—barriers.

The ability of jazz to represent change in the 1920s is best reconstructed through social and cultural analysis that locates jazz performance in its historical context. Jazz was related to several patterns of oral and musical performance particular to Afro-American culture. As such, it emerged from a cultural tradition that literary critic Houston Baker has called an Afro-American vernacular composed of the "material conditions of slavery in the United States and the rhythms of Afro-American blues which combined and emerged from . . . an ancestral matrix that has produced a forceful and indigenous American creativity."[9]

When black audiences and performers migrated to urban centers they hastened the spread of blues and jazz. Black Americans found, in turn, new performance environments and commercial markets for electrically and mechanically reproduced jazz that catapulted the vernacular into a national rage. Beginning in the 1920s, many Americans identified jazz not only as a popular music they loved, but also as a symbol of the nation's coming of "jazz age" in a modern world.

Listening and dancing to jazz was not, therefore, merely an entertaining pastime. Despite commercialization and exposure to new audiences, jazz maintained the participatory qualities of its origins. The rich exchange between performers and their audiences became a definitive feature of jazz entertainment and is the key to understanding the larger drama of the jazz controversy.

Although this study is aimed at improving our understanding of the jazz controversy—and our assessment of the cultural significance of jazz—I do not begin with the controversy. Instead, I first describe the social and cultural milieus in which jazz appeared, giving special attention to form and content in performance. My reasons for this approach are partly methodological—I am intrigued by the difficulties and rewards of trying to analyze the context and meaning of past performances. But I also have substantive reasons. It was the expressive quality of jazz that made it controversial. Although critics projected their own fears and values on it, they could not have done so had it not had striking social and musical characteristics, if, in other words, it had not been played in certain places and in certain ways. By themselves, those characteristics of jazz performance say something about cultural change. But they also lead to my end point, which is a remarkable debate about jazz and—ultimately—about America in the 1920s.

Reconstructing jazz performances in the early twentieth century poses several problems. Jazz music provides a valuable but elusive primary source because written scores reveal little about how a piece of music sounded to its audience. In the case of jazz, performances are often notated after they have been played and simply reflect what a transcriber thought the musicians actually did at any particular moment. Studio recordings from the twenties preserve some wonderful performances, but the recording technology was rudimentary and many performers were either never recorded or recorded inadequately. In any case, recordings usually cannot capture the excitement of live music. It is especially difficult to reconstruct the interaction between audience and performers without live recordings of the sort only possible with present-day technology.

Nevertheless, a performance history of early jazz can be reconstructed by combining the many fine musicological studies of classical jazz with an analysis of how the experiences of performers changed at the turn of the century, how the locations and settings of live performances influenced performers and musical entertainment. The experience of jazz performance can be reconstructed not only from print media, secondary sources, and jazz recordings but also from business and trade publications relevant to the broadcasting and recording industries. The perspective of performers is well documented in biographies, autobiographies, and a growing number of oral histories.[10]

This study, which is based on both traditional and newly appreciated sources, treats the years in which the controversy emerged, 1890–1930. It focuses primarily on the cities most identified with jazz: New Orleans, Chicago, and New York, and secondarily on locations like Kansas City, Los Angeles, and San Francisco. Jazz was played in many other locales, but these were the leading urban centers for jazz performance.

Jazz virtuoso Sidney Bechet understood well the power of jazz performance to symbolize changing American life. "My story goes a long way back," wrote Bechet in his autobiography *Treat It Gentle*, "It goes further back than I had anything to do with. My music is like that . . . I got it from something inherited just like the stories my father gave down to me." Bechet's music never belonged exclusively to him, and he described how the improvisational dynamic between an individual performer's skill and the community created a musical road open to many travelers:

> The music, it's that road. There's good things alongside it, and there's miseries. You stop by the way and you can't ever be sure what you're going to find waiting. But the music itself, the road itself—there's no stopping that. It goes on all the time. It's the thing that brings you to everything else. You have to trust that.[11]

Jazz was controversial because it symbolized the changing and often contradictory character of American entertainment. Bechet's jazz road was paved with Afro-American participatory musical traditions, and in the 1920s that represented the transience and transformations of modern American life.

1/ *"Comin' Down the Same Drain": Performance Practice of Bluesmen, Minstrels, and Jazzmen*

In the late nineteenth and early twentieth century, Afro-American music played a dual role. It spoke to the unique experiences of black Americans and, at the same time, became the dominant influence on American popular music generally. Black music evolved from older folk music, including African and slave musical traditions, which it transformed into powerful expressions of the black experience in new settings, especially in the industrial cities of the North. Although it was a child of racial separation, black music, by its new-found commercial success after 1900, made it clear that black culture, like black people, could not be kept on the margins of American society.

By the 1920s, jazz—the most distinctive form of modern black music—was influential enough to pose an unmistakable challenge to white cultural domination. The threat was especially serious in the minds of traditional moralists because a significant number of whites themselves found jazz exciting. Indeed, the first contact many northern white audiences had with ragtime and jazz came from early white bands out of New Orleans, like Tom Brown's Dixieland Jass Band, which performed in Chicago in 1915, or Nick LaRocca's Original Dixieland Jazz Band, which played in Chicago and New York.

However successful such groups may have been, jazz was

obviously a music in which blacks were the primary creators and whites often the imitators. Black and white musicians generally did not play in the same ensembles during jazz's formative years, although performers often heard each other's performances. Equally obvious, jazz was a music of raw emotions—of hard luck and good times, of lust and loneliness. At first, neither jazz nor the places where it was played fell under the control of respectable whites. The morally and culturally subversive aspects of jazz stirred anxieties that fueled a long-running public controversy in the 1920s. Understanding the debate over jazz enables us to journey into the past meaning of the music for those who played and heard it and—equally significant—to a deeper knowledge of American values in a time of transition.

Before treating that controversy, however, we must trace the course of jazz as it made its way northward and to a larger audience among blacks and whites. Reconstructing *where, how,* and by *whom* jazz was heard is crucial to our task, because the music was fundamentally shaped through interactions between performers and audience.

Students of black American culture emphasize the pervasive and continuing influence of oral performance on Afro-American speech, folklore, literature, and music. Because slaves from Africa lacked a common spoken language and because written literacy was restricted for many blacks until well into the twentieth century, music served a crucial role as a medium that conveyed the history and values of black culture. Consequently, it is easy to see many of the distinctive aspects of Afro-American oral performance in jazz. Jazz writer Charles Nanry underscored the communicative power of jazz when he described it as a distinctive "language."[1]

The most important "ways of speaking" in jazz were shaped by musical traditions that relied on significant interactions between performers and audiences. This exchange encouraged spontaneity and culminated in the defining features of jazz: improvisation, call and response techniques, polyrhythms, syncopation, and blue tonalities. I shall briefly describe each of these

characteristics of the jazz language and analyze the role of participatory performance in their development.

Improvisation is perhaps the best-known musical element in
jazz. All musical creativity develops, at least in part, because composers or performers alter the rhythmic, harmonic, or melodic
ideas of musicians who preceded them. Improvisation is central to
all jazz performance, however, and virtuosity is measured not
merely by the technical proficiency of players but also by their
ability to perform new musical ideas consistently. Improvisation
can also take place collectively in the exchange of musical ideas
between instruments or sections of a jazz band or combo. In the
earliest jazz performances, improvisation was developed through
a heterophonic ensemble style.[2]

One important early source of improvisation was the "call
and response" tradition of Afro-American sacred and secular
music, in which musical ideas developed out of exchanges between a leader and chorus. This process encourages audience
participation in the creation of music.

In addition to pervasive improvisation, Afro-American music
has a complex rhythmic base which originated in Africa and
which distinguishes it from European music forms. "The essential principle of African music," according to jazz historian and
biographer James Lincoln Collier, "was the setting of two or more
time schemes against one another. At its simplest, this might mean
playing three beats on one drum against two on another. Rarely
was it this simple, however. More often three to six instruments
would each be playing a complex rhythmic figure in a different
meter or "beat" at the same time."[3] Polyrhythms, particularly
when combined with syncopation and swing, give jazz much of its
rhythmic pulse.

Polyrhythmic musical performances depend on an accurate
yet flexible "metronome sense," which one critic compared to
"an automatic feeling for what the pulse ought to be in some
musical piece."[4] Once this metronome sense is understood by
performers and audiences, the beat can be rushed or slowed
down, and competing rhythms introduced. Several musicologists
and linguists suggest that the metronome sense common to black

speech and music differed significantly from that known to white Americans.[5]

At the turn of the century, black musicians began new experiments with polyrhythms in their ensemble playing. Early jazzmen often began their careers by playing ragtime, which, for pianists in particular, provided important training in polyrhythmic music. Music officially labeled "ragtime" was first heard by the general public in the 1890s at exhibitions and in saloons and dance halls. Ragtime probably derived from plantation banjo music, where it may have accompanied the cakewalk and similar dances. As musicologist Eileen Southern writes, "The earliest rag music players were anonymous drifters in the Mississippi River country and on the eastern seaboard who played piano music in cheap eating-places, honky-tonk spots, saloons, and riverside dives. . . ." Much of the white public, however, would have heard ragtime songs performed in minstrel shows rather than in the venues described by Southern.[6]

The earliest composers to transcribe rags often performed, like Scott Joplin, from the honky-tonks of midwestern and southern towns like St. Louis, Louisville, and Texarkana. The pianist created novel effects by altering the emphasis expected in a song's meter, hence, "ragging" a tune came to mean that it was performed in an unpredictable and percussive manner. Ragtime bands also performed this improvised syncopation off the written scores for hymns, cakewalk marches, two-steps, schottishes, polkas, and waltzes.[7]

Jazz historian Marshall Stearns explained that the rhythms in ragtime came from a "steady beat in the left hand and a syncopated beat in the right hand." The left hand usually played a 2/4 rhythm while the right hand, according to Stearns, "plays light beats in the same interval, but accents every third beat, an effect that may well have been taken from the minstrel banjo."[8] Virtuoso ragtime performers improvised on this framework by suspending rhythms or providing unusual accents. This playful alteration of the music helped earn for ragtime a reputation as an exciting new sound.

Gilbert Seldes, in his 1924 study *The Seven Lively Arts,* recalled that ragtime "has torn to rags the sentimentality of the song which preceded it."[9] The name of the music itself emphasized the role of meter as a defining characteristic, and *Opera Magazine* noted in 1916: "Ragtime has carried the complexity of the rhythmic subdivision of the measure to a point never before reached in the history of music."[10]

The use of syncopation was not unprecedented in European and American music; but, as ragtime historians Rudi Blesh and Harriet Janis explained, syncopation in ragtime was used continuously, not merely for "a few measures" as it had been in European styles. Blesh and Janis described the effect produced:

> Continued syncopation, however, far from limping builds up greater and greater momentum hence the old English term for syncopation is deeply stimulating and exciting, and European masters seem always to have been wary of it. So the thorough use of these delayed and misplaced accents (misplaced, that is in the sense of our regular meters) and their employment with regular meters to set up complex multiple rhythms, or polyrhythms, were never seriously explored in our music.[11]

The adjectives Blesh and Janis used, such as "disturbing," "upsetting," "stimulating and exciting," and "misplaced," indicate accurately syncopation's effect on listeners accustomed to Western rhythms.

Ragtime engendered a controversy among listeners that presaged the 1920s debate over jazz. A typical article in the May 23, 1900, issue of *Musical Courier* reported: "Louis Blumenberg, the 'cello-virtuoso,' reports to us that ragtime—a rag-weed of music—has grown up everywhere in the Union and that its vicious influences are highly detrimental to the cause of good music." In his ragtime history, Edward A. Berlin concluded that ragtime was attacked primarily through "ridicule, appeals to racial bias, prophesies of doom, attempts at repression, and suggestions or moral, intellectual and physical dangers." Ragtime's defenders pointed to its "popularity, innovation," and American origins.[12]

Negative estimations of ragtime compared it to an irresistible force or contagious disease. One enraged critic commented:

"Ragtime is syncopation gone mad, and its victims, in my opinion, can only be treated successfully like the dog with rabies, namely, with a dose of lead." A ragtime proponent praised the music for similar qualities:

> Suddenly, I discovered that my legs were in a condition of great excitement. They twitched as though charged with electricity and betrayed a considerable and rather dangerous desire to jerk me from me seat. The rhythm of the music, which had seemed so unnatural at first, was beginning to jerk me from my seat. It wasn't the feeling of ease in the joints of the feet and toes which might be caused by a Strauss waltz, no, much more energetic, material, independent as though one encountered a balking horse, which it is absolutely impossible to master.[13]

In these arguments regarding ragtime—and as we shall see in the jazz controversy—the participatory and improvisational characteristics of the music are often the salient features acknowledged by fans and foes alike. The music is loved or loathed because it forces a response from or seduces a participant.

Harlem stride and boogie-woogie piano also made major contributions to the evolution of jazz and encouraged performer-audience interaction in some contexts. Pervasive syncopation characterizes both keyboard styles. Nanry described boogie-woogie as being "closest to the vocal blues in conception and execution." We shall return to the blues shortly, but boogie-woogie shared the same 12-bar structure and "a persistent, percussive *ostinato* bass figure in the left hand of 'eight beats to the bar'." The right hand in boogie woogie then improvised against the left. This piano music was louder and more percussive than vocal music, inspiring the nickname "the horses" because it sounded like trotting.[14]

Similarly, stride piano, which developed in Harlem and other Northeast cities, drew on both blues and ragtime traditions. Stride performers, however, developed the possibilities of the left hand more thoroughly so that each hand played quite distinctive and different melodies. Willie "the Lion" Smith described how he used competing songs with different rhythms in each hand: "A good pianist had to be able to play with both hands performing in perfect unison . . . We had such control that we could play a different song with each hand at the same time."[15] The term "stride" evoked the driving momentum built up in the music—much like the brisk walk it was named after.

In addition to the rhythmic energy of ragtime and stride piano, jazz also incorporated the blues. A distinct secular music, the blues probably emerged from work songs, shouts, and spirituals in the rural South following the Civil War. It would be misleading to try to pinpoint an exact origin for the music, however, since tonal flexibility is the distinguishing feature of the blues. "It is an aural music, intended to take on its shape and style during performance," writes Eileen Southern.[16]

Several jazz historians and critics suggest that the first blues songs were based on English ballads and might have been 8, 10, or 16 bars long. But they were also characterized by three-line stanzas that were probably an African-derived "inner form." Jazz musician and poet Amiri Baraka offers one plausible explanation for the process by which blues took on their "classic" 12-bar form out of these antecedents: "The three line structure of the blues was a feature of the shout. The first two lines of the song were repeated, it would seem, while the singer was waiting for the next line to come. Or as was characteristic of the hollers and shout, the single line could be repeated again and again. . . . " Baraka suggests that repetition might be a result of the musicians' desire to repeat favorite phrases, but a warm audience might also encourage certain stanzas. The communal production of music like the spirituals or work songs was modified in the blues because an individual performs by himself or herself. But the audience might well contribute to the blues performance by their acceptance or rejection of each improvisation made by the performer.[17]

Listeners who were unaccustomed to blues considered it disturbing or dissonant because the tones sounded flat when compared with conventional European harmony. When blues were written down, their West African pentatonic-based tones were

adapted to the European diatonic-based system of pitch and notation. "Blue notes" were represented by flatted thirds, sevenths,
and later fifths on the diatonic scale. This notation does not, of
course, capture the wide range of pitches that might be "bent" or
"worried" in instrumental and vocal blues performances.[18]

White Americans often believed the blues conveyed sad or sor-
rowful messages exclusively, when in fact, the blues expressed a
wide range of emotions and descriptions of Afro-American life.
The development of the blues clearly points to the relevance of
seeing this form of black music as a means of communication
that expressed the history and values of the black community—
particularly since certain blues took as their subject matter local
or current events. In fact, Amiri Baraka suggests that early blues
may have been a language specific to the acculturation of ex-
slaves to a tenuous American citizenship. "I cite the beginning of
blues as one beginning of American Negroes," writes Baraka,

> . . . The stories, myths, moral examples, etc., given in African were
> *about* Africa. When America became important enough to the Afri-
> cans to be passed on, in those *formal* renditions, to the young, those
> renditions were in some kind of Afro-American language. And fi-
> nally, when a man looked up in some anonymous field and shouted,
> "Oh, Ahm tired a dis mess/Oh, yes, Ahm so tired a dis mess," you
> can be sure he was an American.[19]

Jazz, like the blues, is not a "pure African tongue." Early jazz
incorporated the several parts of musical speech described here,
as it became a music that communicated the stories of black
Americans, as well as many others who found themselves in
transition at the turn of the century.

Jazz developed most directly from the ragtime, blues, brass
and marching band and dance music popular at the turn of the
century. Some aspects of its performance style can also be
traced to the early contact between African slaves, their European and (later) American masters. White observers of the African Diaspora gave music and dance performance prominent

mention in travel accounts, diaries, missionary reports, and early histories. These commentators passed varied—and typically ethnocentric—judgments on the practices they witnessed, but all of them attested to the expressive power of black musical performance.[20]

Although it is impossible to be completely accurate when generalizing about performance practices typical to slavery, common musical traditions have been documented, even though some African music practices, particularly communication via drums, were outlawed by southern whites who did not want slaves signaling each other. Performers sang at festivals and holiday gatherings. On some plantations, skilled musicians were asked to perform for their masters on social occasions. Similar opportunities existed in towns at inns and later at saloons and dance halls. Syncretism between European and African musical practice took place, depending upon the amount of contact blacks had with whites and their music.[21]

The distinctive qualities of black music were expressed regardless of whether it was used primarily as a "sacred" or "secular" form of expression. Much music was communally created and drew on the experiences of both observers and participants. The spirituals are the best-known example of this kind of communal music expression, but the same process probably also inspired work songs, ballads, and shouts. One nineteenth-century description of a shout illuminated the practice of communal creation:

> The true shout takes places on Sundays or on "praise" nights through the week, and either in the praisehouse or in some cabin in which a regular religious meeting has been held. Very likely, more than one half the population of the place is gathered together . . . The benches are pushed back to the wall when the formal meeting is over, and old and young, men and women . . . all stand up in the middle of the floor, and when the "sperichil" is struck up, begin first by walking and by-and-by shuffling around, one after the other, in a ring. The foot is hardly taken from the floor, and the progression is mainly due to a jerking, hitching motion, which agitates the entire shouter, and soon brings out streams of perspiration.[22]

As this description indicates, dance was an important part of musical expression, and often music was created by the interchange between a group of dancers and singers. These performance events encouraged individual and group spontaneity, as well as the repetition of standard formats.

Slaves used a similar interactive style in music that accompanied work on the docks and levees and in the fields. The songs used rhythmic accompaniment appropriate to various tasks and treated topics ranging from love to the oppressive conditions of slavery. Frederick Douglass recalled one such satirical work song he knew from the plantation:

> We raise de wheat
> Dey gib us de corn;
> We bake de bread,
> Dey gib us de cruss;
> We sif de meal,
> Dey gib us de huss;
> We peal de meat,
> Dey gib us de skin;
> An dats de way
> Dey takes us in.[23]

The "call and response" between a leader and chorus common to such songs reinforced antiphonal traditions in both West African and European music. Most Afro-American music, including jazz, echoes this dynamic form.

According to anthropologists, music was "among those cultural traditions most readily maintained under slavery," and its performance was closely related to verbal arts such as toasts, folk tales, and joke-telling. Participatory performance practices that relied on communal creation, call and response experiences, and a strong tradition of improvisation provided a means of accommodating oneself to a dominant white culture without being completely absorbed by it. These early developments constituted the participatory performance heritage out of which jazz developed.[24]

Freedom challenged, but did not destroy, the participatory

style of black music by breaking down some communal forms (such as the work song), and by increasing the diversity of life-styles of Afro-Americans. Black music after the Civil War expressed the experiences of ex-slaves as they struggled to define an identity under freedom. Some songs described new kinds of work—in lumber mills, factories, on western cattle drives. Others described the route to new jobs and lives on the road, the steamship, and the train. The prison song arose as a new genre depicting the limits of freedom as vagrancy laws and black codes restricted the movement of blacks in the South, and as jail replaced the private "justice" of the plantation. Many of these new forms were highly personal expressions of individual experiences—as the blues have always been—and far distant in that respect from more participatory forms such as the work song and church music. But even the blues could often capture shared versions of the world, especially in an era of dramatic change for the black community like the one just before and after World War I.

Commercialism and technology also affected black music after the Civil War, and in ways that likewise tended to make it less communal and regionally unique. Traveling professional musicians partially replaced local songsters who knew and performed with their audiences. After the turn of the century, phonograph recordings (and later radio) completed the process of separating performers from their audiences.

The participatory style, nonetheless, did not die among blacks. It would even survive and adapt to the rise of the phonograph record. At the turn of the century it helped shape ragtime, blues, and early jazz as they were performed in several cities prior to the First World War, particularly New Orleans, New York, Kansas City, Los Angeles, and the Mississippi port towns. Among blacks migrating to these areas were musicians who created exciting new forms of musical entertainment with roots in earlier, more communal styles.

Although not alone as an early twentieth-century center for black music, New Orleans offered a rich combination of perfor-

mance opportunities that made it one of the foremost environments in which musicians created jazz. The city, according to
some jazz historians, was more tolerant of Afro-American slave
culture than cities dominated by Anglo-Saxon values.[25] More
important, New Orleans had a rich and varied musical life, including street bands, theatre orchestras, and amateur musical
societies, and the opera. The musical traditions and institutions
of New Orleans were important not simply because musical performances were available to many residents, but also because
they provided employment, some private music instruction, and
inspiration to the earliest ragtime and jazz musicians.

Prominent jazz musicians from New Orleans recalled a city
pervaded by music. The large number of social clubs and benevolent societies in New Orleans helped foster this musical ambience. Pianist Jelly Roll Morton said: "I have never seen such
beautiful clubs as they had there—the Broadway Swells, the Iro-
quois, Orleans Aides, the Bulls and Bears, the Tramps, and the
Allegroes—that was just a few of them, and they would parade at
least once a week." Sidney Bechet described the effect of these
club parades on the community: "There used to be these big
parades all over New Orleans—a band playing, people dancing,
and strutting and shouting, waving their hands, kids following
along waving flags." Organizations sponsored brass bands for
Mardi Gras and other holidays, parties, special occasions and of
course, funerals.[26]

The music of bands in the street was complemented by other
sounds that inspired musicians. Guitarist Danny Barker remembered numerous outdoor sounds from his childhood that provided him with musical inspiration. He described "peddlers: the
ice cream man, the snowball man, the crab man, each with a song
or some noise to identify them and their wares." In addition,
Barker heard "night and day people walking along singing popular jazz songs, sad mournful spirituals . . . virtuosos whistling jazz
songs just like their favorite musicians played. . . ." Barker speculated that this music was audible at great distances because of

"different kind of acoustics" created by the water under and around the city.[27]

In addition, Barker attributed the carrying power of the music to the relative absence of tall buildings and automobile sounds that would muffle musical strains later in the twentieth century. Percussionist Paul Barbarin agreed with Barker and reported hearing bands from a mile and a half away when Barbarin, too, was young.[28]

Stories about cornet player Buddy Bolden symbolize well people's memories about the legendary drawing power of music in New Orleans. According to biographer Donald Marquis, Bolden performed in a number of bands between 1894 and 1906, and his influence was perhaps exaggerated by subsequent generations of musicians. But Marquis has established that Bolden sometimes played loud and "ratty," which apparently prompted many New Orleanians to claim that they could hear him over great distances.

Bolden left a strong impression on younger musicians. Paul Barbarin said he remembered hearing Bolden, who "sure could blow"; and horn player Harrison Barnes heard Bolden's sound carry from the Globe Hall near the old Congo Square. Trombonist Kid Ory pictured Bolden starting a dance by saying, " 'Let's call the children home.' And he'd put his horn out the window and blow." Although everyone who claimed to have heard Bolden may not really have had the privilege, the frequent association of his siren cornet song with early twentieth-century New Orleans music attests to the pervasiveness of music "in the air."[29]

Much music was performed outdoors in New Orleans, when marching bands played for holidays, parades, Mardi Gras, and the renowned funeral processions. The popularity of marching bands was accelerated by the national craze for military bands before and after World War I. Some bands had servicemen or veterans in them, but many dressed in military-style uniforms regardless of the past military service of members.

Military bands not only heightened public awareness of the contributions of black musicians, but also like street bands, pro-

vided training for musicians. Guitar player Nathan Robinson
and trumpet player Punch Miller both chose music to avoid
more monotonous duty. Robinson switched from guitar to trombone, for example, when he discovered that playing in the band
exempted him from digging foxholes. Both men went on to play
professionally after the war.[30]

Music performed outdoors nurtured several performance
practices important to jazz. Musicians in marching bands had
"bucking contests" to test each other's skills and to advertise themselves to the public. Trumpet player Wingy Manone recalled:

> Down the street, in an old sideboard wagon, would come the jazz
> band from one ballroom. And up the street, in another wagon would
> come the band from another ballroom, which had announced a
> dance for the same night at the same price. And those musicians
> played for all their worth, because the band that pleased the crowd
> more would be the one the whole crowd would go to hear and dance
> to at its ballroom later.[31]

Competing from the tailgates of wagons or on foot, these "advertisements" tested audience preference and tried to win business
away from other performers.

According to Manuel Manetta, the furniture wagons used in
these contests were pulled by mules. Some had tops and others
were open. Musicians sat on folding chairs with the "drummer
sittin' behind the driver facin' the rear . . . the trumpet and trombone opposite him . . . and clarinet and violin [on the other
side.]" The bass player faced the drummer and the trombone
player faced off the tail of the truck. This is where "tailgating" or
"vamping" was easiest. Manetta said bands played only when
they stopped on "business corners" near saloons. According to
bass player George "Pops" Foster, barkeepers encouraged this
proximity because it helped business.[32]

The sides of the truck might be hung with a sign listing the
particulars for the evening's performance and sometimes the
band arranged for notices to be handed out. Kid Ory advertised
his band on a rented wagon when he first moved from LaPlace,
to New Orleans, and Ory believed that he was the first to put his

phone number on the sign. He used the technique to drum up business rather than promoting a job that was already set.[33]

Feuds took place between bands from across the Mississippi River in Algiers and those based in New Orleans. Some contestants formed intense rivalries. Clarinet player George Lewis recalled one between a band he was playing in and Buddy Petit's. Lewis's band beat Petit's one Saturday—probably because Petit was drunk. "The following Saturday," Lewis remembered, "we drove up and saw Buddy sitting there with his head hanging down and his hands floppy, so we set up to go after them again." Unfortunately for Lewis, Petit was faking, "and then somebody sneaked around and chained the wheel of our truck to theirs so we couldn't get away, and Buddy jumped to his feet, and that Saturday they really wore *us* out."[34]

Advertising could promote individual musicians as well as bands. Manetta was "called off the truck" while playing one Sunday and offered a job playing in a nearby saloon. Street and saloon performances can be seen as part of a continuum in these descriptions, and other performance locations were similarly related. Louis Armstrong, for example, credited one of these contests with attracting the attention of bandleader Fate Marable, who hired Armstrong for his first riverboat excursion trip in 1919.[35] Similar "cutting contests" or band battles took place at picnics, in the parks, and at nightclubs and dance halls, where two bands performed at opposite ends.

Many musicians performed at the camps at Lake Pontchartrain, where predominantly white picnickers brought their lunches on Sunday afternoons. John Handy described a typical contest that took place from 9:30 a.m to 5:00 p.m.: "They had at least five bands out there every Sunday, on different wharfs . . . Every time you'd turn around you could hear a trumpet blowing through the window at each other." Paul Barbarin took the "Smokey Mary" train out to the lake to play at Lucien's Pavilion at the Milneburg camp, and Punch Miller remembered four or five bands competing there, too.

George "Pops" Foster counted many more bands—as many as thirty-five or forty on an afternoon at Lake Ponchartrain.

"The clubs would all have a picnic and have their own band or hire one," he wrote. "All day you would eat chicken, gumbo, red beans and rice, and drink beer and claret wine." The food "was mostly every tub, that means everybody takes what he wants and waits on himself." "Mondays at the lake," according to Foster, "was for the pimps, hustlers, whores, and musicians. We'd all go out there for picnics and rest up. At night they had dances in the pavilions out on the piers." Clearly, musicians combined work with pleasure at the lakeside jobs.[36]

Other performers remembered battles that took place in the parks around the city. Kid Ory and Frank Adams both described the excitement of music combined with hot air balloon exhibitions featuring Buddy Bottley in Lincoln Park. Johnson Park was about two blocks away from Lincoln Park—close enough for bands to compete within hearing distance of all park patrons.[37]

In each of these settings, the bucking contest served several purposes. It helped build a reputation for the most successful performers, based both on the judgment of other performers and audience reaction. In addition, competitive playing required polished individualized technique and made improvisation a central feature of the musical style. Cutting contests didn't pit just one band against another—audiences became an important part of the performance. The band knew it had won a bucking contest, Manetta recalled, when it received the most "excitement and applause" from the audience that gathered in the street.

Youngsters and other aspiring musicians joined marching bands as part of the "second line." Social club members walked, danced and carried items like umbrellas, baskets, and cabbages with cigars stuck in them. Barney Bigard described the role of the second line in one funeral procession. "The band turned away," from the vault he recalled and "the second line get together and all of a sudden they start out with 'Didn't He Ramble' and . . . then they carry on and they dance all through the street, and at the second line, that's when the fun starts."[38]

Second liners might help carry instruments at the end of a long parade, and Sidney Bechet observed that the second line was one way that observers joined performers in a spontaneous assemblage:

> One of these parades would start down the street, and all kinds of people when they saw it would forget all about what they was doing and just take off after it, just join in the fun. You know how it is—a parade, it just makes you stop anything you're doing; you stop working, eating, any damn thing; and you run out, and if you can't get in it you just get as close as you can.

Jelly Roll Morton, however, remembered the second line as a defensive group armed with "basketball bats, axe handles, knives and ammunition" needed to protect bandsmen from attack when they crossed the ward lines of the city.[39]

Sometimes the second line interfered with the musicians and became too participatory. Danny Barker told the story of a bass drummer Black Benny, who served as a second liner bass drummer in Barker's grandfather's (Isidore Barbarin) Onward Brass Band. The "polite Creole members" of the Onward Brass band, according to Barker disliked second liners who got "belligerent, sarcastic . . . who would get carried away by the music and dance in the path and in and about the musicians." Benny solved the problem by "beating heads as well as drums" with a drumstick that doubled as a blackjack. It is also possible that "polite Creole" musicians disliked the participation of those considered lower class.[40]

Novices with little or no musical training also joined the second line and, if they proved themselves, might stay and play. Harrison Barnes, for instance, started out in a plantation band composed of his brother and a few friends. At first, he could not read music so he learned cornet by imitation. Later he received some formal instruction and studied method books. When he moved to New Orleans, Barnes still had relatively little training and was embarrassed to perform in public. Eventually he was persuaded to join in and found many kinds of jobs, frequently at private parties. "They didn't have these radios and things," he remembered, "when people would give birthday parties and everything they would ring me."[41]

Kid Ory also started out in a plantation band in LaPlace. He and his young friends on the Woodland Plantation made a banjo, guitar, bass, and violin out of wooden or soap boxes strung with fishing cord. The youngsters caught their own fish and then organized fish fries to feature the band. Since the homemade instruments wouldn't carry well outdoors, the band performed in empty houses lit by candles. Ory explained that his cousin gave him beer and food to help his venture along, and the band soon played concerts following baseball games.

When he had saved enough money, Ory and the band bought new instruments and Ory chose the valve trombone. He had taught himself basic breathing techniques by watching adult musicians—sometimes while hiding under a bed during rehearsals. Ory also learned from the bands that came to play at the sugar cane plantation on payday, and he heard excursion bands who passed through La Place on their way to and from Baton Rouge.[42]

Other early New Orleans jazz musicians began playing on their own at a young age—sometimes in "spasm bands" that brought a hot style of playing to more conventional groups. Danny Barker, for example, had a spasm band called the Boozan Kings, a name derived from the Creole word "boozan," which means party. He got the idea after watching strolling entertainers, including young children, perform in the District. According to Barker, spasm bands:

> . . . played all sorts of gadgets that produced sounds: musical saws, washboards, spoons, bells, pipes, sandpaper, xylophones, sets of bottles (each with a different amount of water), harmonicas, jews harps, one string fiddles, guitars, small bass fiddles, tub basses, kazoos, ram horns, steer horns, bugles, tin flutes, trombones, and many others . . . These performers and musicians were welcomed by the patrons in the joint, although the first time it was mainly out of curiosity . . . If the fool was an artist and performed well, he was always welcome to walk through the swinging doors and perform. Some of these performers were hired to keep the joint jumping.[43]

Barker and his friends survived the loss of one performer whose irate father took him home in the middle of an early performance, and they tolerated numerous racial slurs from rowdy patrons. The Boozan Kings became local celebrities, wrote Barker, because they could "imitate the songs featured by many of the city's jazz bands."[44]

Barker, like many other jazz musicians, came from a musical family which encouraged formal lessons. In several cases, brothers formed their own bands or parents taught their children how to play an instrument. Some children learned to play in bands organized at schools, churches, and orphanages. Louis Armstrong began performing in a child's vocal quartet for nickels and dimes on New Orleans street corners and then learned to play an instrument in the Colored Waifs' Home (also known as the Jones Home). The wide variety of opportunities to hear and join the music-making helped these young players pick up musical skills. Many of the musicians took some formal lessons or studied method books, but in many cases it was after they'd already been performing for several years.[45]

Musicians in other locales, although exposed to fewer opportunities, also learned from a combination of formal training and informal observation or apprenticeship. Percussionist Sonny Greer learned some basics in his Washington, D.C., high school, but he credited Eugene Holand, who played on the Keith Vaudeville Circuit, with teaching him how to play the drums in return for Greer's instruction in pool. Dicky Wells joined the Sunday School band at Booker T. Washington Community Center in Louisville.[46]

One of Chicago's best known twenties ensembles was named for the high school where they all met. The Austin High School Gang began when the McPartland brothers and their friends started playing at local fraternity parties. At the same time, Milt Hinton was performing in the Wendell Phillips Gang—named for his Chicago high school—and featuring Eddie Cole, Nat Cole, Dan Burleigh, Ray Nance, Lionel Hampton, and Scoville Browne.[47]

Lawrence Brown had his first exposure to music in his father's church choir in Oakland, California. Brown rejected the idea that he should play only sacred music. He was inspired to learn jazz after playing at Pasadena Junior College. He snuck out of the house and down to Los Angeles to hear groups like the Sunnyland Band.[48]

Regardless of the mixture of ideas and experiences that helped train the earliest generation of jazz musicians, most of them emphasized the pre-eminence of ear training. Some performers learned music fundamentals by simply listening to and imitating other performers. Reb Spikes paid close attention to other children's piano lessons, for example, and began to play piano on his own. John Handy said that he taught himself clarinet "note for note; feeling for them 'till I found them." Nick LaRocca took this process one step further by putting the songs he'd heard on paper and then marking "whatever valve corres- spond[ed] with the tones I had in my ear." Although all of these men are describing approximate ways of playing or scoring exact sounds, their experiments nevertheless prepared them to play and improvise without reading written music.[49]

Performers frequently described the values of these aural skills. Clarinetist Barney Bigard explained that when a violist was the lead melody instrument in a band: "he'd play the melody to the tune . . . and then the trumpet player would pick up . . . because he could play it, then the clarinet player, he'd listen and he'd put his own melody to it. So would the trombonist, see? And that's the way they formed the band, and that's how they got the melody." John Casimir, also a clarinet player, described a similar process in which he and other members of the Original Tuxedo Band would follow Louis Armstrong's lead.[50] In their autobiog- raphies and oral accounts, many musicians explained the impor- tance of this skill in jazz by distinguishing between those who could read music and those who played by "head" or faked a part. Johnny Lala remembered that his fellow clarinetist Alcide "Yellow" Nunez was a "wonderful faker," unlike some other "legitimate" musicians who could read. Another typical way to explain the differences in musical training was conveyed by Har- rison Barnes, who said, "When you would go in a band and . . . you got a new fella say he can play pretty good, see the other fella wanta know could he see. Say no, he's blind as a bat. Know what that means? He plays by ear."[51]

Many other musicians used a reading analogy for analyzing or explaining musical styles and skills. Bass player Albert Glenny told an interviewer that "I'm not a reader, I'm a speller, but I know my instrument." Ed Allen explained that all the bands he played in as a young musician in St. Louis were "reading" bands and that "faking came later."

Peter Bocage, a musician who could read music, used the most common metaphor signifying the relationship between head training and jazz when he commented that Buddy Bolden "was a fellow, he didn't even know a note as big as this house, you understand what I mean; and whatever they played, they caught or made up . . . they made their own music and they played it their own way. . . . so that's the way jazz started." What musicians "caught" of course was the metronome sense of the group they played with and, in so doing, they perpetuated improvisation and developed it into an art form.[52]

Differences in music-reading ability led several of the New Orleans performers to describe themselves in two different ways: those who could read music were nicknamed "musicianers" and those who could not—who "ragged" or "jazzed" it—were, of course, jazzmen. Pops Foster believed that musical taste gradually changed in the early twentieth century and that audiences demanded livelier music:

> . . . the dicty people got tired of hearing that violin scratchin' all night and started to hire some bands who'd play some rough music for them. Jack Carey's band, the Tuxedo Band, and some others who could read and play some sweet music too started getting some of the jobs. The Magnolia Band and the Superior Band could play anything, too. The bands that couldn't read made the most money and were the biggest talk of the town. They were the gutbucket bands like Ory's band and for a while Dusen's Eagle Band. They played hot all the time.[53]

Significantly, an accomplished musician was not necessarily the one who had taken formal music lessons and learned to sight read. According to these performance expectations, a *literate* performer might read music, but was required to play hot or sweet, to swing and improvise, and to deliver a ratty blues upon audience request.

Some of the evidence from New Orleans suggests that the different valorization of musical skills derived from caste and racial tensions. Black Creole musicians were more likely to receive formal training in sight-reading and other skills than non-Creole black New Orleanians. The black Creoles identified with French Caribbean cultural traditions, taking pride, for example, in their familiarity with opera and related musical genres that originated in Europe. When the racial codes in Louisiana were intensified in the late 1890s, black Creoles lost their special status as descendants of the nineteenth-century *gens de couleur libres.* Black Creoles found that many opportunities they enjoyed based on their half-caste status were abolished.

As musicians, black Creoles were gradually forced into more contact and competition with black performers. Jazz critic Martin Williams provided a succinct summary of the musical results of these changes:

> It has been said that New Orleans jazz resulted from the juxtaposition of the Creoles' musicianship and the freed slaves' passion and feeling. Downtown sophistication plus uptown blues. To the downtown sophistication belongs a transplanted European musical tradition, ranging from the opera house to the folk ditty. And to the uptown tradition belongs the work song, spiritual, field holler—an already developed African-American idiom.

Hence "downtown" and "uptown" referred not merely to the geographical centers of the two ethnic communities, but also to the differences in musical style between musicianers who had some connections to the earlier black Creole traditions and jazzmen who played "ratty" or hot.[54]

In his biography of Louis Armstrong, James Lincoln Collier pointed out that "uptown" and "downtown" also referred to two different sections of the famed Storyville red light district that employed musicians in commercial clubs, dance halls, saloons, and brothels. The close association of early jazz with the seamy side of New Orleans nightlife gave truth to the association in the public mind between jazz and illicit activities. One estimate suggested that by 1902 there were "85 important jazz clubs, 800 saloons, and over 200 bordellos."[55]

For the most part, brothels and bordellos provided employment to pianists rather than ensembles or bands. Jelly Roll Morton, Eubie Blake, James P. Johnson, and others took these jobs because they paid well. Their repertoire included ragtime, blues, popular songs, and some jazz piano. In brothels, as in clubs or saloons, tips made the difference for performers. Louis Armstrong explained how high tips affected the musicians' attitude toward wages:

> In those days a band who played for those places didn't need to worry about their salaries . . . their tips were so great until they did not even have to touch their nightly gappings . . . Most of the places paid off the musicians every night after the job was over instead of the weekly deal . . . that was because those places were threatened to be closed any minute. So the musicians and performers didn't take any chances.[56]

Dependence on tips predisposed musicians to adjust their music to audience tastes. Pianists in some clubs also had the added responsibility of drawing in business and divvying up the kitty among waitresses, waiters, and other performers when the night was over.

By the turn of the century, many of the New Orleans clubs were owned by Sicilian immigrants with ties to organized crime. A 1938 guidebook to New Orleans recorded the dual legacy of Italian immigrants to the city: "The importation of Italians, many of whom turned out to be first-class musicians and teachers, and the legalization of gambling in Louisiana after 1869, both gave impetus to the musical and night life scene which aided in the later development of jazz." Italian-Americans taught music and controlled much of the illicit activity in New Orleans, especially in the French Quarter. In one study of this relationship, Ronald Morris speculated that Italian-American patrons were appreciative of black music because it was reminiscent of cafe music in Italian towns. He concluded that all these factors produced a form of "patronage" that allowed jazzmen security necessary for creative work.

It is possible that a rapprochement between gangsters and jazz musicians in New Orleans existed. Certainly, black musicians remembered some gangsters fondly for handsome tipping. Black and Italian-American immigrants shared some of the same experiences of struggling for work and security in urban areas, and both groups valued entertainment as one possible road out of poverty.

Like blacks, Sicilians were reputed to see "music as a highly personalized affair, a reflection of an individual's feelings, although born of a collective experience." This affinity for the communal creative tradition, however, should not be exaggerated. Italian-American patrons did not always outnumber others at popular New Orleans jazz clubs, nor for that matter, did blacks and Italian-Americans make up a common audience in many clubs.[57]

The emergence of jazz clubs where a band might get a predictable salary rather than having to rely on tips was a welcome development for some musicians. But nightclubs also marked changes in the performance of street music, in large measure because when music "moved indoors," some of the spontaneity created by out-of-doors audiences was curtailed. Furthermore, musicians would increasingly perform for entrepreneurs who considered the bandsmen professional entertainers.

By contrast, the outdoor performances of white as well as black bands, and the Creole-black musical fertilization that took place in New Orleans were unique to early jazz performance practice. Audiences were not separated from a band marching down the streets or riding in a sidewagon, consequently, some aspects of an older communal creative tradition persisted. Performances combined with commercial and private social events also encouraged spontaneous and improvisational performer-audience interactions. The impoverished backgrounds of musicians likewise ensured that their musical training would come primarily from family connections or apprenticeship relationships with more skilled band performers.

In the clubs, of course, apprenticeship would remain a major avenue of training. Audience participation remained possible for both black and white patrons. But listening to a performer in a nightclub was not exactly the same as following him on the street and possibly joining in if you had an instrument. Clubs, nonetheless, represented a new stage in the commercialization and professionalization of jazz—and put it into a setting where it would be more accessible to whites.

It is impossible to pinpoint the exact person or moment when popular tastes demanded jazz instead of ragtime and other syncopated black music. James Lincoln Collier succinctly describes the central rhythmic "discovery" that produced jazz: "In the very first years of the twentieth century, some person or persons in the black and black Creole subculture tried the epochal experiment of making the double speed secondary pulse in ragtime explicit—that is to say, putting a four-beat tap under a two-beat rag."[58] Jazz emerged from collaborations like those previously described—between blacks and black Creoles, instrumentalists and pianists, street musicians and club performers.

In spite of the importance of New Orleans, musical experiments in other cities paved the way for jazz. Ragtime and stride pianists performed in honky tonks from Kansas City to Atlantic City. Brass bands performed Chicago to Los Angeles, and points in between. In New York, James Reese Europe dazzled New Yorkers with his syncopated orchestras and dance bands. When New Orleans musicians left Storyville they brought their music to areas already primed for hot jazz.

Syncopated dance music, in particular, had grown popular all along the eastern seaboard before World War I, and it encouraged New York musicians to experiment with new sounds. Public dancing increased dramatically in the teens, and Afro-American dances provided the basis for new ballroom fads that swept the dance hall, theatre and revue, and cabaret. "The decade between 1910 and 1920," wrote popular culture critic Sigmund Spaeth, "can be identified primarily as the period in which America went dance mad." Spaeth pointed out that music publishers made danceability a criterion for sheet music.[59] By the twenties, dancers discovered the rhythmic power of jazz and celebrated it in newly designed cabarets. Jazz dance as a popular nighttime entertainment would—as we shall see—fuel criticism of jazz itself.

The dances popular in the teens and twenties varied in complexity, and not all were accessible to "dance mad" white youngsters. The cakewalk, for example, was strenuous and difficult. Other dances, like the animal-inspired turkey trot, grizzly bear, monkey glide, chicken scratch, kangaroo dip, and scratchin' the gravel were condemned as overly sensuous in "nice" ballrooms. These dances were performed primarily in honky-tonks, dance halls, and brothels. They were automatically labeled—like jazz itself—conducive to promiscuity.

This salacious reputation was encouraged by the names of some dances, which had suggestive meanings in black slang. The name of the pre-World War I dance "Ballin' the Jack" is based on a "railroad expression," according to Willis Laurance James, who grew up in Jacksonville, Florida. "Jack is the name given to the locomotive . . . on the analogy of the indestructible donkey or jackass, while 'ballin' comes from *high ball*, the trainman's hand signal to start rolling. Hence, 'ballin the jack' means travelling fast and having a good time."[60] As plausible as James's interpretation is, slang allowed other meanings that were less technological and more physiological.

Risqué dances spread to new enthusiasts, despite the outcry against them. Ragtime sheet music listed dances appropriate to each piece like the cakewalk, march, and two-step. Edward Berlin points out that there was "no orthographical consistency" in the dance names and that several dances might be grouped together as in the 1899 composition "The Rag-Time Sports. Cake Walk-March and Two Step."[61] This catholicity about applicable dance steps for lively music created opportunities for marketing new dance ideas.

Black vaudevillian Perry Bradford wrote several songs that had a strong influence on the dissemination of dance. Bradford appropriated steps from vernacular dances he saw while touring the South. "Once in a while if the step went over big," Bradford said, "I'd work up a tune and lyrics that explained how to do it, have it printed, and sell it to the audience after my act."[62] The lyrics of Bradford's sheet music might then explain how to do the dances. Take, for example, Bradford's "Bullfrog Hop" of 1909:

> First you commence to wiggle from side to side
> Get 'way back and do the Jazzbo Glide
> Then you do the Shimmy with plenty of pop
> Stoop low, yeah Bo', and watch your step
> Do the Seven Years' Itch and the Possom Trot
> Scratch the Gravel in the vacant lot
> Then you drop like Johnny on the Spot
> That's the Bullfrog Hop.[63]

Another song by Bradford called "Rules and Regulations" acknowledged the public concerns that certain dances and dance steps be restricted from polite dance floors:

> The first rule was now you can Jazzbo Glide
> You must do it neat and have a gal by your side,
> Scratchin' the Gravel and Ballin' the Jack
> If you do them rough dances you musn't come back
> If you Shimmy inside you will Wabble outside
> If you break these rules now Jim will break your hide.
> The next rule was you can Stew the Rice
> Do the Bullfrog Hop and you must do it nice,
> On the Puppy's Tail so neat and slow
> Get way back and do the Georgia-Bo-Bo,
> No Shimmy dancing on the inside
> Or there will be some cryin' and a mighty slow drive,
> No rough dancing, smile and grin.
> Rules and regulations, signed Slewfoot Jim.[64]

Animal dances and dance songs were also popularized by Broadway shows such as *Darktown Follies,* produced in Harlem's Lafayette Theatre in 1913.

    Although they did not always acknowledge their sources, white professional dancers gained acclaim by their experimentation with black vernacular dance. For example, Vernon and Irene Castle—who rose to fame with their performance in the

film *The Merry Widow* in 1907—learned many dances from black
vaudeville and used these steps in their early career. They attracted patrons and dominated the market for dance instruction
by performing on Broadway, establishing dancing schools, publishing instructional books, and finally, opening their own cabaret, Castles in the Air.

One of the main inspirations for the Castles' innovations
came from the accomplished black bandleader James Reese Europe, who accompanied their performances and exposed them
to the latest black band music. Europe was one of the best-known
black bandleaders in the nation. He was a founding member of
the Clef Club—a professional organization for black musicians
in New York—which helped sponsor his 1914 performance at
Carnegie Hall. Europe directed a 125-member orchestra playing
ragtime and syncopated dance music on that date. James Weldon Johnson, who counted the composition of ragtime music
among his many talents, reported that "New York had not yet
become accustomed to jazz; so when the Clef Club opened its
concert with a syncopated march, playing it with a biting attack
and an infectious rhythm, and on the finale burst into singing,
the effect can be imagined."[65] Europe's band was a popular success and public tolerance for the dances associated with syncopated music also improved.

When Europe enlisted in the 15th Infantry in World War I,
he was asked to organize a first rate brass band. Europe's band
went to France as the 369th Infantry Band. Audiences in Europe
soon joined Americans in applauding the "Hellfighter's Band,"
although one French band leader accused the musicians of using
special instruments to create their unique and fast-paced sounds.
When Europe's band led the Fifteenth Regiment of New York's
National Guard through the New York Streets in 1919, Harlemites rushed into the streets to welcome them home.[66]

Once their popularity grew, the Castles abandoned some of
the dances they first performed. Serving as arbiters of taste for
the dancing public, they published their own rules and regulations. "Do not wriggle the shoulders," they admonished, "Do not

shake the hips. Do not twist the body. Do not flounce the elbows. Do not pump the arms. Do not hop—glide instead. Avoid low, fantastic, acrobatic dips . . . Drop the Turkey Trot, the Grizzly Bear, the Bunny Hug etc. These dances are ugly, ungraceful, and out of fashion."[67] Like Bradford, the Castles responded to the critics' demand that uninhibited Afro-American dances be toned down. Nevertheless, the dances popular in the twenties, especially the Charleston, conformed more closely to Bradford's less restrictive scheme than to that of the Castles.

While white dancers could learn approximations of black music and dancing from sheet music and model themselves after dancers like the Castles, new opportunities were developing for less-directed intimate dancing in bars and cabarets. New York City, predictably, offered many opportunities for black musicians. Prior to World War I, the center of black musical entertainment was San Juan Hill, located west of Broadway from 59th up to 64th Street. Jim Marshall ran a hotel on West 53rd Street that catered to black musicians and entertainers. The headquarters for the Clef Club was across the street.

Willie "the Lion" Smith and James P. Johnson both recalled that there was a range of clubs in New York. Those clubs that catered primarily to migrants from the South were instrumental to some of Smith's piano innovations. He described how the dancing tastes of these recent arrivals became part of his own musical style when he performed at the Jungles Casino:

> These people came from around the Carolinas and Georgia sea islands. They were called Gullahs and Geechies. . . . The Gullahs would start out early in the evening dancing two-steps, waltzes, schottishes; but as the night wore on and the liquor began to work, they would start improvising their own steps and that was when they wanted us to get in the alley, real lowdown.[68]

It was from this dancing, according to Smith, that the Charleston was born. It was "a variation of a cotillion step brought north by the Geechies." Johnson verified this perception when he said that the Charleston was "just a regulation cotillion step without a name." Johnson credited some of his compositions, including "Charleston" to the music he played for these "southern dancers."[69]

Because there were varieties of the dance popular with patrons, Smith and other piano players had to "make up their own musical variations to fit the dancing." Collaboration between audience and performers was encouraged in these dance halls—unrestrained by "rules and regulations." Many performers in New York and elsewhere had expectations about the rhythmic skill of the dancing audience. Danny Barker complained about dancers who were "out of step" because "these sort of dancers are an annoyance to rhythm players in bands. If you watch them closely they will confuse and throw you off tempo." Dancing remained a central feature of participatory music creation.[70]

Many of the entertainers who brought stride piano and the jazz band to northern audiences had been a part of the great black migration out of the South. It would be a mistake, however, to regard them or the music they played as coming from a relatively non-commercial folk tradition. Often they had perfected their craft in minstrelsy, theatre, and vaudeville. Professional entertainment networks for blacks had already begun to shape performance styles before World War I and before jazz began to reach white audiences. Minstrelsy was the most important field of entertainment that opened to blacks after the Civil War. In antebellum America it had been the domain of white musicians in blackface. Those who did enter minstrelsy after the war were artistically constrained by white audiences, who expected them to demonstrate demeaning racial stereotypes characteristic of antebellum minstrel shows. In addition, white theatre-owners in the 1860s and '70s often would not book black-owned companies, forcing at least one black owner, George Hicks, to sell out to a white manager, George Callender. As many music and dance historians emphasize, however, minstrelsy, along with circuses, tent shows, medicine shows, and similar acts provided openings in professional entertainment.[71]

Although most black professional musicians after the Civil

War were not formally educated, they perfected their music and dancing skills through an apprentice system. Dewey "Pigmeat" Markham, who would dance on the American stage for the better part of fifty years, compared his musical education to the public schools:

> In the old days show business for a colored dancer was like going through school. You started in a medicine show—that was kindergarten—where they could use a few steps if you could cut them, but almost anything would do. Then you went on up to the gilly [traveling circus] show—which was like grade school—they wanted dancers. If you had something on the ball, you graduated to a carnival—that was high school—and you sure had to be able to dance. College level was a colored minstrel show, and as they faded out, a vaudeville circuit or even a Broadway show. Vaudeville and Broadway sometimes had the best, although a lot of great dancers never got out from under the rag, never left the tent shows.[72]

Blues performer W.C. Handy also attested to the pivotal role of minstrelsy for turn-of-the-century entertainers. "It goes without saying that minstrels were a disreputable lot in the eyes of upper-crust Negroes," he noted, adding, "but it was also true that the best composers, the singers, the musicians, the speakers, the stage performers—the minstrel shows got them all."[73]

Minstrel bands varied in size and in the scope of their circuit. Jack "Papa" Laine who sponsored several bands in New Orleans, also had a minstrel show. Eddie Durham was part of a black band that traveled a southwestern circuit in and around Texas. Durham was in a fifteen-piece black band that performed for a "Doug Morgan's Dramatic Show" and the "101 Ranch" which he described as a circus or wild west show. At night, the band broke into a smaller group for the minstrel performance. Durham said that he learned to read and arrange music while working on this circuit.[74]

For black minstrels, as for black jazzmen, "respectability" mattered less than experience and income. There were few other channels besides minstrelsy open to black performers, especially those seeking exposure outside a local area. Minstrel shows also provided rare opportunities to learn from and emulate black performers.

In addition to minstrel companies, musicians also found work in extravaganzas, variety shows, and vaudeville. The Fisk Jubilee Singers, who were in the first troupe to perform spirituals on tour for large audiences, stole the show at Boston's World Peace Jubilee in 1872. At the 1876 Centennial of American Independence in Philadelphia, one exhibit featured a "plantation scene" of Afro-American singers and dancers who performed the cakewalk. Similarly, the 1893 World's Columbian Exhibition in Chicago featured a "Colored American Day" on which Harry Burleigh sang, Paul Lawrence Dunbar recited verse, and Joseph Douglass, grandson of Frederick Douglass, played the violin. The "Dahomian Village" featured African music at the Columbian Exhibition, which was quickly associated with "coon songs" and ragtime by the popular press.

The predominantly white audience for these extravaganzas was quite large and expected variations on the minstrel show format. Song and dance acts set on plantations, for example, characterized both minstrel shows and extravaganzas. In Brooklyn, New York, in 1894, an all-black extravaganza called "Black America" was produced by Buffalo Bill's agent, Nate Salisbury. Set in a large park, the extravaganza was designed:

> . . . into plantation scenes with real live cabins, livestock, cotton fields, and cotton gins, about which people could wander until the show began. The performance itself took place in a huge ampitheatre. The first part of the show was devoted to a re-creating of African episodes in dance and song; the second part consisted of American songs and dances and for the finale there was a grand cakewalk contest.[75]

The plantation setting would haunt black entertainment long after minstrelsy and extravaganzas were supplanted by new forms of entertainment. Many jazz nightclubs, for example, would later have names, and sometimes decor, along southern or plantation themes. Cities featured Club Alabams, Plantation clubs, and of course New York's Cotton Club. Southern settings may have expressed nostalgia for home on the part of a black migrant clientele, but for whites the nostalgia probably was for a place and time remembered less fondly and more realistically by blacks. By the 1920s, as we shall see, the "plantation" and "primitive" merged in significant ways to shape both the decor of clubs and white perception of jazz.

The opportunity to perform in a minstrel company or for a traveling circus or gilly was available only to some entertainers. For many others music took place a greater distance from white ears. In all the cities where jazz was first performed—New Orleans, Chicago, Kansas City, and New York, as well as in hundreds of smaller ones—black musicians found part-time and poorly paid employment in bars, brothels, and dance halls. Instrumentalists often played a mixture of these kinds of local engagements combined with some traveling shows.

Music performed in bars and dance halls or in theatres supplied by the traveling road shows was quite insulated from the nineteenth-century European styles that had dominated the rest of American popular music. The result was that separate and generally segregated black entertainment encouraged unique styles that did not have to conform to white tastes. Both ragtime and blues evolved from this separateness and were the most immediate precursors of jazz.[76]

Black entertainers continued to find employment in either local theatres and bars or in regional and national networks. Vaudeville, new road shows, and traveling theatres replaced minstrelsy as the most popular musical entertainment in the teens and twenties. Some performers learned their music from exposure to vaudeville performances while others played on the circuits. Willie "the Lion" Smith, for example, said he learned to read music by trading ragtime instruction for lessons in sight reading from vaudeville pianist Arthur Eck. While growing up in Parsons, Kansas, Buck Clayton found inspiration in the trumpet players of the traveling circuses.

Eubie Blake was part of the vaudeville team "Sissle and Blake," who performed on the very popular Keith Circuit. Keith was a predominantly white circuit, and Blake believed that the

blacks' acts were purposefully booked in the second act in order
to prevent them from getting a good review from the newspaper
critics, who always came in the third act.[77]

Most musicians described more modest vaudeville show experiences than Blake's. Red Norvo played in a marimba band on
the Chautauqua the summer before he went to college and he
toured from Illinois to California. In the Far West, saxophonist
Reb Spikes and his brother performed as the Spikes' Brothers
Novelty Stars in a seven-piece band which traveled on their "own
little circuit" that went from Bisbee, Arizona, to the Mexican
border, Tuscon, Phoenix, and "up to Bowie and Stafford and all
around."[78]

Several musicians from the Southwest migrated to Los Angeles and San Francisco for jobs, and New Orleans musicians
worked there too. Spikes played at Purcell's So Different Saloon
in the "Barbary Coast," and for Baron Long in Watts. When
drafted in World War I, Spikes played in army bands while
located in Hawaii and Nogales, Texas. The commanding officer
was "crazy" about jazz and let the band charge for the punch at
their dances.[79]

After the War, Spikes played with Jelly Roll Morton in Oakland. Morton was just one of several New Orleans musicians who
traveled west to play music. Mutt Carey and Kid Ory went west
in 1919 and King Oliver's Original Creole Jazz Band followed
them there in 1921. George "Pops" Foster described a variety of
dance halls and clubs in Los Angeles where many of the musicians played.[80]

The most influential circuit that hired black performers was
the Theatre Owners Booking Agency. Kansas City pianist Mary
Lou Williams's first professional job, for example, was in
T.O.B.A. vaudeville, where she performed alongside "Buzzin'
Harris," a blackface comedian and owner of the show. In the
teens the Theatre Owners Booking Agency (T.O.B.A.) was
formed by retired comedian Sherman Dudley. It served as a
main circuit for black vaudeville, dancers, musicians, and singers, reaching from the deep South to locations like Cleveland
and Kansas City. Like earlier road companies, T.O.B.A. wages

were low and life on its circuit could be brutal and dangerous. Not surprisingly, black performers claimed its initials stood for "Tough on Black Artists" and "Tough on Black Asses."[81]

T.O.B.A., nonetheless, was an early twentieth-century equivalent of the minstrel companies of the late nineteenth century. It helped promote blues stars such as Bessie Smith, Ma Rainey, and pianist James P. Johnson. The increasing spread of Jim Crow at the turn of the century left black performers with few options outside segregated entertainment. "Toby time"—another term for T.O.B.A.—served as a new avenue down which young blacks advanced towards careers as professional performers. In doing this, T.O.B.A. maintained some of the separateness of black musical traditions, and according to one scholar it "provided places where black talent could develop fully at its own pace and it own direction, unhampered by the demands of commercialism and unconcerned with the standards of white America."[82]

T.O.B.A.'s ghettoization of musicians may not have been to their benefit, but the network moved some stars into even wider exposure through recording careers on "race" labels aimed at black audiences in urban areas. Ma Rainey and Bessie Smith were among the first classic blues singers to make these recordings. As we shall see, urban black fans quite possibly already knew of Rainey, Smith, and other recording stars, having been to T.O.B.A. shows before migrating north.

The most successful T.O.B.A., minstrel vaudeville, or other black professional performers might, with luck and skill, develop national reputations, even if few reached Bessie Smith's popularity. One could "break into" the business with very slim resources—a good voice, dancing shoes, a used cornet. There were relatively few requirements for advancement other than the ability to imitate and improvise, and a willingness to work long and perhaps dangerous hours for small pay. (This was not what defenders of white standards and classical training had in mind when they thought of proper preparation for career in music.) But even if one did not make it on "Toby time," there were opportunities at more local levels of entertainment—social clubs, parties, and gin joints looking for music.

The increasing professionalization of live entertainment, reflected in T.O.B.A. and other kinds of black entertainment, resulted in a less intimate relationship between audience and performer. But the participatory nature of black music remained in some forms, especially when audiences danced or voiced their comments on musical acts. Improvisation and interplay between audience and performer persisted as distinguishing characteristics.

The teens and twenties, nonetheless, did witness significant changes in performance styles. Some of these were the result of technology and will be treated in a separate chapter. Others came with changes in demographic patterns and in the settings in which black music was played. Urban markets for black performers grew, in part as a result of World War I migrations and postwar consumerism. New locations for music, like the speakeasy or the movie theatre, partially eclipsed the popularity of music in the street. In any case, northern cities did not share the New Orleans traditions of frequent fetes and parades. Musicians, however, still competed to create the best new riffs and dance tunes. Increasingly, young white musicians sought to imitate them, and white audiences flocked to listen and dance. Jazz spread beyond the black community, but with change and controversy.

Much of the creative experimentation in jazz took place in Chicago. The "Windy City" was especially attractive to impoverished black farmers and sharecroppers from the agriculturally depressed South. European immigration virtually ceased during the war, diminishing the supply of unskilled labor at a time of high demand for it. Between 1910 and 1920 approximately 50,000 blacks migrated to Chicago to find work in the meatpacking and steel industries. Many southern states were so alarmed at the exodus that they passed ordinances controlling, licensing, and jailing labor recruiters. Banned in many southern communities, the Chicago *Defender,* a nationally prominent black newspaper, extolled the virtues of Chicago while vilifying the lynching-prone Jim Crow South. By the end of World War I, however, the "land of Canaan" on the shores of Lake Michigan proved bitter, as the pressure of returning servicemen, recession, segregated and undersupplied housing, and postwar political conflicts fueled a major race riot in 1919.[83]

For musicians the war years mark the shift of jazz performers from New Orleans north to the "Windy City," and New York, and west to Los Angeles. A group of notable New Orleans musicians moved to Chicago in the late teens and early twenties, including Joe Oliver and Louis Armstrong, while others like Freddie Keppard and his Original Creole Orchestra had gone west in 1912. Sometimes the closing of Storyville in 1917 by orders of the Secretary of the Navy is cited as the main event to force musicians out—a time when trombonist Bill Matthews said the "wolf began riding the red lights. . . ."[84] But shutting down the red-light district only accelerated an emigration begun earlier. The center for black music in Chicago was—predictably— the tenderloin section. In 1939, Frederick Ramsey provided this typical description of the area:

> Down State Street from the Loop the red-light district began, centering around 22nd Street. The two big places were Pony Moore's and the Everleigh Club. There was music by Negro piano players who travelled from city to city, getting their keep from the management and their pay from the clientele in tips and drinks. A good town on the circuit, they hit Chicago oftener and stayed longer. Tony Jackson, Benjamin Harney, and Jelly Roll Morton could be heard in the "district" regularly in the years around 1919.[85]

The distinctive music of the New Orleans musicians set them apart from the older practitioners, although the piano-playing of Morton certainly contributed to the mix that became the Chicago sound.

Musicians may well have been unusual among migrants because many had already traveled to urban areas, including Chicago, as part of their entertainment careers. Several had worked on riverboats or excursion trains that exposed them to new cities and spread their reputations. Riverboat excursion companies based in New Orleans, St. Louis, and in other Mississippi River towns brought music to patrons on the boats as well as audiences at the pier. The most influential company was that organized out of St. Louis by Joseph Streckfus and his sons.[86]

Streckfus hired black pianist Fate Marable to organize bands for the line and many musicians remembered Marable with special admiration because of the opportunities he gave new performers. According to Zutty Singleton: "There was a saying in New Orleans when some musician would get a job on a riverboat with Fate Marable they'd say 'Well you're going to the conservatory.' That's because Fate was such a fine musician and the men who worked with him had to be really good." John Handy, on the other hand, disliked Marable's frequent rehearsals and complained: "I don't like that much playing—just to be playing to the empty walls." George "Pops" Foster played for Marable on nightly trips that lasted from 8:00 to 11:00 p.m. with two ten-minute intermissions, and for Saturday matinees and some Sunday all-day trips.[87]

Louis Armstrong and other New Orleans musicians were among those talented enough to play with Marable and gain exposure to new audiences and cities. Several of the bandsmen, including Armstrong, learned the rudiments of sight-reading from Marable's band.[88]

Danny Barker considered Fate Marable's calliope-playing one of the most distinctive features of the riverboats. Barker could hear the calliope "all over town," and he described it as an instrument requiring considerable caution and skill to play:

> It was worked by a steam boiler and had copper on it, and you had to play it with gloves on and a raincoat and rainhat over your band uniform because the steam came from all directions. The keys got real hot and you had to be careful or the copper would get into your skin.[89]

Barker said the hot keys forced the calliope performer to play staccato. Most music on the riverboats, however, was dancing music played by ten-piece bands. Both black and white bands performed on different nights of the week in front of audiences that were typically segregated by race.

Musicians described different audience expectations on the

riverboats. George "Pops" Foster said that St. Louis blacks patronized the steamer *St.Paul* on Monday nights, and that the band could then play "how we wanted." Foster believed they were the first band to play before whites in St. Louis. On the steamer *Capital*, Ed Allen remembered that they could literally "rock the boat" by playing New Orleans numbers like "Panama," and that Captain Joe Streckfus would ask the band to tone it down. Just as in nightclubs and dance halls, audiences interacted with musicians on the riverboats.[90]

Migration affected the themes of black music. This was especially true of blues lyrics, which had earlier depicted the migratory experience of farm laborers and translated easily into traveling north. Blues musicians in the South often performed in locations where they met migrants: "A favorite hangout [of blues musicians] was the railroad station." W. C. Handy wrote, "There, surrounded by crowds of country folks, they would pour out their hearts in song while the audience ate fish and bread, chewed sugar cane, and dipped snuff while waiting for trains to carry them down the line." Danny Barker described a similar encounter as a young child visiting the docks of New Orleans with his grandmother. There he saw "Blind Tom" sing the "Ballad of the Titanic," which Barker felt was popular with stevedores and others working on the river.[91]

Literary critic Houston Baker finds particular significance in the association between blues and travel, especially by railroad: "The railway juncture is marked by transience," he notes. "Its inhabitants are always travellers—a multifarious assembly in transit . . . Like translators of written texts, blues and its sundry performers offer interpretations of the experiencing of experience. To experience the juncture's ever-changing scenes, like successive readings of ever-varying texts by conventional translators, is to produce vibrantly polyvalent interpretations encoded as blues."[92] Blues performer Cow-Cow Davenport explained that some of his blues had a literal reference to trains: "When I began playing the 'Cow-Cow Blues' I was trying to imitate a train, . . . I was trying to get in a part where the switchman . . . boarded the train from the cowcatcher on the front of the train."[93] Jazz musicians passed through the same junctures as those described by Baker and Davenport. And as they played blues, accompanied blues singers, and incorporated the blues into their own interpretations of the "experiencing of experience," jazz, too, emerged as a product of this matrix.

Many of the great early jazzmen emphasized their own wanderings. Louis Armstrong left New Orleans on the Mississippi River excursion boats—a trip he compared to Huck Finn's raft trip—and then traveled on to Chicago and New York. Jelly Roll Morton has been called a nomad because he lived and worked in so many places: New Orleans, Meridian, Jacksonville, St. Louis, Kansas City, Chicago, San Francisco, Detroit, Los Angeles, Memphis, Vancouver, Casper, Denver, Las Vegas, Tijuana, South Bend, Seattle, Davenport, Houston, Pittsburgh, Baltimore, Washington, D.C., and New York. Duke Ellington left Washington for New York, and Willie "the Lion" Smith left New York for Chicago. Although the history of jazz is often portrayed as a long migration up the Mississippi from New Orleans to Chicago (a geographic impossibility) followed by a trip to New York, it was a long and round-about journey. Travel is frequently a way of life for most musicians, but what made turn-of-the-century black musicians and their music special, was that the music captured and carried the experiences of migrating black audiences, and eventually, the shifting fortunes of the nation at large.[94]

Black musicians found both critics and an expanding audience when they reached the North, particularly in Chicago. One such critic was Dave Peyton, a black bandleader who wrote a weekly column on music and musicians for the *Defender* during the teens and twenties. Payton advised musicians on the attitudes they should take to their music, the behavior appropriate to their community standing, and the standards of professionalism he believed they should adopt. These had very little to do with the experiences of southern blues and jazz musicians, which combined communal performance traditions with professional experience. Peyton argued for behavior that conformed to white professional standards and middle-class values, rather than the rough and tumble of the black entertainment circuits.

Peyton warned against "clown music" and defined "musicianship" as "the . . . addition by white musicians of symphonic elements to the modern syncopated score." He and other members of the black music "establishment" also led Local 208 of the Musicians' Union, which gave them some authority in arranging jobs for members. New Orleans-based players, by contrast, seemed uninterested in the union; they were pleased to receive significant increases in salaries and tips in Chicago.

Despite higher incomes, all black performers worked in a community in which segregation strongly circumscribed employment and attitudes towards black entertainment. Playing opportunities were further divided between New Orleans-type bands, who "controlled the cabarets and recording sessions," and established bands, who "dominated the ballrooms and theatres."[95]

Despite Peyton's advice, Chicago audiences liked hot jazz and believed that it enlivened the atmosphere of clubs and theatres. Milt Hinton recalled that New Orleans style jazz created new respect for black music among black audiences. He pointed out that Louis Armstrong evoked the participatory tradition and provided a refreshing alternative to the typical "European" theatre atmosphere:

> Black people wanted to be like white people because they felt this was the way to be: that you were right and you were white and this was the only way it could be. . . . Louis had enough of the academic thing to read the music properly, and so this was the style. We were going to be just like downtown. And we'd sit and listen to this overture which had a European environment. Then the people would be a little restless, and say "Hey Baby, play so and so," and when Louis stood up and played one of his great solos, you could see everybody letting their hair down and say, "Yeah, that's the way it should be. This is it."[96]

Hinton pointed out that the contrasting performance styles represented by the very different traditions of white and black musical entertainment—one regimented and predictable and one spontaneous and participatory. Peyton and his supporters obviously did not understand the power of music to communicate a positive self-image to black audiences. The variety of musical entertainment contributed to Hinton's belief that Chicago was a "paradise for black folk" in the twenties, especially when compared with a southern town like Vicksburg, Mississippi—the town that Hinton and his mother had happily left behind.[97]

In addition to theatres, the cabarets and nightclubs became the prominent locations for hot jazz in Chicago. Most clubs in Chicago, like those in New Orleans, were owned by men with connections to organized crime, especially when Prohibition made speakeasies lucrative. Ronald Morris argues that in Chicago, as in New Orleans, patronage paid well and provided an environment conducive to experimentation. He also found that Sicilians were more likely to hire blacks than Irish owners were.[98]

But patronage had its risks. Performers attested to gun battles and cabaret violence as nightly possibilities. Jimmy McPartland was working at Tancil's when Al Capone moved it. McPartland remembered: "All over the place people were gashed and bleeding. The mobster would break a bottle over some guy's head, then jab it in his face, then maybe kick him. They made mincemeat of people. . . . But we just kept playing—period."[99] The relative economic security provided by a steady club income had to be weighed against the risks of underworld competition. There were abundant opportunities for popular musicians like Louis Armstrong to reach black and sometimes mixed audiences:

> Things were jumping so around Chicago at that time, there was more work than a cat could shake a stick at. I was doubling from the Dreamland for awhile. Then I stayed at the Vendome for only a year before I decided to double again.

> Then came Carroll Dickerson, the leader who had that fine band at the Sunset Cafe, owned by my boss, Mr. Joe Glaser. He hired me to double from the Vendome Theatre. After the theatre I'd go over to the Sunset at Thirty-fifth and Calumet Streets, and swing there with them until the wee hours of the morning. 'Twas great I tell you.[100]

Many musicians agreed with Armstrong, and doubling was a common practice.

The participatory performance qualities that were preserved

from early Afro-American music through bucking contests and street parades in New Orleans continued in the North, although in indoor locations. Musician Garvin Bushell remembered one technique that took some of the movement of street performances into a popular New York club. "This happened only in Leroy's," Bushell recalled; ". . . often when we played blues, each instrument would be in a different corner. The trumpet at the far end; the clarinet in the back room, etc. You'd take a solo from where you were in the room, and then when it was time to start the ensemble, you'd come back to the bandstand." Other musicians captured some of the flavor of a band marching in the street by leaving the bandstand to parade around a room or concert hall.[101]

Another form of improvisational music contests was the jam session that took place in after-hours clubs or musicians' homes. Percussionist Sonny Greer explained how jam sessions developed at New York's famous Rhythm Club. "It was a place to hang out after you would get through work," he said. "A lot of guys would come in there and sit down and jam . . . play cards, play pool and eat . . . It was just a social club for musicians." Danny Barker, too had fond memories of his first entrance to the Club, where "A wild cutting contest was in progress, and sitting and standing around the piano were twenty or thirty musicians, all with their instruments out waiting for a signal to play choruses of Gershwin's *Liza*."[102] Clearly, jazz clubs became new and in some cases segregated, environments for improvisation.

The "second line" in Chicago did not march behind a street band. Instead, young musicians sat in on club dates or eavesdropped from balconies. Muggsy Spanier—who was white—recalls "sitting in a dark corner of the balcony to listen to the music. I was only fourteen then, still not old enough to be allowed in a public dance hall." Many of the other performers listening in were white, like Paul Mares of the New Orleans Rhythm Kings. "We did our best to copy the colored music we'd heard at home," Mares explained. "We did the best we could, but naturally we couldn't play real colored style." NORK, and later the Wolverines, featuring Bix Beiderbecke, learned by imitating both black and white bands and proved especially popular with young college audiences, providing fuel for the controversy in the twenties that would swirl around the allegedly corrupting nature of jazz.[103]

The Chicago years also established a national following for performers like Louis Armstrong. Their recording careers began there, and many moved to the next center of the national music scene—New York. The experiences of musicians in Chicago demonstrated that it was increasingly important to be connected to national recording companies or booking agencies to have employment. Lil Hardin came to Chicago trained to read music and got her break as a demonstrater in a music store that also housed a booking agency. When the New Orleans Creole Jazz Band came to town, she was sent to audition and discovered her training was not nearly as important as picking the music up in performance: "When I sat down to play," Hardin remembered, "I asked for the music and were they surprised! They politely told me they didn't have any music and furthermore never used any. . . . the leader said, 'When you hear two knocks, just start playing'." Lil Hardin did just that and was hired. She "never got back to the music store—never got back to Fisk University."[104]

Chicago jazz careers were characterized by opportunities that mixed openings in national booking or recording agencies with local experiences. Strict adherence to professional training or codes of conduct like those advocated by Peyton were of secondary importance. The hot jazz that Armstrong popularized in clubs, jam sessions, and on records became the music preserved as most illustrative of the Chicago jazz scene of the twenties. But the recording and broadcast industries certainly never followed Peyton's advice. Instead, record promoters and club owners took the country blues and New Orleans-inspired jazz and made them national phenomena—squawks and all.

Early jazz developed from participatory performance traditions that began in Africa and continued among blacks during slavery. The dynamic created between performers and audiences in the streets, clubs, honky-tonks, and private parties continued polyrhythmic and improvisational styles in new settings. But early jazz also had social as well as musical aspects. Both the promise and uncertainty of migration were encoded in black music, especially the blues and later in jazz. New performance locations and job opportunities in northern cities sustained improvisational musicians, permitting survival of techniques and audience-performer interactions as salient characteristics of black musical entertainment. Black music itself came to fascinate white musicians while meeting resistance from white critics as well as black critics like Dave Peyton.

What jazz was—for friends and foes alike—was not just a matter of where it came from, but also of how and where it was performed.

2 / "All the Lights Were Tinted Green or Red": Location and Setting for Jazz Performance

> I was most impressed by the story of a friend who told me that after four successive parties he found himself dancing in a subcellar joint in Harlem. The room was smokey and sweaty; all the lights were tinted green or red and, with smoke drifting across them, nothing had its proper shape or color; it was as if he were caught there and condemned to live in somebody's vision of hell. When he came out again on the street, he said it was bathed in harsh winter sunlight, ugly, and clear and somehow reassuring. An ash-colored woman was hunting for scraps in a garbage can.
>
> —Malcolm Cowley in *Exile's Return*

Cultural critic Malcolm Cowley's description of a Harlem night-club captured the disorienting economic and social collapse that ended the 1920s. Although Cowley's vision of this "subcellar joint" exaggerated its netherworld qualities, his is a typical twenties portrayal of the nightclub. The passage captures well the special and exotic worlds of musical entertainment that emerged between 1900 and 1930 and that significantly influenced both the performance and perception of jazz.[1]

The provocative unity of jazz music and the cabaret described by Cowley marked the culmination of several changes in American popular music theatre, middle-class tastes, and black entertainment. By the 1880s a wide range of musical entertainment was available in the theatre and concert hall, minstrel and variety shows, saloons, cafés, dance halls, and sporting houses. Spontaneous and intimate interactions between audiences and performers heretofore characteristic of working-class amusements—and especially black ones—spread to middle-class and mixed audiences.

Clubs, hotels and restaurants, theatres, ballrooms, and cabarets began to feature syncopated ragtime and jazz in the teens and twenties. Performers migrating to New York, Chicago, Kansas City, Los Angeles, and smaller cities discovered new audiences primed for jazz entertainment. All the locations associated with jazz in the 1920s represented a transition between turn-of-the-century working-class entertainment and new middle-class urban leisure activities. The brothel, bawdy house, and honky-tonk gave way to the cabaret and nightclub. Some jazz locations also developed in response to the needs of black migrants from the South. These environments can be seen as marginal zones in which patrons, particularly from the middle class, could escape normative social expectations and experiment with new public roles. Just as performances on the streets and in honky-tonks or stride piano bars helped shape early ragtime and jazz, so too, did new locations in the urban areas shape exchanges between performers and audiences.[2]

When reconstructing the physical landscape for jazz performance, one must begin with its overall contours. Many twenties nightclubs, cabarets, and ballrooms were located in entertainment districts. In these enclaves of vice and excitement, danger and mystery, audiences participated in real or ersatz jazz performance. Many of the entertainment locations were to be found grouped in distinct districts within major cities. When visually stimulating club designs and decor combined with musical performance, these places created opportunities for extraordinary musical experiences.

Although by 1920 no longer legally defined as a vice district, New Orleans's Storyville is the entertainment zone first associated with jazz. Storyville, also known as the "District," was established in 1897 and closed by orders of the Secretary of the Navy in 1917. Bounded by Basin, St. Louis, North, Robertson, and Iberville streets, the area was the only one in which white and a few black prostitutes could legally ply their trade. These streets enclosed about twenty-three square blocks of restaurants, bars and saloons, brothels, cribs, and the St. Louis No. 1 and 2 cemeteries.

A smaller area of about four square blocks contained the "uptown district" for black prostitutes, which was opened in accordance with city ordinance in 1917 and lasted only a few months before being officially closed down along with the larger

Storyville. In reality, the area located between Locust, Perdido, Gravier, and So. Franklin streets, was open for business long before and after its official creation.[3]

Storyville, like tenderloin and vice districts in many other cities, was controlled by collusion between politicians and entrepreneurs. In New Orleans, it was Tom Anderson who negotiated among the patrons, police, political machines, and city government. Anderson ran a number of establishments including saloons, cafes, and brothels. As the political boss of the Fourth Ward, Anderson served in the state legislature for sixteen years as well as ruling over the diverse interests of "Anderson Country."[4]

According to pianist Jelly Roll Morton, who performed in several Storyville establishments, this small principality of vice was considered second only to France, "meaning the second greatest in the world." Morton explained why:

> . . . this Tenderloin District was like something that nobody has ever seen before or since. The doors were taken off the saloons there from one year to the next. Hundreds of men were passing through the streets day and night. The chippies in their little-girl dresses were standing in the crib doors singing the blues . . .
>
> The streets were crowded with men. Police were always in sight, never less than two together, which guaranteed the safety of all concerned. Lights of all colors were glittering and glaring. Music was pouring into the streets from every house. . . .
>
> They had everything in the District from the highest class to the lowest—creep joints where they'd put the feelers on a guy's clothes, cribs that rented for about five dollars a day and had just about room enough for a bed, small-time houses where the price was from fifty-cents to a dollar and they put on naked dances, circuses, and jive. Then, of course, we had the mansions where everything was of the highest class. These houses were filled up with the most expensive furniture and paintings. Three of them had mirror parlors where you couldn't find the door for the mirrors, the one at Lulu White's costing thirty thousand dollars. Mirrors stood at the foot and head of all the beds. It was in these mansions that the best of the piano players worked.

Fond memories of vice districts typically emphasize sensuality, as well as visual and musical stimulation. The areas had an exotic appeal akin to that of a foreign country.[5]

Musicians and others who made a living in the District, of course, were not tourists with a temporary visa. Bands played in saloons and restaurants and pianists were most likely performed in brothels. Storyville historian Al Rose estimates that 214 jazz musicians performed in the District during its twenty-year life span. "On an average night . . . ," writes Rose, "Storyville employed about fifty musicians, including the solo piano players working the mansions and parlor houses." Most musicians worked for tips and still the piano "professors" could earn as much as a thousand dollars a week. Rose adds that although "jazz was not born in Storyville, many of its early greats flourished there," because of "steady employment."

In addition to the financial rewards of the District, Rose asserts that the musicians had "almost unlimited freedom to experiment and to work out stylistic qualities of their own in circumstances less demanding than those experienced by performers in other milieus." Musicians responded to patron requests, too, and a certain amount of performer-audience interaction took place, particularly when the pianists offered bawdy renditions of popular songs.[6]

Musicians saw a great deal of the trade that took place in saloons, dance halls, and brothels and many recalled the seamy side of the sporting life. Albert Glenny, for example, described "naked dances" that he accompanied at Lulu Whites's Mahogany Hall, and Jelly Roll Morton watched "uncultured things" from a slit in a screen at Emma Johnson's Studio. Some musicians became pimps themselves, and George "Pops" Foster claimed that they kept their music jobs because the "cops didn't want no man living off a woman; they wanted you to work."[7]

By the 1920s, Prohibition and other major Progressive moral crusades had tried to clean up vice districts. But drinking, prostitution, and gambling continued in most cities—often under the auspices of men with ties to organized crime. New York's Harlem took on a risqué reputation as it was the place to go for bootleg liquor and other entertainments. Restaurateurs, however, disassociated themselves from the entertainment business because of prohibited liquor sales and increased licensing restrictions following World War I. Establishments featuring nighttime amusements were often clustered together in easily identifiable parts of the city. Entertainment historian Lewis Erenberg writes that "adventurous urbanites could hie themselves to 'bohemian' Greenwich Village in New York . . . or up to 'darkest' Harlem, over to Culver City outside dry Los Angeles, or down to Chicago's Southside to return to a primitive Garden of Eden . . ." Revellers continued to find vice areas set aside from everyday life, and many of them hummed to the strains of jazz bands and orchestras.[8]

Jazz was played in several areas of Chicago and its suburbs, for example. Residential zoning laws designed to regulate commercial development and racial segregation often combined, however, and forced blacks and other inner-city residents to live in the same areas that supported vice. Geographically designated entertainment areas persisted in the twenties and often appeared to have a deviant ambience comparable to that of the old "districts" because of their gangster owners or their location in black neighborhoods.

For example, in Chicago the South Side neighborhood where most black-owned businesses were located was packed with entertainment. Willie "the Lion" Smith described the "Stroll," several blocks centered on State Street, where "You'd pass the Vendome Theatre, across the street from the Grand . . . it was the movie palace of the South Side. . . . And down near the corner of 35th and State was the New Monogram Theatre, the official Chicago house for the T.O.B.A. circuit." Smith also remembered the States Theatre, Lincoln, Owl, Indiana, Avenue, and the Peerless. His list of the "big-time" cabarets in the vicinity of 35th and State Sts. included the Elite No.2, Deluxe Gardens, Bill Bottom's Dreamland Cafe, Entertainer's Cafe, LaFerencia, Paradise Gardens, and the Sunset Cafe.[9]

Other musicians remember this as an area where music seemed to play continuously—a little bit like the New Orleans of

Danny Barker's youth. Eddie Condon said the "midnight air on
State Street was so full of music that if you held up an instrument
the breeze would play it." The music in the air was small consola-
tion to those black Chicagoans forced by segregation to live and
work in the same area as the vice district. "State Street was both
Wall Street and Broadway to the black community in the 20s,"
long-time resident Travis Dempsey recalled; "The white lights of
South Street went on after the red lights of New Orleans'
Storyville section went out in November, 1917."[10] Black Chicagoans had been forced to tolerate brothels and saloons long
before the closing of Storyville, according to a 1911 Chicago Vice
Commission report, and hostility toward interracial mingling in
the "black and tan" cabarets purportedly contributed to the 1919
race riots. Nevertheless, the population explosion that accompanied black migration to the area before and after World War I
made it seem like Storyville to Dempsey.[11]

Early twentieth-century New York, of course, had its share of
vice and entertainment. New Yorker James Weldon Johnson
patronized a typical "sporting house" and used it as a basis for
his description in the 1912 novel *The Autobiography of an Ex-
Coloured Man:*

> . . . in the basement of the house there was a Chinese restaurant.
> The Chinaman who kept it did an exceptionally good business; for
> chop suey . . . is a food that, somehow has the power of absorbing
> alcoholic liquors. . . . On the main floor there were two large rooms:
> a parlour about thirty feet in length, and a large, square back room
> into which the parlour opened. The floor of the parlour was car-
> peted; small tables and chairs were arranged about the room; the
> windows were draped with lace curtains, and the walls were literally
> covered with photographs or lithographs of every coloured man in
> America who had ever "done anything." . . . The floor was bare and
> the center was left vacant for singers, dancers, and others who enter-
> tained the patrons. In a closet in this room which jutted out into the
> hall the proprietor kept his buffet. There was no open bar, because
> the place had no liquor license. In this back room the tables were
> sometimes pushed aside, and the floor was given over to general
> dancing. The front room on the next floor was a sort of private
> party room; a back room on the same floor contained no furniture

and was devoted to the use of new and ambitious performers. In this room song and dance teams practiced their steps, acrobatic teams practiced their tumbles, and many other kinds of "acts" rehearsed their "turns." The other rooms of the house were used as sleeping apartments.[12]

Like many of the entrepreneurs in Storyville, this owner set up shop in a converted domestic residence—thus blurring the distinction between private, "domestic" space and public behavior. By the 1920s, "sporting houses" had largely given way to newer, more commercial performance environments (although not necessarily *better* ones) of the sort Cowley had in mind.

In New York several areas supported jazz music and many clubs were operated by Jewish, Italian, or Irish entrepreneurs with ties to organized crime. Harlem became the best known with clubs on Seventh Avenue, on 135th between Lenox and Fifth, in the "jungle alley" along 133rd Street, and elsewhere. The "jungle" was home to clubs like The Nest, Spider Webb's, Shim Sham, Basement Brownies, 101 Ranch, Catagonia, Orient, Livia's Blue Club, Green Cat, The Paradise Inn, Bamboo, Garden of Joy, Clam House, Club Swanee, Bucket of Blood, Baltimore, Hole in the Wall, Congo, Lenox Club, Saratoga, Yeah Man, Log Cabin, and the Oriental. Such clusters of clubs gave patrons several choices in a relatively small area as well as maintaining the aura of a "district."

Some Harlem clubs came from midtown Manhattan. Bank's, Barron's, Little Savoy, and Edmund Johnson's all relocated from the Tenderloin and San Juan Hill. The perception of Harlem as an after-hours pleasure capital for "slumming" adventurers points to its reputation as a marginal zone.

Broadway boasted club entertainers like Tex Guinan and Jimmy Durante. "Ragtime Jimmy" also performed in Brooklyn and Coney Island. One of the five Reisenweber restaurants, located on Columbus Circle, hosted the Original Dixieland Jass Band(ODJB) in late 1916 and early 1917. It was the band that introduced many white New Yorkers to jazz.

In Kansas City, political boss Tom Pendergast kept an old-time entertainment district going until well into the Depression. According to pianist Mary Lou Williams, there were fifty cabarets where live jazz was performed in a downtown area six blocks square. Jo Jones claimed you could hear music "twenty-four hours a day" because "practically all the little places had a piano and a set of drums." Kansas City jazz historian Ross Russell described "thirty-odd cabarets" where Kansas City jazz was played "during the good years" of the twenties and thirties. Russell named the clubs and their locations:

> The complex of nightclubs near the intersection of Twelfth and Paseo included the Sunset, Boulevard Lounge, Cherry Blossom, and Lone Star. In the Eighteenth and Paseo area were located the Panama, Subway, Lucille's Band Box, Elk's Rest, and Old Kentucky Bar-B-Que. Farther downtown, somewhat out of the district, in the vicinity of Twelfth and Cherry, were clustered the Reno, Amos and Andy, Greenleaf Gardens, and Hey Hay Club. Scattered throughout the general area were the College Inn . . . Bar Le Duc . . . Hole in the Wall . . . Hi Hat . . . Elmer Bean's Club . . . and Novelty Club. All were within walking distance of one another and were the best known. . . . Others in the area were the Vanity Fair. . . . Wolfe's Buffet, the Spinning Wheel, Hawaiian Gardens, Blue Hills Gardens, Hell's Kitchen, Jail and the Yellow Front Saloon.[13]

Russell pointed out that these were only a "fraction of the total number of nightclubs, bars, speakeasies, taverns, saloons, and music lounges" in Kansas City, but these were the ones where jazz was played. It also had stage shows "that rivalled Chicago's and New York's" at the Vanity Fair, Club Harlem, and the Cherry Blossom. Descriptions of Kansas City's musical atmosphere are similar to those of New Orleans, where music pervaded the Storyville district.

Before Prohibition, the West Coast had several famous vice districts including the Barbary Coast in San Francisco, and the Central Avenue area between 5th and 6th in Los Angeles. Performers played up and down the West Coast—often as part of the Pantages entertainment circuit. In Los Angeles, pianist Jelly Roll Morton led an early migration of New Orleans players to

Los Angeles, arriving in 1917. Before moving on in 1922 he had
played at the Cadillac on Central Avenue, which appears in
many reminiscences as the best early place in which to hear the
pre-World War I syncopated music that would become jazz. Morton also ran a dance hall briefly and, with Pops Woodward,
opened Wayside Park Café, where King Oliver was introduced
to the West Coast in 1922. Morton also invested in a gambling
place and pimped for a group of women he called the "Pacific
Coast Line."[14]

In the twenties, bands performed in Los Angeles hotels like
the Ambassador and in Central Avenue and Main Street locations, but a vehement Progressive campaign to enforce the
Volstead Act sent many music fans outside the city limits to the
row of clubs along Washington Boulevard in Culver City, and to
West Hollywood. Frank Sebastian's Cotton Club was especially
popular. Lawrence Brown recalled that the places still operating
on Central Avenue were small or located in private homes so
entertainment was restricted to a piano player at best.

In San Francisco, Purcell's Elite Cafe became what historian
Douglas Henry Daniels called the "most important Black night
spot on the west coast in the twentieth century." One of Purcell's
other clubs, the So Different Saloon, rivaled the roughest spots
in any other tenderloin. According to Daniels: "bouncers were
on hand to eject the rowdies as well as mere spectators. The
proprietor of Spider Kelley's, a place next door, reportedly lined
the back of his bar with iron boiler plates to keep the bullets shot
by Purcell's patrons from ripping through the walls." The Turkey Trot was reputed to have been invented there.[15]

In addition to these well-known entertainment neighborhoods in America's large cities, small tenderloins also provided
some limited exposure to jazz music. Willie "the Lion" Smith
played in the Atlantic City "Line," for example, which featured
the Boat House, Philadelphia House, New World, The Pekin,
and Kelley's Cafe. The Elephant Cafe, especially notable, because "the front of the cafe was fixed up to look like an elephant's ass and one entered by passing under a big long tail
hanging between the animal's legs."[16]

Opponents of jazz underscored the importance of its environment by lodging numerous complaints against the neighborhoods where it was played with policemen and relevant city authorities. As critics recognized, many jazz clubs were located in vice districts against which white and black reformers had crusaded without success.

Individual establishments within these geographically separate vice zones enhanced the communication of playful, exotic, and salacious themes through floor plans, decor, and activities. As we shall see, each entertainment spot could have distinctive environmental features, but taken collectively all of them represented a part of a special world set apart from everyday life, and primed for leisure, consumption, and sensual pleasures. Many of the smaller clubs reflected their seedy origins through their ties to the mobsters providing alcohol. But these same mobsters also bankrolled the largest and most respectable cabarets and clubs. In many cases, owners were continuing improvements begun by prewar cabaret owners and they hoped to attract a clientele from the respectable element that had discovered ragtime and jazz.

Changes in both the variety music theatre and black theatre were one source of white exposure to ragtime and jazz. In these locations, audiences found more active and participatory entertainment than was available to them in the circus, melodrama, or concert hall. Beginning in the 1890s, minstrel and "Tom shows" had been replaced by all-black musical theatre and vaudeville companies like *Black Patti's Troubadours*. These shows often featured ragtime and early jazz music.

Troupes like the *Troubadours* signaled their departure from earlier black theatre formats. These all-black shows featured black musicians—performers who did not appear in black-face makeup—and beautifully dressed women. The *Troubadours* broke with the tradition of completing a show by featuring a cakewalk, and chose to spotlight Sisieretta Jones's arias instead. Shows like Bob Cole's 1898 production *A Trip to Coontown* and musicals like *The Creole Show* (1891) and *The South Before the Civil*

War, The Octoroons (1896) likewise eliminated some of—but not all—the demeaning aspects of minstrelsy. The public derisively labeled them "coon shows" and the ragtime music they featured as "coon songs." Although whites were exposed to black music through these theatrical ventures, the racist stereotypes remained intact.[17]

Langston Hughes believed shows like *Black Patti's Troubadours* benefited black performers because they "laid the groundwork for public acceptance of the Negro women and of the Negro male on stage in other than burlesque fashion." Talented songwriters and instrumentalists like Will Marion Cook and J. Rosamond Johnson adapted ragtime and other Afro-American music to Broadway theatrical formats in these shows. In the 1920s, numerous black musical comedies hit Broadway, led by Eubie Blake and Noble Sissle's *Shuffle Along.* Blake believed these shows further exposed white producers as well as audiences to black musical skills.[18]

By 1900, vaudeville supplanted minstrel and variety shows as staples of white variety theatre entertainment. Circuits like Keith, Proctor, Considine, and Pantages brought singers, dancers, and comedians to new audiences. One method of attracting the middle class was to construct vaudeville "palaces," designed as "temples to conspicuous consumption," according to vaudeville historian Albert McClean, that were marked by marvels such as "a dozen large electrical lamps . . . placed along the arch and also high among the pilasters and gargoyles of the second and third story façade."[19]

Immigrant assimilation was also facilitated by vaudeville, according to McLean, because the wealth and opulence of the vaudeville palaces made it possible for newcomers to share vicariously in the American success myth. In the new century, however, the vaudeville audience looked elsewhere for entertainment. Some patrons switched their allegiance to movie palaces, while others sought out the more mysterious and dangerous cabaret and dance hall—both designed to encourage participation as well as observation. Jazz proved the perfect music for these locations.[20]

Restaurant owners may have benefited from what the vaudeville entrepreneurs lost. Restaurateurs introduced dancing and floor shows into their establishments, which would inspire similar changes in the nightclub and cabaret. Eateries featuring nightly entertainment displaced the popular "lobster palaces" like Murray's Roman Gardens in New York. Erenberg attributes this transformation to the changing tastes of New York's bourgeoisie. Specifically, Erenberg argues that in the first decade of the new century, middle-class diners rejected the formal "palaces" and chose instead informal restaurants offering intimate and active settings. Cabaret owners drew their ideas not only from the increased legitimacy of public dancing, but also from the bohemian Parisian cabaret and the American dive.[21]

Introducing live performances into restaurants significantly altered the physical features and design of entertainment environments. Respectable cabarets opened "atop hotels or theatres" to distinguish them from a cheap underground bar. "Indulging in these pleasures no longer required venturing beneath the street," according to Erenberg. "That which had been permitted only in the dark now did not seem so wicked. The cabaret had made a symbolic evolution from a hidden aspect of life to one accepted as a phenomenon of human existence." Other aspects of cabaret interiors made it possible, however, to evoke some of the mysterious intimacy of older saloons or clubs. Restaurant owners created "action environments" by clearing out areas to use for patron dancing and professional entertainers. Patrons found themselves seated on the same level as the show because the barrier normally provided by a proscenium stage had been removed. Obstructive pillars or potted palms also gave way to the desire for maximum floor visibility. This transference of "performance from the theatre stage to the floor proved a novel experience for patrons accustomed to the formal distances of theatre entertainment."[22]

Restaurant owners were primarily motivated by financial concerns. They wanted to attract more customers, but they did not want to make large investments of capital in theatre stages. They could also avoid theatre licensing fees since dining continued to be the primary—or at least stated—function of these establishments. Nevertheless, a wide variety of entertainment, including dancing, musical acts, comedy and theatrical revues eventually appeared on the cabaret floor. The participatory environments of the old dives and honky-tonks began to lose their dangerous associations as cabaret owners sought middle-class audiences.[23]

These new cabarets promoted a version of participatory performance because patrons shared the entertainment space with performers. Vernon and Irene Castle entered the floor from the tables in the audience, for example, thus using proximity to add excitement and informality to their dance routines. Comedians assimilated unsuspecting audience members in their acts, although at least some of the "unsuspecting" diners may have been plants. Managers encouraged participation by providing noisemakers to the audience. One cabaret owner revealed his unsympathetic view of jazz by posting a sign encouraging patrons to bang their "knives, forks, and plates," to "make their own jazz" if the band went on strike.[24]

Placing tables alongside the cabaret floor made it possible not only for the audience to see and feel a part of the performance, but performers could also move through the tables to the audience. This practice had been standard among black blues and jazz singers. Alberta Hunter remembered how this worked at the Dreamland in Chicago: "Singers then would go around from table to table singin' to each table, hustlin' dollars in tips. But nobody at the other tables would get mad when they couldn't hear you. I made a lot of money that way."

Both Lawrence Brown and Garvin Bushell remembered certain advantages that came from this arrangement. Brown played at the Club Alabam in Los Angeles and he said band members played individual solos at tables, too. Similarly, Bushell described the kind of influence this had on the musicians accompanying the vocalists: "Most cabarets had a five piece band and seven or eight singers. The singer would sing one chorus at each table and would make every table in the joint. If you didn't know the song when she started, you would by the time she'd completed her rounds. The pianists could improvise very well; for one thing, they got a lot of practice, working from 9:00 p.m. to 6:00 a.m."[25]

Respectable cabarets discouraged tip solicitation, presumably because of its association with prostitution in old-time saloons. But this technique of interaction still served as one model for cabaret entertainment. When the most ambitious cabarets introduced Broadway revues and chorine acts into their clubs, the chorus girls might circulate through the audience as part of a song and dance routine. Although they collected no tips, acts like the Balloon Girls from Ziegfeld's Midnight Frolic "moved among tables, allowing men with cigars and cigarettes to pop the balloons" attached to their costumes. Other acts featured chorus girls who "fished" from a platform atop the diners by letting down their fishing line into the tables below.[26]

For some critics, provocative behavior from scantily clad chorus girls proved the cabaret had not sufficiently broken with its dubious origins. "To a public accustomed to the old and well-recognized pitfalls—the saloon the brothel—the cabaret was a new and more intriguing form of moral hazard," a 1933 study of *Vice in Chicago* pointed out. Warnings failed to prevent many middle-class pleasure-seekers from embracing the new entertainment. The earlier legitimization of vaudeville, musical theatre, dancing, and black theatre had prepared white audiences for experiments in cabaret entertainment.[27]

Many of the dangerous or disreputable connotations of the cabaret were modified or eliminated in the development of new middle-class nighttime amusements before World War I. Erenberg suggests that the cabaret ceased to represent bohemia: "rather than being a rejection of the values of success, the cabaret was pictured as its reward." With the advent of Prohibition in the twenties, unfortunately, many clubs and cabarets no longer proved financially viable. White audiences seeking participatory and intimate evening entertainment were often limited to vice districts where blacks lived and worked, and where "successful" club owners were often connected to organized crime through bootlegging. In these predominantly black neighborhoods, jazz was bolder and closer in performance style to its Afro-American origins.[28]

A good example of the polite jazz whites were accustomed to hearing is provided by New York jazz historians Samuel Charters and Leonard Kunstadt:

> The New York cabaret musicians were playing songs, with a single melodic line usually played by the violin. Ensemble arrangements were usually simple harmonizations of the melodic lead. The orchestrations were published for full orchestra, usually eleven pieces, but the publishing houses were aware that there were few cabarets or dining rooms that could hire an eleven piece orchestra. The music was scored so that almost any kind of small ensemble could play it. The first violin, clarinet, and flute parts were usually identical, with the same melody sketched into the piano part in case the orchestra dwindled to one musician. Since the cornet wasn't used much, the cornet part was secondary. . . . Often the trombone part simply doubled the cello part. . . . It was this music, with its single melody and simple orchestrations, that was the stylistic source of the New York syncopated orchestra.[29]

The syncopated orchestra soon competed with New Orleans, Chicago, Kansas City, and New York jazz musicians who performed much hotter, unpredictable, and swinging music. Whites, however, would have to venture away from society cabarets and go "slumming" in Harlem or Chicago's South Side to hear it. And that is what they began to do in the 1920s.

Descriptions of twenties nightclubs and cabarets indicate that many of the characteristics of the levee and the dive never left the older tenderloin district cabarets and saloons. Although some clubs were owned by "legitimate" businessmen, most were not. Prohibition favored the bootlegger and his speakeasies, thus accentuating the association of jazz with illicit activities. Gangster club owners lent an aura of mystery and excitement to their establishments, which intrigued the adventurous. (Patrons of the prestigious clubs were protected by their disreputable hosts from any truly threatening experiences.) Clubs that allowed both black and white patrons were criticized for fostering miscegenation and racial violence, prompting many to maintain a racially exclusive policy to avoid trouble from patrons and/or the police.

Nightclubs, cabarets, and speakeasies continued to offer intimate opportunities for hearing music. In Chicago you could visit "gin-soaked little joints" like the Sunset Cafe, the Plantation, the Dreamland, the Panama, the DeLuxe, the Fiume, and the Elite. Typically, musicians entertained the guests and provided music for dancing. These places did seem a bit different from the earlier corner saloon with dancing in the back. Louis Armstrong had grown up in New Orleans's ragged Third Ward and compared it with the clubs he later saw up north:

> . . . Every corner had a saloon and honky-tonk in the rear . . . They call them lounges up North. Of course, those honky-tonks weren't as elaborate either. . . . But I'm just trying to give a fast picture of how a lounge would look in the rough without all of that swell ta doo stuff they put in nowadays. Decorately speaking—[ellipses in the original].[30]

Despite the cleaner decor of new (or improved) clubs, an environment conducive to participatory entertainment was created through names, decor, seating arrangements, and floor shows or other kinds of live entertainment. Chicago pianist Art Hodes describes a typical Chicago "cafe": "If it was a real class spot, it sported a five-piece band and an intermission piano player and singers. A floor show would consist of an M.C., a line of girls, the singers in the place—the band was strictly for background and a little dancing." Kid Ory described the Plantation Club in Chicago as "about 25 years ahead of its time" because it was "nice-looking . . . had good acoustics . . . a nice bandstand . . . and nice rugs on the floor."[31]

A popular Chicago jazz club, the Dusty Bottom, took its name from its unique physical features. It featured a Sunday afternoon dance "under a large tent, in the middle of which was placed a wooden floor, but around this floor there was only earth, and there was such an amount of dust kicked up that, by the end of the afternoon, the feet and the bottoms of the pants of the dancers were covered with dust." Pianists at the Dusty

Bottom were very loud in order to carry over the open air. Chicago's Subway Club was placed in sightseeing trips and the tourists were warned to watch their valuables before entering. George Lugg said the club definitely resembled a subway with "catacomb-like alcoves and passageways." A "cafe" could be quite large. Frank Sebastian's Cotton Club in Culver City, California, was the "only cafe in the world with three dance floors . . ." according to its publicity copy, and it featured "dancers, singers, actors, and entertaineners."[32]

Kansas City was well known for its intense and long-lasting jam sessions that took place in the "small, intimate type of club." Like Chicago's gin mills, these places had a "decor" that "was the product of the owner's imagination." Customers sat on bales of hay in some establishments and in one the bandstand was made up out of an old antique huckster's wagon.

Kansas City clubs, except "the largest and most elegant" had a kitty, which Russell describes as "a large metal can surmounted by such original shapes as cats, tigers, spooks, or pickaninnies, all with grinning mouths and sometimes electric lighting systems that produced winking eyes—the idea to encourage customers to throw coins (happily folded money) into the receptacle." Some clubs, notably the Reno, had back areas where prostitutes plied their trade and took tricks upstairs into their quarters above the club. Gambling dens were also located close by.[33]

In New York's Greenwich Village the "nightclubs capitalized on the area's bohemian reputation," according to Erenberg. Cafe Montmarte, for example, used "red table cloths, spiderwebs in the corners, and wine bottles on the tables to create a Parisian atmosphere." The Plantation Club took its inspiration from the minstrel stage and surrounded patrons with "log cabins, Negro mammies, picket fences around the dance floor, a twinkling summer sky, and a watermelon moon. Aunt Jemima herself stood in one of the cabins flipping flapjacks." The search for exotica was easily transferred to Harlem, where the number of clubs expanded dramatically during the 1920s.[34]

One section of Harlem along 133rd and on Lenox Avenue described previously as a "jungle alley," got its name because of the astonishing number of clubs located there. But the idea for a "jungle" may well have come from the earlier black section of Hell's Kitchen, which James P. Johnson described as "the toughest part of New York. There were two or three killings a night." Willie "the Lion" Smith concurred in his description of an early Hell's Kitchen saloon:

> The saloons all had "Family Entrances." Inside, each one had a long bar, sawdust on the floor, and the familiar round-top beer tables with pretzel backed chairs. All around the place were shining brass cuspidors with a sign over them on the wall reading, DON'T SPIT AT EM, SPIT IN EM. . . . . . . Against the side wall opposite the bar would be an old upright piano, sometimes flanked by a Regina music box . . . The walls would be covered with pictures of naked queens and . . . all the big time prize fighters."[35]

In 1913, Johnson performed at "Drake's Dancing Class," which he called the "Jungles Casino." Since it was hard for blacks to get a dance-hall license, Johnson said they resorted to the dance-school ruse.

The Casino was certainly an unusual looking dancing school. It was in a cellar "without fixings." Guests could "stash their liquor" in a nearby coal bin if "the cops came." Johnson remembered that: "There were dancing classes all right, but no dancing teachers. The pupils danced sets, two-steps, waltzes. schottisches, and the 'Metropolitan Glide'."[36] Harlem's 1920s jungle alley had few dancing schools like the Jungles Casino. Instead, the clubs ranged from large enterprises to small after-hours bars. But it may well have benefited from the notoriety of the earlier establishments.

By contrast, Baron Wilkins opened Harlem's Executive Club, which became one of the area's most exclusive spots. Wilkins served a predominantly white and light-skinned black clientele and many sports and entertainment stars. Smith said you could tell that it was a "high class" place because Wilkins forbade the removal of dresses and underwear—an old bawdy house trick. On weekends tuxedos and other formal attire were required.[37]

One of the most popular clubs was Small's Paradise, located

underground at 2294½ Seventh Avenue. Harlem clubs may have operated in basements to keep their owners free from complaints by people living nearby. Willie "the Lion" Smith said that "Irish cops patrolling the neighborhood were afraid to venture down the dark stairways for fear they wouldn't get back up in one piece during Prohibition." Small's Paradise had waiters who roller-skated between tables and it was considered one of the hottest clubs in New York. Patrons reserved their seats by the year, according to Dicky Wells, and "all the waiters danced with their trays, and they put on a little show by themselves." Locating nightclubs and cabarets in cellars reversed the earlier trend aimed at disassociation with the tenderloin atmosphere.[38]

Small's was especially popular as an after-hours place. Jazz aficionado John Hammond gave this detailed description of the advantages of Small's over two of the other leading Harlem night spots—Connie's Inn and the Cotton Club:

> You went downstairs, under a modest marquee, into a standard night-club setup; a room holding about two hundred and fifty persons, with a bar at one end, a bandstand at the other, and banquettes against the wall surrounding a dance floor. Ed [Small] had a line of girls—dark-skinned; the Cotton Club and Connie's Inn catered to whites and featured light-skinned Negroes—and had original music written for his shows. He served good Chinese food, another plus. Connie's had no kitchen and the Cotton club menu was bad and expensive.[39]

A place like Small's became an institution and its appeal included the possibility of meeting the rich and famous.

One estimate suggests there were eleven "premiere" black and white clubs in Harlem featuring jazz, as well as theatres and ballrooms. Many clubs catered to white patrons looking for "exotica" in Harlem, although at least one reporter from *Variety* complained in 1926 that the "Black Belt" was not "a wild place at night." Small's was the only place in which he found white patrons and he concluded: "The Black and Tans are staged for the whites, like Paris is staged for the Americans."[40]

Perhaps the *Variety* reporter had visited Pod and Jerry's,

where Danny Barker witnessed a classic performance designed for the slummers from downtown:

> New York clubs were the haunts of crafty night people. They used to put on the act: set a trap to catch the day nine to five people. I first saw the drama cleverly enacted at the old Nest Club, where there was not much action until after the big joints closed at the curfew time—3 a.m. Some officials were paid off and the after-hours joints stayed open until after daylight, not bothered by the police. It was a night when the place was empty. Everybody sat around like half asleep. [When the doorman rang the buzzer,] it meant some live prosperous looking people, a party, were coming in.
>
> Like jacks out of a box the band struck up *Lady Be Good.* Everybody went into action; the band swinging, waiters beating on trays, everybody smiling and moving, giving the impression the joint was jumping. . . . The unsuspecting party entered amid finger-popping and smiling staff . . . This was kept up until the party was seated and greeted and their orders taken. Then on came the singers, smiling and moving; then another singer, a dancer. Then it was off to the races—action—"Let's get this money . . .".[41]

Black vaudeville, minstrelsy, and other kinds of staged performances had prepared white audiences for the kind of act described above. As historian Nathan Huggins notes, the persistence among whites of stereotypes about black entertainment may have trapped both blacks and whites in roles that were not "authentic" but staged. In these cases, jazz performance became part of a contrived tradition.[42]

New York's Cotton Club probably put on the most lavish and well-known "exotic" shows. Like many large clubs, the Cotton Club was laid out with two levels of seating around the dance and/or stage floor. It originated as the Douglas Casino in 1918. By the time mobster Owney Madden and his backers opened it in 1923, the Club seated 700 patrons on "two levels" with "some tables surrounding a dance floor in front of a proscenium stage." There were also tables in the back and along the walls. Connie's Inn, another prestigious and expensive club, had a round performance space surrounded by tables all on one level. Both featured elaborate floor shows.[43]

The Cotton Club used graphics patterned after African sculpture or interspersed with palm trees and bongo drums. The entrées were supposed to represent exotic cuisines from China, Mexico, and "Harlem" (chicken and ribs). Performers wore revealing shirts with palm adornments. One act used women with bongo drums attached to their bodies. When Duke Ellington opened there in 1927, his promoter, Irving Mills, encouraged him to lead a "jungle band." Some observers recalled a different set at the Cotton Club, which was a ". . . replica of a Southern mansion with large white columns and a backdrop painted with weeping willows and slave quarters. . . . The entire scene created a *Gone with the Wind* atmosphere."[44]

The gyrations of the dancers and the rhythmically exciting Ellington music were supposed to provide primitive entertainment to the Cotton Club's white patrons. But the size and physical structure of the club does not suggest that it encouraged participation as much as voyeurism. Patrons assumed they were part of the emotionally unrestrained practice of black music and dance when in fact they observed carefully orchestrated floor shows. Jimmy Durante explained that for some members of the audience, that was sufficient: "It isn't necessary to mix with colored people if you don't feel like it. But it's worth seeing. How they step." Participation at the Cotton Club was quite stylized and white patrons entertained themselves by watching blacks be "primitive"—without sharing their enjoyment with black patrons.[45]

Performers could introduce an element of spontaneity in their carefully choreographed acts. Percussionist Sonny Greer described a routine he used to relax singer Ivie Anderson on stage:

> She was singing a song . . . real good, "I'm a little blackbird looking for a bluebird, too" and in back of all them drums, I raised up and said "Don't look no further, baby I'm right here." And the house caved. It shocked her so much, she damned near forgot the lyrics, so the house caved in . . .

Exchanges like these could then become part of the act, and Greer recalled other instances in which he and Anderson bantered back and forth—much to the audience's delight. Historian James Lincoln Collier points out that this kind of theatrical trick could be important to a band's success: ". . . in the early period, when records were strictly a side matter to musicians, the success or failure of a band depended on how audiences reacted to them in cabarets, dance halls, and theatres." Dicky Wells remembered gimmicks created with elaborate props. While playing in Charlie Johnson's Chocolate Dandies band, Wells and the other band members met the crowd by emerging out of a giant chocolate box.[46]

Clubs built for large crowds provided a wide-open space for jazz. The Panama, had an "upstairs and a downstairs," and five girls and a piano player performed on each level. Alberta Hunter recalled a range of entertainment brought under one roof at the Panama: "Now the downstairs at the Panama was more of a quiet reserved type of entertainment. But upstairs it was rougher. Upstairs, we had Mamie Carter, a dancer, the "shake" kind, and Twinkle Davis who danced and sang . . . Then there was Nellie Carr who sang and did splits, Goldie Crosby, and myself".[47] A club designed like the Panama would not focus patrons' attention on one activity or performer and patrons might have a greater choice of entertainment.

Similarly, when King Joe Oliver brought his band to the Lincoln Gardens in 1923, it could hold up to 1000 patrons. Oliver's Creole Jazz Band featuring Honore Dutrey, Baby Dodds, Louis Armstrong, Lil Hardin, Bill Johnson, and Johnny Dodds attracted huge crowd nightly. The Lincoln Gardens size provided a great space for astonished listeners to hear the frenetic New Orleans sound. Among the occasional white patrons at the Gardens was aspiring jazz musician Eddie Condon, who described the explosive combination of the music and its location:

> In the cubicle outside where we paid admission the sound was loud; it came like a muscle flexing regularly, four to the bar. As the door opened the trumpets, King and Louis one or both, soared above everything else. The whole joint was rocking. Tables, chairs, walls, people, moved with the rhythm. It was dark, smoky, gin-smelling. People in the balcony leaned over and their drinks spilled on the

customers below. There was a false-ceiling made of chicken wire covered with phony maple leaves; the real roof was twenty five feet up. A round, glass bowl hung from the middle of the chicken wire; when the blues were played it turned slowly and a baby spot light worked over it. . . . There was a place near the band reserved for musicians who came to listen and to learn; we sat there, stiff with education, joy and a licorice-tasting gin purchased from the waiters for $2 a pint. You could bring your own but it didn't matter much; in the end the effect was the same—the band played Froggie Moore, Chimes Blues, Sweet Baby Doll, Jazzin' Babies Blues, Mabel's Dream, Room Rent Blues, High Society Rag, Where Did You Stay Last Night, Working Man Blues, and everything and everybody moving slid-ing,tapping out the rhythm, inhaling the smoke, swilling the gin.[48]

Another musician remembered that the "chicken wire was the only artificial thing in the place," and that performers felt the Lincoln Gardens "was informal and if the boys in the band wanted to take their coats off and really get comfortable they did."[49]

This sampling of jazz performance locations shows that each created a setting that differed from the outside world, and one in which audiences felt they might participate in the creation of musical entertainment. Names like the Cotton Club, Plantation Club, Club Alabam, and the Panama indicated worlds geographi-cally separate from the North and East, and culturally unfamiliar to many whites. A "nest" or a "hole in the wall" promised intimacy while a "web" denoted both seduction and immobility. Although many of the fancy clubs tried to move out of the cellar and base-ment to attract a new crowd, several of the most successful did not. "Action environments" could be planned or evolve on their own, but in either case, a patron could take the opportunity to perform publicly or witness behavior that was typically "off limits" in the course of a "normal" day. When combined with other primi-tive or exotic trappings on the interior, these locations offered at least the possibility for adventure and intrigue.

Several new ballrooms also provided exciting opportunities to hear jazz in the twenties. Like the nightclub or cabaret, some dancing establishments had seedy origins. Indeed, one of the first new opportunities for participatory entertainment was provided by the public dance hall, which was often connected to a saloon and frequented by amateur or professional prostitutes. Halls were also rented by social clubs, particularly in New Orleans, and the bandstands were sometimes located up near the ceiling.[50]

The taxi dance hall was the target of many reformers in their larger crusade against the brothel and saloon. For example, the 1911 Chicago Vice Commission Report complained: "In many cases public dancing halls are located in the same buildings with saloons . . . the dancers have been seen to frequent the rear room of saloons." Buck Clayton described how one worked in Los Angeles. Clayton played one 32-bar song during each dance: "It was the beginning and the end of a song . . . we would go from one song right into another. Play one chorus of this. As soon as we switched songs, that's another dime for the house and for the girl." Based on the evidence collected by reformers and government agencies, licensing legislation was successfully used to separate the dance hall from the saloon by restricting the sale of liquor, licensing owners, and arresting or discouraging "undesirable characters." In addition, the dancing public apparently became more particular about their musical tastes and increasingly requested specific bands.[51]

The Grand Central Palace in New York was a good example of the new style of ballroom. It opened in 1911 and attracted thousands of dancers who would never have frequented a disreputable or unsafe saloon or club. Municipal dance halls were opened in many places to provide wholesome alternatives to the old dance hall. Cafes and cabarets offered afternoon dances called "*thé dansants*" or "*tango teas,*" which quickly attracted unescorted upper- and middle-class women. Jazz bands found new opportunities for work in all these dancing establishments, as musicians like James Reese Europe introduced both jazz and jazz dances to New York's affluent society in these new locations.[52]

Ballrooms encouraged improvisation and variety among performers and patrons. Some acts combined music, comedy, and dance—much like a theatre revue. Louis Armstrong provided

one of the richest descriptions of the lively nature of a twenties
ballroom jazz performance:

> The Sunset had Charleston contests on Friday night and you
> couldn't get into the place unless you got there early. We had a great
> show in those days with Buck 'n' Bubbles, Rector and Cooper, Edith
> Spencer and Mae Alix, my favorite entertainer, and a gang of now
> famous stars. We had a finale that just wouldn't quit.
>
> The Charleston was popular at the time until Percy Venable, the
> producer of the show, staged a finale with four of us band boys
> closing the show doing the Charleston. That was really something.
> There was Earl Hines, as tall as he is; and Tubby Hall, as fat as he
> was, little Joe Walker, as short of he is; and myself, as fat as I was at
> that time. We would stretch out across that floor doing the Charles-
> ton as fast as the music would play it. Boy, oh boy, you talking about
> four cats picking them up and laying them down—that was us. . . .
>
> On the drums in this orchestra was my boy, Zutty Singleton. We
> would play an overture and then run into a hot tune. Sometimes
> Zutty and I would do a specialty number together. . . . Zutty, he's a
> funny guy anyway, would dress up as one of those real loud and
> rough gals, with a short skirt, and a pillow in back of him. I was
> dressed in rags, the beak of my cap turned around like a tough guy,
> and he, or she [Zutty] was my gal.[53]

Armstrong's act combined dance and vaudeville comedy with
jazz music. The playful quality of his stage antics encouraged
audience participation and established an expectation of spontaneity rather than a rehearsed act.

In New York, dancers had hundreds of ballrooms to choose
from. The Roseland featured jazz, as did the Cinderella, where
the Wolverines played. At the Renaissance, described as a "red
brick building with Arabic decor," Fletcher Henderson played to
packed houses. The Manhattan Casino held 6000 dancers when
full. Eddie Barefield recalls playing in many ballrooms because
"in those days there was a ballroom every place you went, they
had a ballroom and a house band. And the road bands would
come in and play opposite them in 15-minute sets. Usually the
dances were from 8:30 to 11:30.[54]

Harlem's newest ballroom also featured Henderson's orchestra when it opened in 1926. The New York *Age* announced that the block-long Savoy was superior to all other uptown ballrooms. It had a "spacious lobby set off by a marble staircase and cut glass chandelier" and a hall "decorated in a color scheme of orange and blue." The Savoy's size allowed for a 200-foot-long dance floor and ample seating for observers. There were two band-stands that facilitated battles for the dancers' acclaim—bucking contests survived in this swank new ballroom.[55]

A participatory dynamic continued even here between the bands and dancers and led both to new dances and to new jazz styles. Dancers competed just as musicians did, and created many steps that would be known by their Savoy origins. Jean and Marshall Stearns described the rich "routine" of the Savoy: "Saturday was known as Squares' Night, because everyone squeezed into the ballroom and there was no room for great dancing." Monday (ladies' night) and Thursday (domestic service workers') were the least crowded. Tuesday was reserved for expert dancers only.[56]

Star dancers improvised from each other—much as tap dancers competed at the Hoofer's Club. Shorty Snowden claimed credit for inventing the Lindy during a dance marathon at the Manhattan Casino. "I was really doing the regular steps, just like we did them at the Savoy, several of us, only maybe a little faster," recalled Snowden. "I used to dance seven complete choruses of 'Bugle Blues' or 'Tiger Rag' in a minute and three quarters." During one of his fast-paced routines, Snowden executed a breakaway that so impressed onlookers that he was pressed to name it. Thus the Lindy or Jitterbug was born.[57]

Snowden and other frequent dancers staked out a section of the ballroom called Cat's Corner for themselves. Interlopers were discouraged with Charleston kicks to their shins. The dancers required jazz that was fast and always changing—like their steps. In the late twenties and thirties, swing bands in particular perfected their sound through interaction with the dancers. The Stearnses explained that "swing music and the Lindy flowed more horizontally and smoothly" than New Orleans jazz. "Swing music and the Lindy were more complicated," according to them, "for while a Lindy team often danced together during the opening ensembles of a big band, they tended to go into a break-away and improvise individual steps when the band arrangements led into a solo."[58]

The ballroom environment clearly perpetuated this kind of participatory practice. The space was large and not bounded by tables or other obstacles. Entrance fees to ballrooms were modest and few Harlemites found the Savoy prohibitive. The bands were also not restricted by formal programs or routines.

Improvisation also characterized the performances in more secluded clubs and private locations. Like Kansas City, New York had many clubs noted for their after-hours jam sessions. Musicians hung out at the Rhythm Club waiting for work offers, and, as Duke Ellington described, others roamed from club to club looking for a chance to play: "And at night everybody used to carry their horns around with them and wherever there was a piano you'd find hornblowers sitting in and jamming." Dicky Wells provided a memorable account of the cutting contests at the Hoofer's Club.

> They sent out these cards—"You Are Invited To a Trombone Sup-per, or a Saxophone Supper." The Hoofer's Club was below Big John's bar, in an empty hall he rented for these sessions, mostly at weekends. Anyone could go, but mostly performers went, mostly musicians. There was no admission charge, and we weren't paid. No money was involved at all. . . . All musicians would be sitting around the walls, all around the dance floor, maybe there would be forty guys sitting around there. The floor was for dancers only, and they would be cutting each other, too, while we were cutting each other on the in-struments. Everybody would be blowing—maybe six trombones. . . . changing keys and going on, everything happening. You'd stomp your foot or hold up your hand if you wanted another chorus.

Like the pre-World War I Clef Club, places like the Rhythm and Hoofer's Club provided musicians with much-valued opportunities to escape the public eye, relax, and perform for each other.[59]

Private rent parties provided other more intimate opportunities for musicians and their audiences. Langston Hughes described typical ones in his autobiography *The Big Sea:* "The Saturday night rent parties that I attended," he wrote, "were often more amusing than any nightclub, in small apartments where God knows who lived—because the guests seldom did—but where the piano would be augmented by a guitar, or an odd cornet, or somebody with a pair of drums walking in off the street." The party hosts and hostesses sold or furnished bootleg liquor, fried fish and chitterlings, and the festivities lasted until dawn. Legendary performers, including Duke Ellington, James P. Johnson, Willie "the Lion" Smith, Fats Waller, and Eubie Blake, were especially welcome.[60]

Smith believed rent parties began as parlor socials put on to raise money for the preacher, and Johnson remembered being asked to play before the war: "Most people who had pianos couldn't play them, so a piano player was important socially . . . if you could play piano good, you went from one party to another and everybody made a fuss about you and fed you." Pianists often called these affairs "jumps or shouts" according to Smith, terms derived from the communal tradition of Afro-American sacred shouts. Southern social and benevolent clubs in cities like New Orleans also raised money through fish fries, so migrants found rent parties a new variation on old sacred and secular themes.[61]

Performers might hit several parties in an evening. Eddie Barefield recalled that in Chicago he might attend ten or fifteen in one weekend. He and a man teaching him to play "got paid a dollar and plate of food like [chitlins] or fried chicken. . . ." Barefield and his friend were also allowed to make "three passes on the crap table . . . By that we would make ourselves five or six maybe ten dollars in each place."[62]

Some apartment owners discovered that the rent parties could become good business. Bernice Gore, an immigrant from Bermuda, explained that she "thought rent parties were disgraceful" until her husband ran off and left her "with a sixty-dollar-a-month apartment on my hands, and no job, I soon learned, like everyone else, to rent my rooms out and throw these Saturday get-togethers." Gore and her boarders provided "corn liquor," gambling, and sex to Saturday-night revellers.

Willie "the Lion" Smith described how some entrepreneurs like Gore advertised their amusements: "It got to be a big business. They would advertise a house-rent party in advance and have circulars printed up and distributed around the neighborhood telling who would be playing and entertaining at the party." Rent parties provided a chance for black New Yorkers to relax and party with the same musicians they might not be able to see in a segregated or high-priced club.[63] For musicians and their audiences, informal settings often promised "carving battles" and impromptu dance contests. The entertainment was lively and unpredictable—and flaunted the possibility of a police raid. Fats Waller's composition "The Joint Is Jumpin' " ends with a reference to the sirens coming to break up the party.

In Chicago, Kansas City, and New York the range of performance environments featuring jazz increased during the 1920s. Sociologists and other contemporary observers calculated their numbers as part of their reform efforts. One study recorded "12,000 night spots" operating in Chicago. New York granted 800 licenses for cabarets and 500 for dance halls. "Estimates for speakeasies, blinds and unlicensed clubs [varied]," according to Ronald Morris, "from 5,000 to 10,000." A survey conducted for *Social Forces* magazine concluded in 1925 that "over 14% of the men in Manhattan and 10% of its women attended dance halls and cabarets three times weekly; and that the number of dance palaces had increased 60% over those of a few years earlier."[64]

Even if these estimates are exaggerated, the number of clubs and cabarets seemed on the rise in the urban North. Jazz, moreover, was introduced to theatres, ballrooms, and scores of other new establishments patronized by whites as well as blacks. The introduction of jazz "wasn't just an innovation," wrote Jimmy Durante, "it was a revolution."[65]

The "revolution" in music accompanied equally dramatic changes in middle-class social mores that were reflected in (and encouraged by) changes in the settings for performance. The entrepreneurs who ran clubs and restaurants catering to whites experimented with seating, floor design, and decoration aimed at creating relaxed performance atmospheres, as well as marketing gimmicks. "Action environments" tantalized middle-class audiences for whom leisure time was an "escape [from] many of the limitations and controls of nineteenth century society, culture, and institutional identity."[66]

White patrons danced and watched the floor shows and revues typical of these cabarets, but remained safe and sheltered from the unrestricted nightlife of the Panama or the Jungles Casino. Fantasy worlds of pirates, plantations, and bohemian Paris may have overdetermined the mood of a cabaret by restricting both imagination and behavior. White patrons, who came from backgrounds very different from those of black performers, may not have known how to respond without strong visual and environmental cues. The gap between the Cotton Club and the rent party was more than racial—it was a gulf separating a participatory culture and a counterfeit one.[67]

Locations that were still "in the rough," as Louis Armstrong put it, continued to provide less-controlled and regulated settings for jazz. Ballrooms, multifloored jazz houses, and some of the more traditional nightclubs were conducive to improvisation and spontaneous audience-performer interactions. The unpredictable mix of musicians, guests, dancers, and bathtub gin provided more variety than Ziegfeld, with half the artifice. Recent migrants found clubs, ballrooms, and rent parties represented an important connection with their past. These were performance milieus that few whites would ever see in the 1920s. The spread of jazz to legitimate clubs helped reduce opposition to the music; but it strengthened at the same time a sense of jazz "taking over" or "infecting" American life.

Characteristic settings and locations infuriated jazz detractors, pleased patrons, and stimulated jazz performance. Large and exciting cabarets and ballrooms promised variety and stimulation to their clientele. Smaller cabarets and clubs enabled people to eat, drink, dance, and mingle in sensuous, intimate, and womblike environs. Club names and decor reflected stylish, "primitive," and exotic themes. The interiors—large or small, lavish or modest—all provided a clear contrast to the streets outside. While small tables around the dance and revue floors removed important barriers to performer-audience interactions, rent and other private parties offered the most informal performance settings. Both environments clearly helped perpetuate the participatory qualities of jazz, at least among blacks, if not whites. For whites, the participatory tradition behind jazz posed a challenge. Either it was something exotic and new, to be experienced to the extent possible, or it was—in the minds of its enemies—a threat to conventional morality.

At the same time new settings for jazz took hold in northern cities after World War I, and electrical and mechanical reproduction of music also appeared—with further implications for the performance of jazz and for the ways in which Americans understood such performances.

3 / Dance-Tested Records and Syncopep for the Millions

Although the roots of jazz were in live performance, technological developments after 1900 made it possible to preserve and transmit black music to audiences far removed from the performer. Player pianos, phonograph recordings, radio, and film brought the sound and sight of jazz musicians to their audiences of millions of Americans. As with the new physical settings for jazz performances—clubs, cabarets, and ballrooms—these media enlarged the audience for jazz, reshaped audience-performer interactions, and provided more fuel for the controversy surrounding black music.

Each new medium relied on standardized formats which determined which performers received recording opportunities and which improvisations were preserved. Aspiring musicians increasingly learned jazz from this pre-selected sample of recordings rather than primarily from live performances as their predecessors had done. Jazz historians and critics agree that as jazz reached a larger audience, the tempos slowed down and larger jazz orchestras replaced the smaller bands and combos, making the music more standardized and palatable to middle-class white tastes. Like certain black dances and "bawdy" blues, vernacular jazz music was "cleaned up" as it was marketed to a mass audience.[1]

The more lively and improvisational jazz performances remained segregated in black communities—known primarily to black audiences. This was as true for phonograph recordings and radio as it was for live performances. "Race records" were produced for black consumers and seldom reached white listeners. One study maintains that the jazz controversy waned precisely because commercial formulas and musically conservative white tastes dominated jazz performance by the 1930s—costing jazz its vitality.[2]

While it is certainly true that the increased popularity of jazz sometimes came at the expense of its most innovative characteristics, records and radio broadcasts both exposed millions of Americans to a new music, and preserved some examples of the participatory styles fundamental to cabaret dancing and live performances. Phonograph records, for instance, conveyed the unique rhythms and tonalities of jazz more effectively than sheet music or piano rolls—both of which preceded phonograph records in disseminating popular music. As we shall see, even a radio broadcast from the Cotton Club shared live performance with thousands of listeners who would never see the inside of a cabaret—at least until Duke Ellington was featured in *Black and Tan* (1930). Radio audiences could hear some of the interaction between performers and audiences, even though they could not participate directly.

All instruments and media that reproduced musical entertainment between 1900 and 1920 boasted of their ability to replicate live musical performance. Pianolas were the first mechanical devices for music-making marketed successfully in the new century. The Aeolian Company introduced the pianola in 1898, and by 1904 "there were more than forty different kinds of automatic piano on the American market." Pianolas retained their popularity for two decades, and it probably peaked in 1925 when half of all pianos produced were "automatic."[3]

Pianolas promised a variety of benefits to consumers. One ad boasted PERFECTION WITHOUT PRACTICE. Another claimed the pianola to be superior to traditional pianos that required human skill and training: "How many thousands of

American parlors contain that shining monument to a past girlhood—a silent piano. Do you wish to enjoy your piano? This can be accomplished by owning a Cecilian Piano Player." This advertisement offered an opportunity for Americans to break with the social custom of buying a piano as a sign of feminine gentility. Other advertisements depicted men playing the pianolas and promised, "you can talk while it plays or play if the talk ends." The player-piano was as much an entertaining amusement as a musical instrument.[4]

Pianola manufacturers, nonetheless, praised the ability of machines to overcome standardized or mediocre sound reproduction. Duo-Art, Ampico, and Aeolian all hired accomplished musicians and concert performers to record the nuances of their personal style on the rolls. The most sophisticated pianos "reproduced not only the notes but also the tempo, rhythm, dynamic changes, phrasing, and pedaling of the recording artist."[5] Consumers could purchase—in theory—perfection and virtuosity. Many pianists, including Scott Joplin, James P. Johnson, and Cow-Cow Davenport made piano rolls and introduced the black musical idiom to new listeners. Davenport said he sold piano rolls featuring his "Cow-Cow Blues" door-t ·-door for the Cincinnati-based Vocal Style piano roll company Pianolas remained popular into the twenties, when they were supplanted by the phonograph and radio.[6]

The earliest commercial recordings were marketed in the 1890s—at the same time as pianolas. The many technical limitations on early recordings may have made player-pianos a more attractive entertainment alternative. Early cylinder recordings were only two minutes in length, could not capture the full tonal spectrum, and could not be mass produced. Each cylinder was individually recorded. According to jazz historian Neil Leonard, these records featured music that "was often scarcely discernible from the surface scratch, squeaks, and snorts that came out of the horn."[7]

With improvements in sound reproduction and invention of the disk-shaped record, sales boomed. By 1921, 100 million records were produced, which represented a "fourfold increase over 1914." Leonard notes that in the same year, 1914, Americans "spent more money for [records] than for any other form of recreation." The popularity of recordings and the taste for jazz grew simultaneously.[8]

From the beginning, phonograph records featured a variety of musical styles, including classical, theatrical performances, and opera. But it was popular music genres that kept sales high. Americans especially liked songs, ballads, ragtime, and marching bands. The dance music that sent patrons into cabarets and night clubs to "shake that thing," also sent customers into record stores.

While it is difficult to assess the availability of phonographs to Americans with modest incomes, the advertising for phonographs reached out for both middle- and working-class consumers. *McClure's, Cosmopolitan,* and *Munsey* magazines, as well as mail-order catalogs directed their wares to a variety of buyers. Cylinder phonographs like the Edison Home Phonograph were available for modest homes and "flourished in small towns and rural areas." More affluent Americans were encouraged to buy elaborate machines that represented an investment in fine furniture. The phonograph became "encased with an eye to decorativeness and fittingness in the room scheme," and a "product" of "recognized cabinet-makers."[9]

Those Americans who did not buy their own phonographs listened to phonograph recordings in bars, dance halls, or the homes of friends. Records provided a basis for shared musical experiences and thereby permitted the continuation of some communal entertainment traditions. Rent parties, for example, used phonographs when live performers were not available. In the rural South, Harrison Barnes, who later played in New Orleans street bands, recalled that people on the Magnolia Plantation congregated at a common phonograph. When the record salesman brought "six or seven records" for them to hear, he would play them at a house and charge ten cents admission. Barnes heard novelty songs and sermons but very little blues or jazz on these early disks. Black music appeared on these early recordings through crude "coon songs" frequently performed by whites.[10]

Tunes like George W. Johnson's "The Whistling Coon" and other ethnic records were aimed at immigrant groups and there is not much evidence that blacks bought these records. It is more likely that whites did—just as white audiences had provided the main audience support for minstrelsy. In the 1920s, however, "race records" succeeded "Negro novelty" songs when record companies discovered a new urban black market.

Race records represented a victory for those black musicians who had tried to break into the recording industry. Blues composer Perry Bradford persuaded Fred Hager of General Phonograph's OKeh label to experiment with a new black vocal offering. "I tramped the pavements of Broadway with the belief that the country was waiting for the sound of the voice of a Negro singing the blues with a Negro jazz combination playing," Bradford recalled. "For our folks had a story to tell and it could only be in vocal—not instrumental—recordings."[11] A white studio orchestra backed Mamie Smith on her first recording, "That Thing Called Love" and "You Can't Keep a Good Man Down." But Smith was invited back, and her second recording, "Crazy Blues" and "It's Right Here for You," featured a black band selected by Bradford. "Crazy Blues" made recording history and sold at a phenomenal rate. In Harlem, 75,000 copies sold in one week. In addition to blues, race records featured sermons, minstrel songs, spirituals and gospel tunes, popular songs, and some early jazz.[12]

All other major record companies followed OKeh's lead and began recording the classic blues singers: Bessie Smith, Ma Rainey, Ida Cox, Clara Smith, Bertha "Chippie" Hill, Sippie Wallace, Lucille Hegamin, Rosa Henderson, and Victoria Spivey. Classic blues recordings helped pull record companies out of the early twenties slump produced by radio competition. The relative lack of blues material on radio broadcasts helped keep recordings popular. Black consumers bought at least five or six million records a year, according to folklorists Howard Odum and Guy B. Johnson, who studied the phenomenon in 1925. Their estimate is low because they drew their data from only three record companies.[13]

Many contemporary accounts attest to the popularity of race records in black communities. Pianist Clarence Williams owned a record story on Chicago's South Side and recalled how the blues records' popularity made them instant sellers: "Colored people would form a line twice around the block when the latest record of Bessie or Ma or Clara or Mamie came in. . . . Sometimes these records they was bootlegged, sold in the alley for four or five dollars apiece." Similarly, Reb Spikes said that the fifty to a hundred blues records he stocked in his Los Angeles store would be "gone in an hour." Spikes posted signs like "Bessie Smith's new record in" and within two or three hours people would be "standing in line half a block waiting to get a record." Blues records were purchased in great numbers, even if it meant a sacrifice for low income families.[14]

OKeh executive Ralph S. Peer chose the designation "race record" because it reminded him of other music marketed on the basis of European or ethnic nationalities. For whites, the term "race record" may have reflected the segregationist assumption that black music was distinct from and inferior to popular music generally. By contrast, black customers, influenced by calls for race pride in the 1920s, probably found the term attractive. Collier points out that race records were segregated into separate catalogs for blacks and whites only by some manufacturers, and he believes that "race" listings issued by the recording companies were produced for the "convenience of record stores that catered to blacks." As we shall see shortly, the appeal to race pride was also an important aspect of marketing strategies stressing "authenticity."[15]

Certainly, they were already familiar with at least some blues songs and performers who had toured the North and South. The popularity of blues prompted many live entertainers to include blues materials in their work. Publishers and record companies released hundreds of new titles. One even published a book probably aimed at whites entitled *How to Play and Sing the Blues Like the Phonograph and Stage Artists*. Pianist Porter Granger and arranger Bob Ricketts advised would-be performers that:

If one can temporarily play the role of the oppressed or the depressed, injecting into his or her rendition a spirit of hopeful prayer, the effect will be more natural and successful. "Blues" are more naturally blue when the melodic movements are treated with minor chords. Though the chords of the diatonic major scale may be employed, the result is not nearly so efficacious as when the minor motive is present. . . . It is possible to properly produce "Blues" effects on any instrument, although the wailings, moanings, and croonings, it can be understood, are more easily produced on instruments like the saxophone, trombone, or violin. "Blues" are sung or played most effectively in crooning or subdued style. Without the necessary moan, croon or slur, no blues number is properly sung.

This volume also included a set of "breaks" to be used to end a performance, with names like: "the Harmony Break, the Jazz Blues Break, the Comedy Blues Break, the Minor Blues Break . . . the Levee Blues Break, Cabaret Blues Break, the Barrel House Blues Break," and more. These publications assumed a novice performer could learn the blues without ever witnessing a live performance, and that improvisation itself could be codified.[16]

Race records were not the only, or even the earliest, source of jazz performances on record. The first instrumental recordings specifically labeled jazz were produced in 1917, thus predating race records. Nick LaRocca and the Original Dixieland Jazz Band recorded the earliest popular jazz hits. This group of white musicians was from New Orleans originally, and, like other jazz musicians before them, the ODJB had traveled to Chicago in 1916 before playing in New York.

ODJB member Eddie Edwards described several attempts to record successfully. He wrote that the first offer came from Columbia in 1917. At that date, "No one knew what we were trying to do, and the date was sabotaged. They were building shelves in the studio and kept hammering away while we tried to play. Also in the middle of cutting a side people kept running in and out, causing all kinds of confusion. . . ." Eventually the band was successful and the public associated the ODJB music with jazz. Actu-

ally, their recordings were based on standard rags and blues
compositions. The ODJB version of "Tiger Rag," for example,
originated as a quadrille and then passed into the basic repertoire of many Storyville musicians.[17]

The ODJB was a smash hit in New York where their white
audiences found the new "jass" a novel entertainment experience, and their first release ("Livery Stables Blues" and "Original
Dixieland One-Step") featured many novelty effects that resulted, in part, from the recording process. Edwards explained
how the recording was made:

> In those days you blew into a four-foot horn with an eight-inch bell
> on the end. The horn led to the receiving wax. You couldn't play
> tests back, and we cut three masters of each tune to make sure that
> one would be good. With this horn you couldn't use a bass drum,
> which vibrated too much, or a snare drum, which came out blurred.
> Tony Spargo had to beat only on the cow bells, wood blocks, and
> sides of the drums. As a result, a great many drummers were influ-
> enced who heard only the record and didn't realize that the bass and
> snares were integral parts of Dixieland drumming.

Their first record sold one million copies and its success forecast
future trends in commercial jazz dominated by white bands and
musicians. Some performers perfected "nut jazz" in which they
"consciously distorted blues notes so that they lost their positive
meaning in grossly exaggerated groans, growls, moans and
laughs." Others followed the opposite strategy and "diluted" or
"refined" jazz by de-emphasizing blue notes. In these processes,
much of the spontaneity in black jazz was lost in the developing
mass market, which marginalized the many black and some
white musicians who remained wedded to participatory and improvisational jazz performance.[18]

The opportunity seized by the ODJB caused some controversy among musicians. Apparently black New Orleans bandleader Freddie Keppard turned down a recording offer from
Victor in 1916, which fueled speculation about his motives. He
told his bandsmen: "Nothin' doin' boys. We won't put our stuff
on records for everybody to steal." Sidney Bechet placed Kep-

pard's reluctance to record in the context of older performance traditions:

> Freddie really understood music; he had a feeling for it. He wouldn't give away any part of the music, and he wouldn't stand for its being played wrong. Freddie, he was a read musicianer. And he had a feeling about that recording thing; he had a feeling that every Tom, Dick or Harry who could ever blow a note would be making records soon. It would get so the music wasn't where it belonged. It was going to be taken away.

With the benefit of hindsight, Bechet believed Keppard's fears had been realized. Other musicians simply tried to retain as much control over the recording process as possible. Willie "the Lion" Smith wrote, "It has always been my opinion that the only way to do oneself any good with records is to make discs of your own composition with a band under your name."[19]

Unlike Keppard, most black jazz bands offered the chance to record did not refuse. King Oliver's Creole Jazz Band, one of the most important in the decade, recorded about forty sides in 1923. Jazz historian James Lincoln Collier explains the seminal influence of these records on later jazz: "No longer did musicians outside of New Orleans have to follow the lead of the Original Dixieland Jazz Band, or the pseudo-jazz put out by popular dance bands. The real thing was at last available in quantity for study, and the impact on musicians was immense." The "real thing" according to contemporary jazz critic Martin Williams sounded "at once spontaneous and deliberate, passionate and controlled, controlled in ways that make its passions all the more convincing." Oliver, Louis Armstrong, and other performers had finally brought the best of the participatory jazz tradition to recorded music.[20]

Hundreds of other musicians recorded in the 1920s, and many of them were associated with the blues craze. Kid Ory, who recorded with Louis Armstrong, explained that musicians were surprised at the recognition produced by recorded jazz:

> We made our first records in Chicago at the OKeh studios, and of course, when we made them we didn't have an expectation that they

would be as successful as they became. . . . Times were good and
people had money to buy records. One thing that helped the sale
was that for a while the OKeh people gave away a picture of Louis to
everyone that bought one of the records. When they did that, the
sales went way up, because Louis was so popular . . .

Recording supplemented live performances, and its first stages,
as Ory indicated, drew upon established talents. Louis Armstrong's prolific recordings in the 1920s convinced OKeh executives he would be a "consistent producer."[21]

The process of making jazz recordings was haphazard in the
teens and twenties. In the acoustic recording process, musicians
played into a recording horn that forced a diaphragm to vibrate.
Then the diaphragm caused the stylus to cut into a cylinder or
wax disk. Cylinders could only be duplicated by repeating the
performance, whereas was disks were more easily copied. Bass
player George "Pops" Foster gave a fairly typical description of
how this process worked from a performer's point of view:

> When we used to make records in St. Louis, they'd hire a loft in one
> of the downtown store buildings. The band would practice without
> the bass and drums. We'd sit over to one side having some fun until
> they were ready for us. Then we'd play with the rest of the band and
> cut the records. They had big megaphones going into the wall. We'd
> stand up to the megaphone and play. The wax was cut on the other
> side of the wall. If you cut a hog you had to start all over and cut the
> wax again.

Wingy Manone remembered standing on top of boxes to get the
correct musical balance in the megaphones, but that was just one
of a number of experiments that might be tried to minimize
vibration.[22]

Manone explained that a band's performance could be somewhat unpredictable in the recording studio. In the same session
described above, Manone said that producer Tommy Rockwell
was almost driven "crazy" because Manone's band, unable to read,
performed differently on each take of the record. Lawrence
Brown reported that when he recorded with Duke Ellington, "All
Ellington would do was strike out the first few bars or so. Some

progressions and we'd know what that number was. . . . There were sort of skeleton arrangements. The solos weren't written." In addition, Brown wouldn't necessarily know the name of the piece because it might be named by the lyricist later. Various kinds of improvisation might take place in the recording studio.[23]

One of the best-known accounts of a recording studio blooper that made music history was Louis Armstrong's claim that he introduced scat singing on records after he had dropped the music for "Heebie Jeebies" and "there wasn't any use in spoilin' this master, so I just went in there and started scattin' and they kep' it." It is certainly plausible that the primitive recording conditions made it possible, for a certain degree of improvisation remained in many recording sessions then—both by accident and design. In other cases, such as some early Ellington recordings, pieces were put together in the studio.[24]

In the early days, recording companies did not have a specific group of musicians hired to provide orchestration. Louis Armstrong's famous "Hot Fives" records were produced because OKeh just "happened to have its portable recording equipment in Chicago at the "time when Armstrong could get together a group of musicians."[25] Particular composers or band leaders hired whomever they felt was appropriate and available for recording dates.

Charlie Gaines remembered that Clarence Williams, for example, "never engaged a man for specific dates." Instead, Williams "had a stable of musicians on a weekly payroll. You might be called for several dates every day of maybe none for a week, but you received a standard sum of about eighty-five dollars each week." Williams would only pay the musicians on a particular day, so those who were out of town had to wait for their next paycheck. Gaines admitted the system could create a "lack of interest in the work you recorded."[26] The arrangement described by Gaines made it possible to add recording work to other performance opportunities.

Composers like Williams published sheet music for the most successful hits. Williams like Perry Bradford and other black middle men, helped blacks break into the white-dominated music business. Williams's organization of studio bands helped several musicians get recorded, and music store owners and composers also hired performers. The Spikes Brothers hired Kid Ory to record with the "Spikes Seven Pods of Pepper Orchestra" in Los Angeles in 1921.[27]

The perfection of electronic techniques in 1924 brought several important changes to the recording industry simultaneously with the rise of jazz and blues to popularity. Electrical recording made it possible to extend frequency range beyond the capability of older mechanical recording devices. Bass tones in particular, could be effectively reproduced for the first time, reducing the reliance on strings and cornet for rhythmic structure in jazz pieces. Since musicians no longer needed to play into recording horns, a studio could be created that simulated, at least roughly, entertainment environments. More sensitive equipment meant musicians did not have to play so loudly and could moderate tone better.

Conditions were still elementary when compared with a modern sound studio. Recording executive Frank Walker remembered an electrical recording session at Columbia in 1926: "We built an enormous tent in the studio on the theory that the conical shape would keep the sound in. There was only one light hanging from the ceiling from a long cord." Walker, Bessie Smith, Fletcher Henderson, and Don Redman were all trapped in a wide "scramble" after a wire broke and the tent collapsed. Many musicians have described the problems that ensued from musicians' stomping their foot to keep time. Eddie Barefield remembered one session with Jimmy Lunceford's band in which a pillow was placed under Willie "the Lion" Smith's foot so he wouldn't jar the microphone. Kid Ory had to do the same thing to Dink Johnson's foot in an early recording. Given these conditions, it is not surprising that even the improved jazz recordings could deliver erratic quality.[28]

Despite the inadequacies of reproduction in early disks, record and phonograph publicity promised to spread authentic performance. A *Defender* advertisement for Mamie Smith demonstrated this pitch:

IT TAKES A BLUES TO CATCH A BLUES! Mamie Smith is sweeping the country with her infectious fluency of humor. She and her Jazz Hounds have a magnificence of color and pulsing rhythm in their music that stirs the senses with its weirdness. They are the greatest Jazz attraction. MEM'RIES OF YOU MAMMY is a plantation song with a southern swinging melody. It is especially well treated by an interlude of recitation by Mamie. The realism of her speaking voice is startling because it is absolutely without affectation. To humor the thousands of requests for personal appearances she is now on a concert tour of the country IF YOU DON'T WANT ME BLUES is pure BLUES! To hear is to Buy![29]

The ad captured the emergence of jazz from blues and other black music idioms, and promised a little of everything: jazz, plantation melodies, novelty (or weirdness), and most important, realistic performance.

Much as in this advertisement from the *Defender,* claims to authenticity were made for the mechanical and electrical reproduction of music in the teens and twenties. For example, the concert performers who recorded piano rolls played at special transcription machines that recorded nuances of phrasing and rhythm. Victor and Columbia cashed in on the dance craze by using photographs and testimonials from dance professionals to verify that the music was danceable. One Columbia advertisement guaranteed performance verisimilitude because the record was pressed "under the personal direction of the greatest authority in this country on modern dancing—G. Hepburn Wilson, M.B., *who dances while the band makes the record.*" As one industry historian has pointed out, "Columbia assured prospective customers that each and every recording would be in authentic dance tempo, and expensive double-track advertisements were taken in the *Saturday Evening Post* to spread the word about Columbia's dance-tested records."[30]

Race records based their appeal to authenticity on a variety of qualities, including musical characteristics, performer reputation, the race of performers, and even the race of company employees and owners. "When you listen to Vocalion Dance Records," one dance ad proclaimed, "you just can't sit still. Vocalion band leaders—King Oliver—Fletcher Henderson—Jimmy Betrand—Elgar—Duke Ellington and others need no introduction to the Race. Their music always sparkles with life, pep and originality—just what you want when you feel like dancing."[31]

Several short-lived black-owned record and sheet music companies also vied for authenticity, and newspapers like *The Defender* encouraged blacks to support them. Because Pace and Handy published the sheet music for one of Mamie Smith's songs, for example, *The Defender* urged its leaders to buy OKeh's recordings of the same songs: "Lovers of music everywhere, and those who desire to help in any advance of the Race should be sure to buy this record as encouragement to the manufacturers who may not believe that the Race will buy records sung by its own singers."[32] Pace made a similar appeal to blacks to promote its products. Pace Phonograph is the "only bonafide Racial Company making Talking Machine records. All stockholders are Colored, all artists are Colored, all employees are Colored."

Pace, incidentally, tried to gain an advantage over its competition by appealing to bourgeois tastes. In the same ad, Pace noted: "Only company using Racial Artists in recording *high class* song records. This company made the only Grand Opera Records ever made by Negroes. All others confine this end of their work to blues, rags, comedy numbers, etc."[33] In this case, "race pride" for the black middle-class meant identification with European classical music rather than with Afro-American cultural creations. Pace's recording represented a victory for *The Defender* who had lobbied for "high class" black artists on records.

Although the white audience for race records was small, it is possible that claims to authenticity were aimed at these white consumers. Blacks were more likely to be familiar with blues singers like Bessie Smith, who had toured on black entertainment circuits. Promises of music reminiscent of minstrel tunes may also have been aimed at white customers. OKeh, for example, advertised the Norfolk Jazz Quartet to distributors as a group popular with white audiences: "You may be interested to know that it isn't the colored race which is responsible for the jump in record sales. The big demand comes from the white people." This kind of advertising continued a pattern set by sheet music, which had promised "authentic plantation melodies."[34]

Recordings supplemented an entertainer's career and were often promoted as part of a concert tour. Ma Rainey, recognizing the role of the phonograph in disseminating the blues, made her entrance on stage out of a victrola. Similarly, Bessie Smith used a stage set that was like a recording studio. Zutty Singleton recalled that Smith would then "explain to the audience how she made records, and sing the tunes she had recorded." Black record buyers knew many of the performers featured in the twenties from theatre and vaudeville. In addition, record companies took road trips in the South to find and record "downhome" or rural blues.[35]

Recorded jazz was soon complemented by radio broadcasts of live performances. In fact, the rise of radio contributed to a serious recession in the recording business in 1922. Electronic recordings improved the industry's outlook slightly during the rest of the decade, but after the Depression the popularity of radio pushed record sales into a deep slump. In 1932 only six million records were sold in the United States, which was "approximately six percent of the total record sales in 1927." Radio rarely used recordings, and as broadcasting historian Philip K. Eberly has concluded, "Live music was the standard. Phonograph records bore the onus of second-rate programming and were to be used only in emergencies or for testing purposes." Listeners could hear the latest musical hits without purchasing the record themselves. One estimate suggests that radio broadcasting reached 20 percent of the public in 1923 and 30 percent by 1928.[36]

Of all the new media, radio provided the greatest capacity for dissemination of jazz. Foster R. Dulles, in his 1940 study *America Learns to Play*, reported that music programming made up "75% of what Americans heard on the air." Initially stations used generic labels such as "sentimental," "comic," or "Irish" to identify programs. Jazz was often included in musical variety segments of a day's programming, but the meaning was unspecific. For many

Americans the term "jazz" referred to all popular music, and might include "pseudo-jazz bands or ordinary dance orchestras using modish effects."[37]

To some extent, it was correct to associate jazz with popular music on the airwaves. As Philip Eberly notes, "white dance orchestras of the period often imitated black models, and in some cases the copies were excellent." Many radio offerings, according to him, were "jazz," which "could mean anything from tearing off an undisciplined chorus of group improvisation to laying down a banjo break; it could mean the studied mannerisms of a moaning saxophone riff or a self-conscious impersonation of Louis Armstrong." There was a truth to the claim of *Etude* magazine in 1924: "Tap America anywhere in the air and nine times out of ten Jazz will burst forth." However far the music might be from jazz at its roots, in the minds of its mass audience it was jazz nonetheless.[38]

The growth of jazz on the airwaves caused some consternation for advertisers who wanted to believe that radio was a force for making public taste more sophisticated. In his study *Advertising the American Dream: Making Way for Modernity, 1920–1940,* historian Roland Marchand describes advertising executives who felt they needed to justify the civilizing properties of radio. One advertising survey, aimed at prospective clients, demonstrated that you could measure the progress of "radio uplift" by comparing the relative popularity of jazz and symphonic music: "Whereas 75 percent of those surveyed in 1923 had indicated a preference for jazz music and only 20 percent for symphonic music, radio had so enhanced public discrimination that by 1925 the preference for symphonic music surpassed jazz by 50 percent to 10 percent." In this climate, it is not surprising that radio broadcaster Meyer Davis sought to dissolve the association of jazz with popular music by offering a $100 prize for another name to replace the term "jazz." Out of approximately 70,000 entries, he selected "syncopep" as the best substitute.[39]

Despite the campaign of the advertising executives, radio continued to carry jazz to millions of Americans. Radio broadcasts brought a sense of jazz locations as well as the music itself to

audiences. Hotel-radio stations broadcast dance bands from ballrooms and quieter combos from restaurants. Duke Ellington and
Cab Calloway performed from the stage of the Cotton Club
cabaret scene. Count Basie attracted Benny Goodman's attention
through broadcasts from the Reno Club in Kansas City. The
Count received his nickname from a radio announcer who
thought his given name Bill was too "ordinary." The announcer
added Basie to the rest of the jazz royalty.[40]

Count Basie remembered how a certain amount of spontaneity was communicated over the air waves. His band's theme "One
O'Clock Jump":

> . . . came out of one of our radio broadcasts. Back in those days,
> when you went on the air, you didn't have to clear songs and titles in
> advance as you do now. In other words, the band would just go on
> the air and play "heads" and anything that came to mind. One night
> we had about five minutes to go on a broadcast and the announcer
> asked me for the title of the closing tune. Well, it just had no title so
> it was up to someone to pick one out in a hurry. I glanced up at the
> clock. It was almost one o'clock. 'Just call it the One O'Clock Jump,' I
> told the announcer. After that we used it for our theme and it's
> unquestionably the record most closely associated with the band.[41]

Radio could not communicate all the excitement of live performance, but it continued to evoke at least some spontaneity and
much excitement in radio audiences.

Some musicians learned or perfected playing styles from the
radio broadcasts. Barney Bigard recalled the sound of Duke
Ellington, and Milt Hinton remembered listening to early "crys-
tal sets" to hear the dance bands broadcasting live from the
Grand Terrace Ballroom in Chicago. Hinton placed the ear-
phones in one of his grandmother's cut glass bowls so that more
than one person could listen at a time.[42]

Unfortunately, the lively jazz broadcasts that inspired a lis-
tener like Hinton to improvise a home-made set of speakers, also
prompted moralist critics to regulate jazz. As the music became
more widely disseminated, industry associations and community
groups intensified their pressures for its regulation. The Musical

Publishers Protective Association was formed in 1921 with the motto "Just keep the words clean and the music will take care of itself." Similar groups formed among piano and music manufacturers. In broadcasting and film, regulations were established to control obscenity or other "offensive" materials. The National Association of Orchestra Directors promised to monitor the kinds of performance in dance halls, nightclubs, and hotels. These private groups were succeeded by the government's regulatory agencies established in the 1927 Radio Act and the 1934 Federal Communications Act. The effect of regulation, whether private or public, was to encourage the transmission of sanitized jazz at the expense of more lively music (although performers still found ways—often non-verbal—to communicate some of the bawdier aspects of jazz).[43]

Regulation was not the only way in which the structure of recording and broadcasting industries influenced jazz performance. The rise of large companies dominating music publishing, recording, and radio opened economic opportunities for musicians—but only for those who conformed to standards set by the corporations.[44]

By the end of the 1920s yet another medium—movies—had joined records and radio in bringing jazz to mass audiences. Indeed, the first "talkie" had the word in its title: *The Jazz Singer* (1927). One measure of the growth of jazz in film is David Meeker's *Jazz in the Movies: A Guide to Jazz Musicians 1917–1977*. Meeker's directory provides a short synopsis of all films that featured jazz musicians. There were few films depicting jazz before the introduction of sound in 1927. The first film to show jazz dance, however, was Biograph's 1907 silent short *The Fights of Nations*. The Original Dixieland Jazz Band performed in the 1917 *The Good for Nothing*. According to Meeker, there were 63 shorts, 80 fuller length features, five cartoons, and two March of Time newsreels that brought jazz performance to the movie theatre between 1917 and 1940.

Silent films would seem particularly limiting on black performance traditions. In *Slow Fade to Black: The Negro in American*

Film 1900–1942, film historian Thomas Cripps underscores this point: "Afro-Americans suffered a major disadvantage during the three decades of silent film. So much black entertainment had a strong musical element and depended upon audience reaction and participation for full effect. The absence of sound restricted the black actor's range." But, as Cripps also noted, black audiences compensated for these shortcomings by greeting "the heroes of the screen" with "rhythmic shouts, clapping, foottapping and yells of encouragement." Black film promoter George P. Johnson used bands and orchestras like Reb Spikes's to promote opening nights at his theatres in Los Angeles and Riverside.[45]

In addition, jazz musicians provided the sound for some of these films by playing in movie-house orchestras. Zutty Singleton felt he had learned valuable tricks of timing and good overall training by playing accompaniment and sound effects for movies. Audiences considered the musical entertainment part of the film. For example, Mary Lou Williams remembered the rave audiences for Fats Waller's performances before the movies: "He was just a sensation in New York, when they'd turn the light on people would scream, when he sat down, people would scream: I never saw such a thing. When he finished, that was the end; they had to let it cool off."[46]

The jazz music in black movie houses did not please everyone. Dave Peyton criticized the liberties taken by musicians in one of his *Defender* columns:

> During a death scene . . . you are likely to hear the orchestra jazzing away on "Clap Hands, Here Comes Charlie" . . . the brass tuba, banjo and saxophones have no business in the legitimate picture orchestra during the showing of a dramatic screen play. The regular legitimate orchestral line-up should be employed . . . During orchestral specialties these instruments are all right for jazz band expression, but only then. There is entirely too much "hokum" played in our Race picture houses. It only appeals to a certain riff-raff element who loudly clap hands when the orchestra stops, misleading the leader to believe that his efforts are winning the approval of the entire audience.[47]

The improvisation provided by these jazz bands was a unique mixture of musical traditions with a new medium—silent film. Peyton conveys the impression that a raucous exchange between performers and audiences was characteristics only of "Race picture houses"—not of those catering to whites.

Many early sound films concerned the world of entertainment. Black musical practice was most directly represented in the shorts produced during the late twenties and thirties. Black musicians featured in these films included the Mills Brothers, Louis Armstrong, Don Redman and his Orchestra, Duke Ellington, Ivie Anderson, and Ethel Waters. Cripps believed the films "helped reshape the black cinema image" by portraying urban life rather than plantation stereotypes. White jazz musicians like Gene Krupa, Benny Goodman, Hoagy Carmichael and Paul Whiteman also performed in these films.

Because the talkies appeared so late in the decade, most of the story of jazz in films lies beyond the scope of this study. Typically, performers made cameo appearances in feature films like *Rhapsody in Blue and Black* (1932), in which a leopard-skin clad Louis Armstrong plays his horn during a dream sequence. Armstrong and Cab Calloway were also cast as primitivist cartoon characters in a series of Betty Boop offerings. In one, Armstrong chases Betty Boop while tooting on his cornet. Duke Ellington appeared in *Murder at the Vanities* (1934) and his band literally pops up out of a concert orchestra audience to play blasts of jazz and drive the classical music out of the concert hall.[48]

Ellington was also the subject of one of the many films that told stories of nightclubs or entertainment life. Dudley Murphy's *Black and Tan* (1930) featured Fredi Washington as a dancer working to support the composing talents of a struggling jazz pianist, played by Duke Ellington. A rapacious club owner shows no remorse when the heroine dances herself to death in a "seedy saloon, with . . . drill team chorus boys in tails against a fake South Seas drop." The film marked the first time a jazz band was given billing, and it exposed audiences to glimpses of the primitive settings typical of a Cotton Club or Connie's Inn. *Black and*

Tan demonstrates that the sophisticated presentation of jazz was possible early in the sound era, but most performance films were not shot with excellent standards like Murphy's.[49]

From the early days of film, movies presented elements of black culture to audiences of both races. By the end of the twenties, movie audiences could hear as well as see jazz performance on the screen. The versions of performance that Hollywood created often diluted some of the energy of live acts, although a few films, notably Bessie Smith's only appearance in *St. Louis Blues* (1929), managed to get past the censor's editing. Movies functioned much like radio and records, however, by providing economic opportunities for musicians (primarily white ones rather than blacks), while requiring them to play acceptable and often stereotyped performances.

Piano rolls, recordings, radio, and film all stimulated the spread of jazz beyond the black community and vice districts to thousands of new listeners who accepted and often praised the music. Historian Nathan Huggins has perceptively explained the popularity of these media: "Sheet music and phonograph records could be taken into the home (though the Negro could not) to undermine the sentimentality of conventional American popular music as well as the un-American formality of the standard classics." Huggins points out that as language, the music was "jazz speech—secretive—, 'in,' causal and fluid" that could "shatter the philistine with its impudence." Unfortunately, many of those listeners who picked up what they knew about jazz and other black music from written or audile media, would not hear collective improvisation and other qualities of jazz performance that derived from live participatory performance traditions.[50]

Race records, combined with the relatively small percentage of black bands recorded, tended to reinforce distinctions between black and white music. The barrier was as difficult for one race to cross as the other. Clarence Williams remembered that few Chicagoans in his South Side Chicago record store asked for records by the popular white band leader Paul Whiteman, whose style was far removed from black musical traditions. Williams concluded that his patrons probably did not know who Whiteman was. (His music may not have suited their tastes either.) Similarly, white customers did not have as much access to race records as blacks. The jazz aimed at the general public was primarily performed by white bands and most of it was more accurately described as popular music with jazz influences.

Musicians like Freddie Keppard and Sidney Bechet had sensed that the growth and consolidation of the recording industry might have an adverse effect on performance. Folklorists and musicologists raised different but related objections to the influence of electronic media. Folklorist Dorothy Scarborough, for example, voiced a common fear in 1925: "I hope that I may sometime spend a sabbatical year loitering down through the South on the trail of more Negro folk-songs before the material vanishes forever, killed by the Victrola, the radio, the lure of cheap printed music." As we shall see, some participants in the Harlem Renaissance expressed similar concerns.[51]

For musicians, however, the recordings actually preserved music styles that could be imitated. Many jazzmen learned from recordings, especially those with limited access to live performance. Danny Barker described "all the alert jazz musicians and local music lovers" who "waited anxiously for each of Louis Armstrong's latest releases"; and Dicky Wells also remembered "everybody was trying to play something like Louis Armstrong." Many musicians heard blues records, Mose Allison said that when he was a child "just about every store had a juke box" and Buck Clayton listened to "a lot of Bessie Smith, mostly blues, because in my home nearly everybody was blues crazy." Joseph "Cie" Frazier learned pieces from playing along with the records.[52]

White bands in particular, benefited from the availability of recorded performance. Jimmy McPartland of the Austin High School Gang described the process he experienced:

> Every day after school, Frank Teschemacher and Bud Freeman, Jim Lannigan, my brother Dick, myself, and a few others used to go to a little place called the Spoon and Straw. It was just an ice cream parlor where you'd get a malted like, soda, shakes, and all that stuff.
>
> But they had a victrola there, and we used to sit around listening to the bunch of records laid on the table. They were Paul Whiteman

and Art Hickman records, and so forth. And Ted Lewis—he was supposed to be the hot thing, but he didn't do anything for us somehow.

. . . One day they had some new Gennett records on the table and we put them on . . . They were by the New Orleans Rhythm Kings, and I believe the first tune played was *Farewell Blues*. Boy, when we heard that—I'll tell you we were out of our minds. Everybody flipped. It was wonderful. So we put the others on—*Tiger Rag, Discontented, Tin Roof Blues, Bugle Call*, and such titles.

We stayed there from about three in the afternoon until eight at night, just listening to those records one after another, over and over again. Right then and there we decided we would get a band and try to play like these guys.[53]

Performers like those in the Austin High School Gang did not have the same apprenticeship experiences as an earlier generation of black jazz men who trained in the saloons—not the soda shop. Nonetheless, recordings made it possible for these aspiring white musicians to discover jazz and to try to imitate their favorites.[54]

The separation of black and white music markets, the domination of performing and recording opportunities by whites, and the nature of the electrical media themselves mitigated against the exposure of audiences, particularly white ones, to participatory traditions in black music. Record promoters may have been responding to this problem when they promised "real blues" and "dance-tested records" harking back to a variety of performance-oriented musical traditions.

Still, the new media brought jazz to a much wider audience—and one which did, after all, have some access to live performance in the cabarets and clubs in many cities. Performers kept participation alive in the midst of increasing mechanical reproduction through their active response to films and, more importantly, their incorporation of records into social events as diverse as rent parties and college dances.

And there is yet another side to the story: the popularity of jazz on phonograph recordings and on the radio, along with the growth of live performance opportunities for jazz musicians, indicated a growing general acceptance of the music. Jazz had come to symbolize not only the journey of black migrants to a troubled new Canaan, but also the passage of the larger society into a modern era. That passage had brought jazz out of the ghettoes of black life. It would, by the early 1920s, bring it to the forefront of controversy over American values in a time of change.

Dink Johnson's Jazz Band, 1920, Los Angeles. (*Left to right*) Claude "Benno" Kennedy (tr), Buster Wilson (pf), Dink Johnson (clar), Ashford Hardee (trom), Ben Borders (d). (*Dink Johnson Coll., William Ransom Hogan Jazz Archive*)

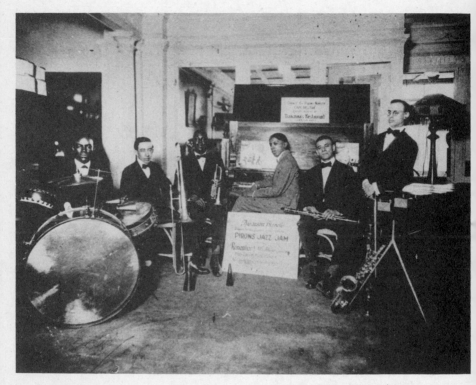

A.J. Piron Orchestra at Maison Blanche, New Orleans, 1921. (*Left to right*) Bill Matthews (d), Peter Bocage (tb), Willie Edwards (tp), Steve Lewis (p), Louis Warnick (cl/as), A.J. Piron (vl). (*William Russell Coll., William Ransom Hogan Jazz Archive*)

Papa "Mutt" Carey's Band, 1924. Note steamship on drum head. Photograph probably taken at a taxi dance hall at 3rd and Main in Los Angeles. (*Left to right*) Leo Davis (s), Bud Scott (g), Minor "Ram" Hall (d), Mutt Carey (tp), L.Z. Cooper (p). (*William Ransom Hogan Jazz Archive*)

Fate Marable's band on the *S.S. Sidney,* 1918. (*Left to right*) Baby Dodds (d), Bébé Ridgley (trom), Joe Howard (tr/cor), Louis Armstrong (tr/cor), Fate Marable (p), David Jones (mel), Johnny Dodds (c), Johnny St. Cyr (banjo), Pops Foster (bass). (*St. Cyr Coll., William Ransom Hogan Jazz Archive*)

Fate Marable and a calliope, around 1907. (*Gene Williams Coll., William Ransom Hogan Jazz Archive*)

Willie "the Lion" Smith, one of the influential Harlem stride pianists. (*Bill Spilka, William Ransom Hogan Jazz Archive*).

Paul Whiteman Orchestra, no date. Whiteman played what some writers called "symphonic jazz" in the 1920s. No date, personnel not identified. (*Neg. #20735. Chicago Historical Society*)

Interior of Artisan Hall, where New Orleans bands performed from the balcony.

Interior of Chicago's Club DeLisa, 1937. Note proximity of stage and tables. (*Neg. #17428. Chicago Historical Society*)

Like many cities in the 1920s, Chicago Jazz clubs sported exotic and/or "Southern" names like the Plantation, 35th and Calumet. (*Neg. # 14428. Chicago Historical Society*)

This 1926 advertisement from the *Saturday Evening Post* for jazz-proof home furnishings captures well the sense of jazz as a invading social force.

4/ *From Devil's Music to Jooking: Jazz Performance and the Black Community*

Black Americans debated the character of their music and musical performance long before the jazz controversy of the 1920s began. The issues were rooted in the evolution of music during slavery. Although much of the music on the plantation was sacred, secular music such as work songs, dance songs, satirical songs, and ballads made up a significant portion of slave music. Slave musicians developed their skills in religious worship and as performers for both their masters and the slave community. Opposition to some music, especially fiddle tunes and blues developed because of bawdy lyrics and the secular themes of some songs. Since the antiphonal forms of Afro-American sacred and secular music are quite similar, it was not primarily differences in song structure that differentiated respectable from disreputable music: it was performance context and lyrics.[1]

The distinction between the song and its performance context is well illustrated in studies of Afro-American music, as well as the reminiscences of blues and jazz musicians. According to folklorist John Szwed, opposition to "fiddle music" probably derived from both Anglo-Saxon and African religious beliefs that precocious musicians received their skills from supernatural forces. Many folktales described performers who met the devil in a churchyard or at a crossroads where they exchanged their soul for musical virtuosity.

In addition, as Szwed points out, blues performers don't sing with their audience. They sing solo which "implies authority" and "although the audience or the guitar may comment support-ively, there is no *song space* for group participation." Bluesmen may have provoked criticism for this authoritarian break with communal music-making practices. Most importantly, it is not the song itself but its "direction" that determines how the com-munity characterizes it. The separation between the sacred and the secular is absolute because "church music is directed *collec-tively* to God; blues are directed *individually* to the collective" (Szwed's emphasis). By the end of the nineteenth century, bluesmen especially represented this tension because they spoke for rural blacks and urban migrants, and thereby competed with preachers and other spokesmen for the black community.[2]

W. C. Handy and other early blues and jazz musicians often confronted community sanctions against playing blues, ragtime, and later jazz. Handy's father was outraged that his son bought a guitar because it was "one of the devil's playthings." The identifi-cation of syncopated secular music with devil's music intensified because many ragtime, boogie-woogie, and stride pianists who later became jazz musicians performed in brothels. Still, many black homes had pianos, and James P. Johnson pointed out that "Most people who had pianos couldn't play them, so a piano-player was important socially."[3]

Jelly Roll Morton's grandmother disowned him when she found out he was playing piano in a New Orleans whorehouse. Eubie Blake's mother monitored his early playing in Baltimore to make sure it reflected the dignity of church playing and not the ragtime he could hear from brothels near his home and in funeral processions through the streets. Blake promised to es-chew both brothels and funeral parades but by age fifteen he was working at Aggie Shelton's "sportin' house." Lawrence Brown had to leave his father's house for playing jazz, and Willie "the Lion" Smith's mother told him when he played ragtime to stay away from the piano.[4]

Eubie Blake, like Jelly Roll Morton, James P. Johnson, and others, found the tips and occasional wages lucrative. Blake was able to win his mother's tolerance of his job because it paid well. He also enlarged his repertoire because "the more tunes you'd know the more money you'd make." Blake insisted that what he played was tasteful: "Those people liked real sentimental songs like "You Made Me What I Am Today, I Hope You're Satisfied," or they liked ragtime. You never heard any *dirty* songs in Aggie Shelton's. It was high class."[5] Clearly, not all blacks saw the work of Blake and others as "high class."

Interestingly, several of the New Orleans musicians suggested that the objections to blues and jazz were not based on characteristics of the music, because it started as church music. Kid Ory said that Buddy Bolden got his tunes from the "holy roller church" and then changed them a little for secular audiences. Bill Matthews compared the effect of Bolden's moans to the feelings that "went through you" when you were in church. Willie "the Lion" Smith extended the individual qualities of a performer like Bolden to the community at large: "All the different [black music] forms can be traced back to Negro church music, and the Negroes have worshipped God for centuries, whether they lived in Africa, the Southern United States or New York City." Danny Barker states simply that jazz "lives on" in New Orleans churches.[6]

Most opponents of jazz and blues did not look favorably upon the similarities among blues and jazz and spirituals or gospel music. One radio program called the "Sheep and the Goats," for example, was forced off the air because the listeners disapproved of having gospel (sheep) and blues singers (goats) on the same show. The strong relationship of jazz and blues meant that jazz, too, was labeled suspect. Since jazz pianists and other instrumentalists accompanied blues singers and performed in shady places, they became practitioners of "devil's music." These criticisms of blues and jazz intensified with the Great Migration, where new complaints were raised against musicians.[7]

When New Orleans and other "hot" style musicians moved north, their status as newcomers produced new objections to jazz. Willie "the Lion" Smith felt the "average Negro family did not allow the blues" precisely because they wanted to distance themselves from the South. In many cities to which southern blacks came before and after World War I, inter-racial conflicts developed over the behavior and life styles of newcomers. More established blacks upbraided newcomers for attracting negative attention to the black community.[8]

The *Chicago Defender* accused migrants of causing increased racism:

> It is evident that some of the people coming to this city have seriously erred in their conduct in public places, much to the humiliation of all respectable classes of our citizens, and by so doing, on account of their ignorance of laws and customs necessary for the maintenance of health, sobriety and morality among the people in general, have given our enemies cause for complaint.[9]

Milt Hinton fondly remembered the head of the music department at his high school, Dr. Mildred Bryan Jones, because she wanted to remedy the situation described in the *Defender* by taking the students downtown to eat in a restaurant. First Jones had to teach the students proper table manners to use when they went out to dinner. "We came from homes where nobody'd ever been out to dinner," Hinton recalled, "She wanted us to know about these things so we wouldn't embarrass ourselves and our community."[10]

Critics in the black community specifically attacked the entertainment choices of migrants and they posed alternatives. Social welfare agencies considered themselves competitors with the saloon for migrant loyalty. The *Christian Recorder* urged its readers to: "Get these Negroes in your churches; make them welcome; don't turn up your nose and let the saloon man and the gambler do all the welcoming." The Urban League tried to be sensitive to migrant tastes by offering "community dances, baseball and basketball." These activities, according to one spokesperson, needed to be "active and practical, to a certain extent primitive. If he [the migrant] does not get it under wholesome conditions, he will seek it under evil ones." "Evil conditions" meant the saloon and dance hall.[11]

The *Defender*'s music columnist Dave Peyton gave musicians extensive advice regarding their careers in Chicago. He suggested that blacks emulate white players, and Peyton defined "musicianship" as "the . . . addition by white musicians of symphonic elements to the modern syncopated score."[12] But it was the jazzman's life-style as much as the music that bothered black critics like Peyton. Peyton advised musicians to stay sober, save money, and invest in real estate because "These days of high salaries will not last . . . Let the automobile alone . . . You don't need them now . . . The thing to do is to invest your money in real estate . . . or gold bonds that mature in from two to ten years. . . . "[13] Peyton's exhortations illustrate the class tensions which intensified between middle- and working-class blacks after migration, and which helped make jazz controversial among blacks as well as whites.

If Peyton had only been a newspaper columnist, his views might be dismissed as those of a black curmudgeon with questionable influence. But his attitudes were echoed by other blacks, and his personal influence extended to Local 208 of the Musicians' Union. It gave him and other members of the music establishment authority in finding jobs and, therefore, of denying them to jazzmen. Peyton was clear in his views that work in the position held by Local 208 members required skills he found lacking in black jazzmen. "The orchestra giving service in the vaudeville theatre," for example, "must be composed of first class musicians . . . ," Peyton argued. He contrasted their ability with that of cabaret (or jazz) musicians who disdained both Peyton's standards and Local 208. "Squeaks, squawks, moans, groans, and flutters . . . make the cabaret musician popular," Peyton believed.

In the cabaret orchestra the "ham" musician finds a comfortable berth. He doesn't have to stick to the score; a mistake can be counted as a "trick figure." . . . The gut bucket orchestra today is what the people want. . . . The hip liquor toter wants sensational noise. They have no consciousness of what real music is.[14]

Black musicians of Peyton's camp wanted to put "Southern," and distinctively Afro-American black performance characteristics far behind them.

Important as Chicago was in the development of jazz—and as an arena of cultural conflict within the black community—New York produced a more interesting and complex debate among blacks over jazz. That was the case in large measure because twenties Harlem was home not only to night clubs and fledgling record companies, it served as the center for the writers, educators, artists, social reformers, and political activists who promoted black art and literature in the Harlem Renaissance.

Some musicians like Roland Hayes were counted among the creative artists of the Harlem Renaissance, but most of them were not given the same recognition as writers. For their part, jazz musicians do not seem to have paid much attention to the manifestos of artistic pride that characterized this fertile decade of Afro-American arts and letters. Participants in the Harlem Renaissance, however, heard—and debated—the merits of jazz.[15]

The Harlem Renaissance itself was characterized by unprecedented discussions of the origins, nature, and goals of black artistic and cultural endeavors. All participants agreed that appreciation and encouragement of black creativity was long overdue. Disagreements arose over means of recognition and appropriate aesthetic principles. Because jazz both embodied and transformed folk music performance traditions, the treatment of jazz in the Harlem Renaissance offered a revealing measure of the movement's character. Harlem Renaissance debates over music had influence beyond the relatively small circle of Harlem intellectuals and fueled the jazz controversy in black communities.[16]

As many scholars point out, Harlem Renaissance leaders generally devalued blues and jazz, at least as usually performed, and preferred the transformation of blues and jazz themes into symphonic arrangements patterned after European art music. Some leaders disdained jazz because of its identification with vice, crime, and migrant "backwardness." When jazz was eventually revalued as part of the rise of a cult of primitivism, some community spokesmen objected to it for reinforcing the negative stereo-types primitivism seemed to encourage.[17]

Harlem Renaissance historian Nathan Huggins summarized the purported myopia towards jazz among Renaissance leaders with a mixture of wistfulness and criticism. "Harlem intellectuals promoted Negro art," he wrote,

> but one thing is very curious, except for Langston Hughes, none of them took jazz—the new music—seriously. Of course, they all mentioned it as background, as descriptive of Harlem life. But none thought enough about it to try and figure out what was happening. They tended to view it as a folk art—like the spirituals and the dance—the unrefined source for the new art. Men like James Weldon Johnson and Alain Locke expected some race genius to appear who would transform that source into *high* culture . . . the promoters of the Harlem Renaissance were so fixed on a vision of *high* culture that they did not look very hard or well at jazz.[18]

Jazz performance, nonetheless, played a much more significant role in the Harlem Renaissance than Huggins suggested, and the Harlem Renaissance, in turn, influenced the jazz controversy.

Many more writers than Langston Hughes appreciated and scrutinized jazz performance. Prominent Harlem Renaissance intellectuals analyzed the history and development of jazz in their aesthetic discussions—sometimes by comparing the formal similarities and performance differences of secular and sacred music. Jazz and blues appeared as theme and language in Harlem Renaissance novels, poems, and paintings, usually with jazz performance depicted as evocative of both the modern sensibility generally and the black experience in particular. These evocations of jazz usually included a recognition of the participatory and expressive traditions of blues and jazz. And while there was no consensus about the influence of jazz among Harlem Renaissance intellectuals, jazz performance became a touchstone of the rich (if uneven) experimentation that characterized their literature and cultural debates.

Prominent spokesmen, especially W.E.B. DuBois, James Weldon Johnson, Charles S. Johnson, and Walter White believed a renaissance would encourage race pride and challenge demeaning stereotypes. These principles formed the basis for their views on jazz. Just as DuBois envisioned a "Talented Tenth" to lead the black masses, so he and others argued that artists had an important role providing a creative "uplift" in the black community. This elitist conception of cultural production was reflected in the National Association for the Advancement of Colored People (NAACP) and the National Urban League (NUL) prize contests. The contests aimed at attracting and promoting young writers and artists and judged them by classical standards. Harlem Renaissance historian David Levering Lewis labeled this philosophy "civil rights by copyright."[19]

W.E.B. DuBois was one of the most articulate of the Harlem Renaissance spokespersons to comment on black music. Although he (like Charles Johnson of the Urban League) clearly saw the political value of art, he warned against seeing "Art and Propaganda as one." He exhorted readers of the *Crisis* to consider what he called "Truth in Art" and not to shirk from considering the "shortcomings" of blacks. Too many writers, DuBois pointed out, "fear to paint the truth lest they criticize their own and be in turn criticized for it. They fail to see the Eternal Beauty that shines through all Truth, and try to portray a world of stilted artificial black folk such as never were on land and sea." What is so curious here is that DuBois could criticize images of "stilted artificial black folk" while repudiating real black folk traditions, such as those embodied in blues and jazz, in favor of white cultural standards.[20] He found a greater measure of "Eternal Beauty" in Beethoven or in spirituals than in the syncopated music of Harlem cabarets and clubs.

DuBois, of course, was a man whose understanding of black folk culture was largely that of an outsider. Raised in rural western Massachusetts, his education, which included the tutelage of William James at Harvard; Gustav von Schmoller, Adolf Wagner, and Heinrich von Treitschke in Germany, prepared him to see folk culture as the essential embodiment of national character. James taught him that the cultural elite of a society had a responsibility to lead the masses. In literature, DuBois studied with Harvard's Barrett Wendell, whom DuBois biographer Arnold Rampersad described as a "charismatic figure disdainful of the problems of a struggling national literature, of the vitality of folk expression, or of the experimentation in forms and themes by which literature revitalizes itself." DuBois's ambivalent attempts to reconcile his belief in folk art and racial creativity with genteel moral and artistic standards formed the basis for his view that artists should improve on folk materials (and judge them) in order to serve as ambassadors for racial pride and understanding.[21]

Although DuBois was not always willing to take black culture on its own terms, he and other Harlem Renaissance leaders appreciated it for its influence in shaping both black identity and the broader American culture. Music especially offered fertile possibilities for tracing the evolution of a larger African and oral folk culture into the many forms of black creativity under slavery and afterward. DuBois himself used spirituals as an organizing theme and as a climax of his renowned study, *The Souls of Black Folk* (1903). (Characteristically, he mingled them with expressions of European culture, such as the poetry of Goethe, to demonstrate the eternal and universal nature of the human spirit.) Many Harlem writers credited *The Souls of Black Folk* with transforming their self-perception. James Weldon Johnson declared it had "a greater effect upon and within the Negro race in America than any other single book published in this century since *Uncle Tom's Cabin*."[22]

Johnson, Joel A. Rogers, and Alain Locke similarly celebrated the folk origins of spirituals, work songs, ragtime, and blues. Johnson introduced his 1922 edited collection, *The Book of American Negro Poetry,* by asserting that Uncle Remus stories, spirituals, the cakewalk, and ragtime "were the only things artistic that have yet sprung from American soil and been universally acknowledged as distinctive American products." The distinctiveness involved their participatory nature. Ragtime, for example, provoked audience response and engaged listeners:

> Anyone who doubts that there is a peculiar hell-tickling, smile-provoking, joy-awakening, response compelling charm in Ragtime needs only to hear a skillful performer play the genuine article, needs only to listen to its bizarre harmonies, its audacious resolutions often consisting of an abrupt jump from one key to another, its intricate rhythms in which the accents fall in the most unexpected places but in which the fundamental beat is never lost, in order to be convinced. I believe it has its place as well as the music which draws from us sighs and tears.[23]

Johnson's appreciation of the participatory distinctiveness of black music was common to Harlem Renaissance treatments of jazz, and its precursors, blues and ragtime.

Johnson's own earlier *The Book of American Negro Spirituals* (1912) was a valuable contribution to black music history and folklore. He followed it with his adaptation of black spirituals in *God's Trombones—Seven Negro Spirituals in Verse* (1927). Johnson explained that the title reflected the resonance of a trombone, which has "just the tone and timbre to represent the old-time Negro preacher's voice—besides there were the traditional jazz connotations provided by the trombone."[24]

Joel A. Roger's essay "Jazz at Home," which Alain Locke included in his *The New Negro* anthology, offered the most comprehensive statement on jazz in the literature of the Harlem Renaissance. Rogers discussed the history of jazz performance, the influence of jazz on other music and entertainment forms, and jazz as a symbol of the modern age. The distinctiveness of jazz, according to Rogers, derived from the performance qualities in folk cultures. Jazz, Rogers wrote, was "of Negro origin, plus the influence of the American environment." Rogers suggested that the "elementals" of jazz had "always existed" in worldwide dance forms:

> It is in the Indian war dance, the Highland fling, the Irish jig, the Cossack dance, the Spanish fandango, the Brazilian *maxixe,* the dance of the whirling dervish, the hula of the South Seas, the *dance du ventre* of the Orient, the *carmagnole* of the French Revolution, and the ragtime of the Negro.

As DuBois did with spirituals, Rogers located the origins of jazz in a worldwide folk culture and asserted a long and dignified heritage for it.[25]

But Rogers, like Johnson, also gave great weight to the participatory qualities of jazz performance. Ragtime, he pointed out, was the "direct predecessor of jazz," and he credited itinerant stride and boogie-woogie pianists with playing the first jazz. Ragtime band performers, he noted, made their own instruments, and if necessary, used their bodies for "patting juba" rhythms.[26] Such performers interacted with a community that contributed to the music. Rogers suggested, for example, that the "spontaneity" required to appreciate jazz came easiest to blacks because they had experienced similar music in religious revivals.

Rogers traced the transformation of the call-and-response form typical of Afro-American sacred music (and he might have added work songs) into blues and jazz. Even his explanation for the word "jazz" emphasized the role of the audience. Rogers credited the term to the exploits of "Jasbo Brown":

> . . . a reckless musician of a Negro cabaret in Chicago, who played this and other blues, blowing his own extravagant moods and risqué interpretations into them, while hilarious with gin. To give further meanings to his veiled allusion, he would make the trombone "talk" by putting a derby hat and later a tin can at its mouth. The delighted patrons would shout "More Jasbo. More, Jas, more." And so the name originated.[27]

Jazz dances like Walking the Dog, the Texas Tommy, and the Charleston also originated in cabarets, according to Rogers. Children on Harlem streets, Rogers insisted, were the "cleverest Charleston dancers . . . keeping time with their hands, and surrounded by admiring crowds."[28]

Rogers pointed out that the excitement and energy of jazz music and jazz dance had inspired Broadway's artists, actors, and producers, as well as influencing modernist European composers. He proudly predicted: "With the same nonchalance and impudence with which it left the levee and the dive to stride like an upstart conqueror, almost overnight, into the grand salon, jazz now begins its conquest of musical Parnassus."[29] For Rogers, the stride of jazz onto Broadway—like the stride of pianists—illustrated that black music was earning well-deserved new respect.

Alain Locke's own essay on music in *The New Negro* was "The Negro Spirituals." He believed spirituals were authentic folk art in danger of disappearing. In that essay, and in his 1936 study *The Negro and His Music,* Locke painstakingly analyzed the formal and performance elements of black music. His treatment of jazz was designed to show how ragtime and jazz embodied "Negro rhythm and harmony" that had been lost through the dilutions of Stephen Foster, minstrelsy, and other popular music.[30]

Like DuBois, Locke hoped black folk music would become a "great classical music" as European folk melodies had become during the nineteenth century. Locke, however, did not approve of art used for propaganda purposes and he exhorted jazz participants with his own manifesto:

> I believe we are at that interesting moment when the prophet becomes the poet and when prophecy becomes the expressive song. . . . We have had too many Jeremiahs. . . . My chief objection to propaganda . . . is that it perpetuates the position of group inferiority by crying out against it. . . . Art in the best sense is rooted in self-expression and whether naive or sophisticated is self-contained. In our spiritual growth genius and talent must more and more choose the role of group expression, or even at times the role of free individualistic expression—in a word, we must choose art and put aside propaganda.[31]

In his study of black music, Locke valued the individualistic self-expression in jazz that evolved out of the dynamic relationship between group and individual creativity.

Central to Locke's analysis was an analysis of the role of performance and participation. In *The Negro and His Music,* he used Abbe Niles's and W.H. Handy's *Blues: An Anthology* to echo Handy's contention that his inspiration for blues composition to the lively response from audiences who heard him play "hot."[32]

Locke likewise located jazz rhythm and improvisation in folk music practice. The "tango rhythm," he wrote, was "characteristically Negro and its popularity among Negroes becomes very plausible when it is realized that it is originally an African Rhythm." It was "basic in the purest and oldest strains of the Afro-Cuban music, in the folk music of Mexico and Brazil . . . and in Negro dances of even the Bahamas and Barbados." Improvisation, Locke wrote:

> . . . came rocketing out of the blues. It grew out of the improvised musical filling-in of the gap between the short measure of the blues and the longer eight bar line, the break in the interval in the original folk form of three line blues. Such feeling in and compounding of the basic rhythm are characteristic of Negro music everywhere, from deepest Africa to the streets of Charleston, from the unaccompanied hand-clapping of the corner "hoe-down" to the interpolation of shouts, amens, and exclamations in Negro church revivals.[33]

Locke's discussion aimed at proving that jazz had a unique structure, history, and musical tone that originated in and continued to express the participatory traditions of black folk music.

Although Locke in some respects appeared to be as much a cultural elitist as DuBois, he nonetheless disputed those who claimed jazz was a "mere set of musical tricks by which any tune whatsoever can be 'ragged' or 'jazzed'." Jazz had a distinctive musical characteristics like other musical genres, according to Locke and could trace its lineage back to secular and sacred black folk music. He pointed out that it took talent and practice to play jazz, and black musicians in particular had mastered the particularities of its creation. Accomplished jazz musicians must be able to improvise, work with fellow bandsmen, and be skilled at head tunes and improvisation. Jazz, Locke wrote, was characterized by a "free-style" that had "generations of experience back of it; it is derived from the voice tricks and vocal habits characteristic of Negro choral singing." He correctly perceived that the distinctiveness of jazz derived from its communal and participatory origins, which continued to be expressed through improvisation.[34]

Harlem Renaissance defenders of jazz like Locke and Rogers had to contend with attacks on its social as well as its musical characteristics. Rogers even turned one of the complaints against jazz into a positive argument in its favor. He accepted the notion that there was a narcotic quality to jazz (as appalled critics suggested) and wrote that it offered a psychological relief that was "safer than drugs or alcohol." Acknowledging potentially immoral influences of jazz, Rogers insisted that its impact depended on the stability of its listeners: "Jazz, it is needless to say, will remain a creation for the industrious and a dissipator of energy for the frivolous, a tonic for the strong and a poison for the weak."[35]

Locke compared jazz to an "epidemic" that spread rapidly and transformed tempo, technique, and themes in popular music. Like James Weldon Johnson, who called ragtime a music that "jes grew," Locke depicted jazz as an infectious sound that had grown quickly to reach a large audience by the thirties. Jazz became a music of "interracial collaboration," according to Locke, and he identified three major playing styles: hot or swing from Chicago, sweet from New York, and classic jazz from Paris. Although Locke was clearly pleased with the international popularity of jazz, he also noted that it had not translated into financial success for the black and white pioneers of jazz.[36]

Locke, however, was not certain that commercialization was a good thing. He feared that the success of jazz might undermine its folk heritage. The "common enemy" of all jazz musicianship was the "ever present danger of commercialization" and the "public taste" which was "a notoriously poor judge of quality." Locke—expressing concerns similar to those of DuBois—hoped jazz "experts" would exert more influence on public taste and encourage listeners to appreciate and thereby protect its folk roots.[37]

In common with Rogers, Locke directly addressed those who criticized the purported immorality of jazz. He concurred with those who found an "erotic side" in the music. But, he explained:

> ... there is a vast difference between its first healthy and earthy expression in the original peasant paganism out of which it arose and its hectic, artificial and sometimes morally vicious counterpart

which was the outcome of the vogue of artificial and commercialized jazz entertainment. The one is primitively erotic; the other decadently neurotic.[38]

Locke carefully defined primitivism by its relation to folk traditions, and in that context, he considered jazz a positive influence on twentieth-century society. Noting that jazz was accused of being both an "emotional escape" and an "emotional rejuvenator" for those trying to cope with post-World War I America, Locke insisted that jazz did not cause immorality. Its popularity was a symptom of larger social changes, he commented, and, much like Rogers, Locke saw jazz as a spiritual child of the twenties, anchored in folk traditions but speaking to modern life.[39]

There was a loose consensus on jazz among W.E.B. DuBois, James Weldon Johnson, J. A. Rogers, and Alain Locke—four of the major figures of the Harlem Renaissance. Each saw black music serving a dual role. Despite their preference for "high" culture, they considered Afro-American music a repository of history and creativity, and a rich potential source of creative idioms for other music forms. In each analysis, these authors acknowledged the power of musical performance to express and encourage emotions through spontaneity and audience participation. As each author documented, the unique strengths of ragtime, blues, and jazz depended on its retention of participatory musical traditions in Afro-American folk culture.

Rogers and Locke rebutted aesthetic and moral accusations against jazz by condemning those with a prurient or commercial interest in jazz that could compromise its folk beauty. Because they believed black music had made and would continue to make significant contributions to American music and society, Locke and Rogers happily accepted the public identification of jazz with 1920s America. They located its controversial qualities in white-dominated commercial culture—not in black performance traditions—and thereby shifted the terms of the jazz controversy.

Fiction and poetry writers of the Harlem Renaissance also discovered a unique creative well provided by jazz performance.

Nathan Huggins suggests that the use of jazz as background was casual—almost a convention required by the cult of primitivism. But for some artists jazz performance was a major inspiration for new themes and language. Three of the many writers who arrived in Harlem used jazz performance in significantly new ways. Claude McKay, Langston Hughes, and Zora Neale Hurston found that music helped them formulate a new art and aesthetics, which in turn challenged political and racial assumptions about art in America.[40]

Claude McKay, a Jamaican-born immigrant, is perhaps the best-known Harlem Renaissance fiction writer to use primitivism as a major theme in his portrait of black life. McKay's poems were among the first published in the Harlem Renaissance. But it was McKay's fiction that depended most strongly on exotic atmospheres derived from jazz performance images and locations. In *Home to Harlem* (1927), which provoked considerable opprobrium from some Harlem Renaissance critics, McKay used jazz, blues, and their performance environments as major motifs for his "primitive" 1920s Harlem. Like Rogers and Locke, he also evoked metaphors of disease for jazz. In *Home to Harlem,* the protagonist Jake returns to Harlem following his desertion from World War I military service. He is entranced by: "The noises of Harlem. The sugared laughter. The honey-talk on its streets. And all night long, ragtime and 'blues' playing somewhere . . . singing somewhere, dancing somewhere! Oh! the contagious fever of Harlem." That tone occurs throughout the novel, with McKay using blues and jazz performance to symbolize the urban primitivism he celebrated.[41]

Much of the novel was set in the cabarets and nightclubs of Harlem. McKay's descriptions of performance locations stressed the exotic and sensational, but nevertheless they were fairly consistent with actual cabarets in the 1920s. McKay explained that some cabarets, like Barron's, relied "on its downtown white trade." Others, like Leroy's, served as "the big common rendezvous shop for everybody." The "Congo" was typical of blacks-only clubs, "it was African in spirit and color. No white persons were admitted there." McKay's fictional Harlem nightlife mirrored actual clubs in the twenties and he used their differences to illustrate class and racial divisions.[42]

McKay was also sensitive to the visual and psychological aspects of jazz. He made effective use of the inner decor of clubs to evoke images of hot-house or jungle-like worlds in which dancing, drinking, fighting, and flirtation were common. The environment relaxed the restraints of everyday life, and performers and patrons responded by expressing emotions normally held in check. In a typical scene from *Home to Harlem,* for example, McKay showed how musical entertainment provided a welcome release for the "common workaday Negroes of the Belt":

> The orchestra was tuning up. . . . The first notes fell out like a general clapping for merrymaking and chased the dancers running sliding, shuffling, trotting to the floor. Little girls energetically chewing Spearmint and showing all their teeth dashed out on the floor and started shivering amorously, itching for their partners to come. Some lads were quick on their feet, grinning gaily while their girls were sucking up the last of their creme de menthe. The floor was large and smooth enough for anything [ellipses in the original].[43]

This scene, like others in McKay's novel, presented the nightclub as a place in which the music and its setting led to release, enjoyment, and participation.

For McKay, working-class and peasant culture contained a beauty relatively untouched by the civilized world. He believed that the Harlem he created in *Home to Harlem* was "similar to what I had done for Jamaica in verse." He used blues and jazz music in the American setting to establish an open, emotional, and participatory ambience—what he considered " primitive." But some reviewers felt *Home to Harlem* strayed too far from folk cultures and pandered to the exploitative tastes of white slummers by glorifying the Harlem underworld. Whatever the merits of these negative judgments, McKay's portrayals of musical entertainment and its meaning for lower-class blacks challenged the assertion of Locke and others that "primitive" virtues belonged only to rural folk culture, and that commercialization distorted "primitive" beauty. Likewise, McKay's suggestion that the power of music came from participatory performances located in dives and cabarets offended more conservative Harlem Renaissance leaders, even though they had also seen participation (although of a more genteel sort) as central to Afro-American culture.[44]

McKay later expressed his disappointment that "many of the talented Negroes regarded their renaissance as more of an uplift organization and a vehicle to accelerate the pace and progress of smart Negro Society." DuBois, in particular, attacked McKay's controversial treatment of blues and jazz performance because DuBois could not accept the moral tone of *Home to Harlem.* McKay depicted an extreme potential of performance that challenged the norms of renaissance leaders and set him apart from more genteel aesthetic values.[45]

Like Claude McKay, Langston Hughes found inspiration in the experiences of common people he saw in Harlem—many of them recent migrants from the South. Hughes, however, did not try to develop a "primitive" vision of modern life. Beginning in the twenties and continuing throughout his career, Hughes based his lyrical craft on the rich oral traditions of Afro-American folk tales and humor, blues and jazz, and sacred music.

Musical performance and performers were prominent themes in Hughes's twenties collections of poetry, *The Weary Blues* (1926) and *Fine Clothes to the Jew* (1927). *Weary Blues,* for example, featured several poems that paid tribute to dancers, including: "Danse Africaine," "The Cat and the Saxophone," "Negro Dancers," and "Song for a Banjo Dance." The poems evoked various kinds of Afro-American dance. All of them, nevertheless, captured the energy and grace of movement, and the relationship of dance to music, reflecting Hughes's appreciation of the richness of Afro-American dance as a performance medium

Performance environments were also important in Hughes's poems. "Jazzonia" and "Jazz Band in a Paris Cafe" captured the alluring world of the cabaret. In "Jazzonia," Hughes equated the effect of the performance atmosphere with that of the garden of Eden and of ancient Africa:

Oh! silver tree!
Oh, shining rivers of the soul!

In a Harlem cabaret
Six long-headed jazzers play.
A dancing girl whose eyes are bold
Lifts high a dress of silken gold.

Oh! shining tree!
Oh, shining river of the soul!

Were Eve's eyes
In the first garden
Just a bit too bold?
Was Cleopatra gorgeous
In a gown of gold?

Oh! shining tree!
Oh, shining rivers of the soul!

In a whirling cabaret
Six long-headed jazzers play.[46]

The performance in Hughes's cabaret is seductive, and the lyrical form nicely echoes the stanzas and refrains of a musical composition. Hughes associates the forbidden with the cabaret in his references to Eve and Cleopatra. The imagery and questioning tone combine to *suggest* the power of music, rather than explaining it directly.[47]

The most innovative aspect of Hughes's jazz and blues poetry was his combination of performance subjects with music idioms—and there he went beyond McKay, who was far less innovative in his prose structure. *Weary Blues* and *Fine Clothes to the Jew* contain a wide range of blues, and many of them express the experience of migration and disappointment: "Bound No' Blues," "Homesick Blues," "Listen Here Blues," and "Po' Boy Blues." Hughes attributed his affection for the blues to his first exposure to them in the seedy district of Washington, D.C. "I tried to write poems like the songs they sang on Seventh Street," Hughes explained in his autobiography *The Big Sea,* "gay songs, because you had to be gay or die; sad songs, because you couldn't help being sad sometimes. But gay or sad, you kept on living and you kept on going. Their songs—those of Seventh Street—had the pulse beat of the people who kept going." Similarly, Hughes, in *Fine Clothes to the Jew*, explained the blues form to his readers and noted: "The mood of the blues is almost despondency, but when they are sung people laugh."[48]

Although Hughes's sustained experiments with jazz forms came later in his career, "The Cat and the Saxophone"[49] offers one of the best examples of a twenties jazz poem:

> EVERYBODY
> Half-pint,—
> Gin?
> No, make it
> LOVES MY BABY
> corn. You like
> liquor,
> don't you honey?
> BUT MY BABY
> Sure. Kiss me,
> DON'T LOVE NOBODY
> daddy.
> BUT ME.
> Say!
> EVERYBODY
> Yes?
> WANTS MY BABY
> sweetie, ain't I?
> DON'T WANT NOBODY
> Sure.
> BUT
> Then let's
> ME,
> do it!
> SWEET ME.
> Charleston,
> mamma!
> !

It is possible that Hughes meant for the alternation of upper-and lower-case letters to create a syncopated effect, and he incorporates jazz lyrics, as well as jazz dance in this poem. "The Cat and the Saxophone, " like other Langston Hughes twenties poems, was his own blues and jazz performance. (Later he would record a reading of *Weary Blues,* with a score by notable jazz musicians, including Charles Mingus.)

The publication of *Weary Blues* did not generate the same outrage as McKay's cabaret world of *Home to Harlem.* W.E.B. Du Bois praised Hughes in a 1924 *Crisis* article on "The Younger Literary Movement," and Jessie Fauset and Dubose Heyward both gave high acclaim to *Weary Blues.* Locke commented that Hughes's poetry did not have "the ragged provincialism of a minstrel but the descriptive detachment of a Vachel Lindsay and Sandburg . . . the democratic sweep and universality of a Whitman." Hughes was less fortunate with *Fine Clothes to the Jew,* which was soundly attacked by the black press. J.A. Rogers, for example, called the collection "piffling trash" that "left him sick."[50]

Countee Cullen also complimented his fellow poet, but offered his reservations about the qualities of jazz poetry. Cullen asked if poems like "The Cat and the Saxophone" should be counted "among that select and austere circle of high literary expression which we call poetry?" Cullen also voiced his concern that Hughes would become like those writers who are "racial artists instead of artists pure and simple."[51]

Cullen's musings were echoed in the more general questions of other critics during the twenties. George Schuyler and Langston Hughes offered sharply contrasting views on the nature of Afro-American art and literature in a famous debate that took place in the *Nation*'s June 1926 issue. Schuyler derided "Negro Art Hokum" and insisted that discussions of a distinctive black folk culture were wrong-headed. According to Schuyler, folk art and folk music, including blues and jazz, could have been "produced by any group under similar circumstances." Black folk art, he suggested, was like that of other "peasant" cultures.[52]

In response, Hughes asserted the position typical of young experimental Harlem Renaissance writers. Hughes began by lamenting the lack of self-worth he felt was expressed by a young poet who remarked "I want to be a poet—not a Negro poet." Hughes attributed the failure of this young man to appreciate his racial heritage to the dominance of black bourgeois cultural values. Hughes castigated the black middle class for "aping things white." Such aesthetic standards, according to Hughes, created "A very high mountain indeed for the would-be racial artist to climb in order to discover himself and his people."[53] Hughes passionately defended the creative qualities of black folk art and insisted that common people continued to offer the best inspiration for great art. They, unlike the middle class, had not been entirely seduced by white artistic standards.

The common people Hughes had in mind were blacks who lived on Seventh Street in Washington, D.C., or State Street in Chicago. "They do not care whether they are like white folks or anybody else," Hughes wrote. "Their joys run, bang! into ecstasy! . . . they are not afraid of the spirituals and jazz is their child." Hughes was proud of the racial themes in his poetry, and he sought to "grasp and hold some of the meanings and rhythm of jazz." The essay expressed Hughes's solidarity with the folks on Seventh Street. His conclusion became one of the most famous manifestos of Afro-American writers:

> Let the blare of Negro jazz bands and the bellowing voice of Bessie Smith singing Blues penetrate the closed ears of the colored near-intellectuals until they listen and perhaps understand. Let Paul Robeson singing "Water Boy," and Rudolph Fisher writing about the streets of Harlem, and Jean Toomer holding the heart of Georgia in his hands, and Aaron Douglas drawing strange black fantasies cause the smug Negro middle class to turn from their white, respectable, ordinary books and papers and catch a glimmer of their own beauty. We younger artists who create now intend to express our individual dark-skinned selves without fear or shame. If white people are pleased we are glad. If they are not, it doesn't matter. We know we are beautiful. And ugly too. The tom-tom cries and the tom-tom laughs.[54]

Hughes punctuated "The Negro Artist and the Racial Mountain" with "tom-tom" rhythms that use music to evoke Afro-

American culture. For Hughes, music was the best language to use when celebrating black creativity. Likewise, jazz and blues gave Hughes a voice with which he could assert his own artistic independence.

Zora Neale Hurston resembled Hughes in her enthusiasm for black folk culture, although her approach was unusual in the Harlem Renaissance and led her to analyze musical performances in intriguing ways. Until recently many critics demeaned her talents and focused instead on Hurston's unconventional life. Hurston's biographer Robert Hemenway pointed out that her flamboyant personal style and storytelling abilities derived in part from her childhood in the all-black town of Eatonville, Florida. She was the daughter of the rural South and a rebel against the repressive nature of its mores. More than many Harlem Renaissance writers, Hurston had first-hand knowledge and appreciation of folk tales and culture. This intimate understanding set her apart from her literary contemporaries and formed the basis for her analysis of musical performance.[55]

Hurston counted herself among the iconoclasts of the Harlem Renaissance who departed from some of the aesthetic ideas of DuBois, Johnson, and Locke. For example, Hurston, along with Langston Hughes and Wallace Thurman, edited the short-lived journal *Fire!*. Much of the innovation in her work came from Hurston's development of a folkloric voice that merged her childhood memories with literary and anthropological interests. She was able to appreciate the relationship between folk materials and the "folk process," according to Hemenway.[56]

Hurston's examples of spirituals, songs, and other music and dance performances are one way that Hurston's collections demonstrated this linkage between folk tales and songs and their performance context. In her contributions to Nancy Cunard's *Negro Anthology* (1934), for example, Hurston delineated "Characteristics of Negro Expression" that included musical performance. As evidence of Afro-American originality, she pointed to the ways blacks "modified" language, methods of food preparation, medical practice, and religion. When Hurston located the dissemination of jazz in this process of modifica-

tion, she used the opportunity to comment on white appropriation of black performance:

> Everyone is familiar with the Negro's modification of the white's
> musical instruments, so that his interpretation has been adopted by
> the white man himself and then re-interpreted. In so many words,
> Paul Whiteman is giving an imitation of a Negro orchestra making
> use of white-invented instruments in a Negro way. Thus has arisen a
> new art in the civilized world . . .

Hurston's did not speculate about what *could* become of folk
traditions, she recorded their transformation. In addition, she
used understatement in this "story" of jazz performers, symbolized by Paul Whiteman, who often obscured black contributions
to jazz.[57]

Like McKay, Hurston was sensitive to the importance of entertainment milieus. Particularly fascinating was her description
of jook, one of the places in the South in which jazz flourished.
"Jook," Hurston wrote, "is the word for Negro pleasure house. It
may mean a bawdy house. It may mean the house set aside on
public works where the men and women dance, drink and gam-
ble." Hurston recorded that the piano replaced the guitar as the
source for music in the jooks, and "player pianos and victrolas"
were following close behind. The significance of jooks, according to Hurston was that "musically speaking, the Jook is the most
important place in America. For in its smelly, shoddy confines
has been born the secular music known as blues, and on blues
has been founded jazz. The singing and playing in true Negro
style is called jooking." Hurston emphasized communal creation
of jook musics, which travel "from mouth to mouth and from
Jook to Jook for years before they reach outside ears. Hence the
great variety of subject matter in each song."[58]

Hurston credited the Jook with providing themes for black
Broadway shows. But whereas black audiences preferred a "girl
who could hoist a Jook song from her belly and lam it against the
front door of the theatre," the white audiences had created a
demand for "the bleached chorus" of light-skinned black women
performers in theatre and cabaret reviews." Hurston also voiced

amusement at another white transformation of rural black culture. "Speaking of the influence of the Jook," Hurston noted that Mae West's performance in the play *Sex:*

> . . . had much more flavor of the turpentine quarters than she did of the white bawd. I know that the piece she played on the piano is a very old Jook composition, "Honey let yo' drawers hang low" had been played and sung in every Jook in the South for at least thirty-five years. It has always puzzled me why she thought it likely to be played in a Canadian bawdy house.

In this analysis, as in the one about Paul Whiteman, Hurston notes the Afro-American origins of a white entertainer's routine. She also described the significance of black women blues singers and the effects of racism on black women entertainers—a topic (and a group) rarely noted by other Harlem Renaissance writers.[59]

Hurston recorded the creation of folk music as she saw it performed, and noted its influence on both white and black music. She did not call for it to be elevated to high culture. In fact, Hurston upbraided the "Niggerati," who would have a renaissance at the expense of what she considered authentic black art:

> To those who want to institute Negro Theatre, let me say it is already established. It is lacking in wealth, so it is not seen in the high places. A creature with a white head and Negro feet struts the metropolitan boards. The real Negro theatre is in the Jooks and cabarets, self-conscious individuals may turn away the eye and say, "Let us search elsewhere for our dramatic art." Let em' search. They certainly won't find it. Butter Beans and Susie, B-Jangles and Snake Hips are the only performers of the real Negro school it has ever been my pleasure to behold in New York."[60]

Hurston's aesthetic differed from the folk abstractions of elitist Harlem Renaissance leaders and she recorded some of the most interesting comments on the value of folk music and black entertainment. Like McKay and Hughes, Hurston's unique style could cause controversy and bring her criticism.

In a 1928 performance description, for example, Hurston cast herself in the role of a primitive whom white companions cannot understand. Contemporary critics complain that Hurston pandered to white stereotypes in this section of the essay "What It Feels To Be Colored and Me:"

> . . . when I sit in the drafty basement that is The New World Cabaret with a white person, my color comes. We enter chatting about any little nothing that we have in common and are seated by the jazz waiters. In the abrupt way that jazz orchestras have, this one plunges into a number. It loses no time in circumlocutions, but gets right down to business. It constricts the thorax and splits the heart with its tempo and narcotic harmonies. This orchestra grows rambunctious, rears on its hind legs and attacks the tonal veil with primitive fury, rending it, clawing it until it breaks through to the jungle beyond. I follow those heathen—follow them exultingly. I dance wildly inside myself; I yell within, I whoop; I shake my assegai above my head, I hurl it true to the mark *yeeooww!* I am in the jungle and live in the jungle way. My face is painted red and yellow and my body is painted blue. My pulse is throbbing like a war drum. I want to slaughter something—give pain, give death to what, I do not know. But the piece ends. The men of the orchestra wipe their lips and rest their fingers. I creep back slowly to the veneer we call civilization with the last tone and find the white friend sitting motionless in his seat, smoking calmly.
>
> "Good music they have here," he remarks, drumming the table with his fingers.
>
> Music. The great blobs of purple and red emotion have not touched him. He has only heard what I felt. He is far away and I see him but dimly across the ocean and the continent that have fallen between us. He is so pale with his whiteness then and I am *so* colored.[61]

Because of her reference to "jazz waiters," Hurston's description suggests a setting like Small's in Harlem. And although it is easy to see why Hurston's characterization might offend some, it can also be read as an ironic parody of the "primitivistic" conventions used by whites to describe blacks.

Hurston's skill as a folklorist enabled her to collect and preserve a wide variety of oral performances in her field work in the South. Her appreciation of performance informs her comments about blues and jazz and she showed a sensitivity to the experiences of black women entertainers that was unique for Renaissance writers. In fact, Hurston's viewpoint has led some recent critics to compare her literary performance to that of the classic female blues singers of the twenties "lamming" their songs against the walls of the theatre.[62]

Hurston illustrates the richness and diversity of thought about jazz among Harlem Renaissance intellectuals, particularly when compared with a far more conventional figure like DuBois. But there was also common ground. Harlem intellectuals were not insensitive to jazz, although it wasn't usually at the center of their analysis of black culture and creativity. Even those whose musical tastes were genteel, like DuBois, found a measure of pride in the folk traditions that helped produce it. Others, notably McKay and, especially Hughes, also glimpsed in jazz the possibility of breaking with white literary conventions in order to speak in a distinctively Afro-American voice. Above all, Harlem intellectuals, in their diverse ways, recognized that performance and participation were essential to jazz and to attitudes toward it. In that insight, they were at the heart of the music and at the heart of the controversy surrounding it.

Behind criticisms of jazz based on moral values and bourgeois taste, a series of more complex issues developed from the particularities of jazz performance itself and was part of the contribution of the Harlem Renaissance. When writers such as DuBois, Johnson, and Locke provided evidence of the artistic potential of the New Negro by documenting the history and development of folk music into ragtime, blues, and jazz, they had to acknowledge that participatory performance was the key to its creative power. Its strong beat and fascinating melodies could also, unfortunately, be trivialized or exploited by whites seeking "primitivism." White patronage could, in turn, seduce black writers into producing commercialized and trite "racial" literature rather than new Afro-American arts and letters of substance.

These concerns about the direction of black aesthetic development put DuBois and other traditional spokespeople at odds with young writers like McKay, Hughes, and Hurston. Transforming the language and voice of musical performance into their art, young creative artists trusted their own emerging aesthetics and were delighted if it captured folk and working-class culture.

Jazz, of course, stirred controversy among blacks outside Harlem and beyond the pages of the Chicago *Defender,* where Dave Peyton held sway. When it did, however, it was with less intellectual sophistication and more predictability than Hurston, Locke, Rogers, and the others brought to it. Indeed, many black Americans found jazz disturbing for the same reasons white Americans were critical of it. Its practitioners performed in brothels and other locations of ill repute that encouraged licentious behavior. In addition, black leaders had special reasons, not shared by whites, for disliking jazz. They objected to zoning practices that located vice districts where jazz and other evils flourished in predominantly black communities. Moreover, they associated jazz and the blues with country ways that they hoped migrants from the South would abandon when they reached the North. It was the contribution of Harlem intellectuals to try and move the debate about jazz away from the conventional moral and racial ground where critics, black and white, tried to keep it. Although influential, they were not fully successful, in part because the debate really was about American values as much as about music and, in part, because, as they perceived, the essence of jazz was what disturbed white (as well as genteel black) critics, just as it was what attracted admirers of the new music.

5 / Prudes and Primitives: White Americans Debate Jazz

Black Americans—especially those active in the Harlem Renaissance—analyzed jazz and blues with the goal of celebrating the unique Afro-American heritage. They also heralded the New Negro of the 1920s who had migrated, literally and metaphorically, from the Old South to the urban "meccas" of the North. For the most part, black critics credited jazz with expressing a historical and cultural record of value. and they tried to understand the relevance to black history of its transmission and performance.

The most prominent discussion concerning jazz, however, took place primarily in white-owned or -managed publications, and among white critics, moralists, educators, and musicians. These commentators and debaters invested jazz with a wide range of meanings, but all pointed to jazz as transforming white as well as black culture.

Some white Americans tried to appropriate the music to their own history or language by stressing a European precedent for jazz or the desirability of using symphonic arrangements to refine jazz. But these critics, too, identified jazz with new entertainment forms, art and literature, and sexual mores. They blamed jazz for the passing of conventions and the relaxation of behavioral restraints. Jazz performance and the jazz controversy provided opportunities for Americans to struggle over both personal and national post-World War I identities.

Jazz bibliographies record an extensive attempt to describe and explain jazz in numerous newspaper, magazine, and journal articles from the teens and twenties. The press accounts ranged from public-interest and feature stories to jeremiads about the music. Even the European reaction to jazz hit the headlines with pronouncements like: "Jazz Pandemonium to Prince Joachim," "Ban Against Jazz Sought in Ireland," "Welsh Invoke Curfews Law As One Way To Stop Jazz," and "Jazz Frightens Bears"—an article explaining how Siberian peasants pounded on pots and pans to scare away bears. All commentators strongly identified it with change and with the emergence of modern sensibility, despite a lack of consensus on the benefits or ills attributed to the music[1]

Numerous articles purported to explain the origins of jazz, particularly the etymology of the word itself. Writers usually acknowledged some jazz antecedents in black musical traditions, but they also speculated on other influences. At one extreme, Jazz was given exotic lineages, such as Siamese or Chinese origins. Other writers insisted jazz was part of Western classical music because it was merely a way of improvising, which Beethoven, Mozart, and Brahms had already perfected. Either strategy played down the role of Afro-Americans and their performance traditions.[2]

Critics analyzing the word reported that it could be a noun, verb, or adjective. Henry Osbourne Osgood, editor of *Musical Courier* in the 1920s, devoted an entire chapter of his book *So This Is Jazz!* to the topic "Jazz That Peculiar Word." Osgood opened the chapter by declaring:

> JAZZ! The word is new and different, just as the thing itself. In the English language it is distinctly *sui generis*. Much to the embarrassment and hindering of the Vachel Lindsay school of poetry, there is no true rhyme for it. Razz? Yes. But razz is plainly a rowdy, low caste word of no standing whereas jazz is to be found in modern dictionaries of dignity and rank. . . . [3]

Osgood cited the inclusion of jazz in encyclopedias as evidence of its growing prominence, but he noted that neither the encyclopedia "nor any body else" can "discover the origin of the word." Observing further that the word "has no relations at all in the English language," and therefore must have originated among some non-English speaking peoples, Osgood concluded it probably came from Africa, where the rhythms characteristic of jazz also seem to have originated. Osgood then summarized the typical explanations for the word provided by twenties critics and writers.[4]

Many of these explanations located jazz in distinctive performance settings, much as writers of the Harlem Renaissance had done. Osgood complimented Walter Kingsley, for example, who wrote an article for the *New York Sun* that explained:

> A strange word has gained wide-spread use in the ranks of our producers of popular music. It is "jazz" used mainly as an adjective description of a band. The group that plays for dancing, when colored, seem infected with the virus that they try to instill as a stimulus in others. They shake and jump and writhe in ways to suggest a return to the medieval jumping mania.[5]

Osgood pointed out that the dances in question were "ring shouts" from Africa—not dances from medieval Europe. But Kingsley's explanation is revealing in its attempt to legitimate the music by comparison with European culture, while still acknowledging some black cultural influences. Kingsley also associated jazz with a virus, which was a common and usually pejorative metaphor.

Ernest Newman, one of the most outspoken and oft-quoted English opponents of jazz, used a similar tactic. Newman compared jazzmen to fourteenth-century musicians who "indulged experimentally in a sort of catch as catch can descant: " . . . the singers-amateurs, like the early jazzers—used to decide upon a given *canto fermo* and then all improvise upon it simultaneously. Writers of the period have told us of the horrible results." Newman allowed that later composers codified these sounds and created "superb polyphonic music of the sixteenth century—an art that has never been surpassed." Jazz was therefore "not a new but a very old thing, " and, Newman implied, not a very good thing at that![6]

Some articles credited jazz to performances closer in time and location to early twentieth-century America. One writer in 1918 published this history in the *Current Opinion:* "In the old plantation days when the slaves were having one of their rare holidays and the fun languished, some West Coast African would cry out 'Jaz her up' and this would be the cue for fast and furious fun." The writer's authority was Lafcadio Hearn, author of *Two Years in the West Indies,* published in 1890 and often cited in jazz controversy literature. A 1919 issue of *Current Opinion* published a revised "genealogy" for jazz based on the Jasbo Brown story that Joel A. Rogers later used in *The New Negro.*[7]

Bandleader James Reese Europe was widely quoted in twenties articles because his prominence had gained him recognition among a wide audience. Europe asserted that an obscure band led by "Razz" had migrated from New Orleans to New York and performed briefly before the "individual musicians [were] grabbed up by various orchestras in the city. Somehow in the passage of time, Razz's band got changed to Jazz's band and from this corruption arose the word jazz." The *Literary Digest* printed Europe's version under the title "A Negro Explains Jazz." Osgood and Europe clearly differed on the suitability of "razz as a precursor for jazz.[8]

Europe's history of the word "jazz" was shrouded in mystery and made an obscure New Orleans band mythical in nature. His anecdote, like all the stories about musicians Brown, was probably based on the exploits of Tom Brown's Dixieland Jass Band, which performed in 1915 in Chicago. Brown claimed that the Chicago unions tried to sabotage his non-union band by labeling the music "jass" or whorehouse music. Brown decided to use the name as a publicity gimmick and turn the tables.[9] This tendency toward using a folkloric past to account for the origins of jazz was typical of many written explanations of jazz, and stood in marked contrast to the more "scientific" or exact explanation provided by interpretors like Osgood.[10]

Musicians as well as critics debated the beginnings and the meaning of the words. Many acclaimed twenties performers, including Sidney Bechet, insisted they played ragtime—not jazz. Others identified particular musical characteristics that distinguished jazz from other music. For example, Garvin Bushell said: "We didn't call the music jazz when I was growing up, except for the final tag of a number. After the cadence was closed, there'd be one bar break and the second bar was the tag—5,6,5,1. Sol, la, sol, do. Dada-da DUM! That was called the jazz." Others identified jazz with a style of improvisation explained by Dicky Wells's comment that "There weren't so many fine names for jazz" when he started playing"; instead, "All we did was try to make a better arrangement than the next band had." Willie "the Lion" Smith defined jazz as a cultural sensibility: "What they call jazz is just the music of people's emotions. It comes from wherever there have been colored people gathered together during the last hundred years." Smith concluded his point by emphasing that jazz, like all black musical forms, came from black churches.[11]

Whatever the origins of jazz, writers and musicians often linked its popularity to changes produced by World War I. Reb Spikes said the term "jazz" came into vogue after the war and replaced the more specific terms "ragtime," "blues," and "hot stuff." Often credited with expressing a break from the past and the introduction of a new time and speed, jazz was directly identified with the war. One source of this perception was the literal spread of jazz and ragtime in the repertoire of military bands that brought the music to greater public scrutiny and popularity.[12]

Other associations of jazz with World War I were more fanciful. Howard Brockway, for example, used weaponry metaphors to describe jazz in the *New York Review:*

> The howitzers of the Jazz band's artillery are stationed in the "traps." Under this heading we find all the instruments of percussion, such as the big drum, the snare drum, symbols, triangle, wooden blocks, played upon with drumsticks, xylophone, cowbells, rattle, whistles for the production of various weird noises. . . . The trombones may represent field guns while the cornets furnish the rapid-fire batter-

ies. The range being point blank, it is easy to see why the effect of the drum-fire is complete.

In the same article, the author also credited jazz with reducing the worries of General Gourland by giving his troops "relaxation and solace and cheer which enabled them to forget what was past and to abandon themselves wholeheartedly to the joyous hilarity, of the present moment." Brockway associated jazz with wartime experiences, while characterizing it as novel and intoxicating.[13]

Jazz also received credit or scorn for the effects it supposedly had on the pace of life. Jazz "sped up" the world, according to many accounts. According to Osgood, Lafcadio Hearn insisted that jazz "had been taken up by the Creoles from the Negroes, that it meant to 'speed things up'; and that it was applied to music of a rudimentary syncopated type."[14] But most twenties commentators compared jazz to the mechanical speed-up commonly associated with industrial production and urban life. Gilbert Seldes, a music critic favoring the refinement of jazz, described it as a "mechanism which at the moment corresponds so tragically to a mechanical civilization," but one, nevertheless, that "may be infused with humanity."[15]

Composer Irving Berlin compared jazz to the "rhythmic beat of our everyday lives. Its swiftness is interpretive of our verve and speed and ceaseless activity. When commuters no longer rush for trains, when taxicabs pause at corners, when businessmen take afternoon siestas, then, perhaps jazz will pass."[16] By indicating that jazz was a music of the city and industrial life, Berlin implied that it was clearly tied to increased mechanization. As historian Stephen Kern points out, the popular perception that jazz literally "sped thing up" was not necessarily based in musical fact. "The new rhythms," Kern writes, "were not simply faster; indeed some innovation delayed or ever stopped the beat unexpectedly. But the mixture of syncopation, irregularity and new percussive textures gave an overall impression of the hurry and unpredictability of contemporary life." Jazz rhythms, in particular syncopation, joined mechanization as a cause of the hectic tempo of the twenties.[17]

Many articles called upon medical or scientific authorities to evaluate the effect of jazz on human physiology. One doctor quoted in a 1927 *Literary Digest* article linked the "motor" qualities of the music to neurological development. The doctor, unnamed in the article but labeled a "specialist, a neuropath," explained that in previous cultures people danced for delight and exercise but in the 1920s tastes had changed:

> The waltz to-day fails to satisfy. Why? simply because the nerves of the present generation are in such a state that they are soon bored by silence. A healthy, normal animal, whether human or not, is not bored by tranquility, rest, silence. A man in a normal state can sit all day fishing or drifting along with a small breeze. When his nervous health begins to fail, he takes to tobacco, to fast motors, to exciting sports; and for those who can not indulge in such things jazz furnished the substitute.
>
> Jazz is rhythmic in the sense that a motor is rhythmic. It is all very well and good to talk about cross rhythms and syncopations in jazz, but these only serve to accentuate the absolute, unchanging regularity of the beat. . . . Jazz devotees resent any irregularity of beat. . . .
>
> . . . The reason the poorly acting motor gets on the motorist's nerves is because he is depending upon rhythmic stimulation. When the beat fails in its perfect regularity it is as if the motorist were deprived of his dope. Thus, also with the jazz lover. The more jaded the nerves are the more rapid and rhythmic the beat must be to soothe them.[18]

Despite his protestations of ignorance about jazz, the anonymous doctor was still willing to offer his analysis of jazz. The doctor identified jazz primarily by its rhythm, and used the narcotic power of the motor, also associated with modern speed-up, to justify his diagnosis of jazz. By comparing jazz to a machine designed to stimulate neurotics, the article echoed many complaints typical of the jazz controversy literature.

Frequently, observers identified jazz with a break or with fissures presumed to have followed World War I. Literary historians, for example, have identified changing conceptions of time as a central sensibility of twenties writers, and the response to jazz supports this observation. Willa Cather's remark that the "world broke in two in 1922" became a familiar epithet for the "lost generation." But, as critic Malcolm Cowley explained, this was not a generation merely despairing its fate, but rather one belonging to "a period of confused transition from values already fixed to values that had to be created."[19] Jazz, already easily associated with transitions from rural to urban, and from slow to faster "times," quickly provided a symbol for the transition to new values. The disaffected flocked to jazz clubs for a first-hand immersion in the "primitive."[20]

White celebration of "primitivism," of course, predated the twenties. American writers created many primitive worlds and characters in early fiction and often used Native Americans and blacks to depict either an idealized noble savagery or fearsome barbarity. Painters and sculptors adopted a primitivist aesthetic to use as inspiration by the late nineteenth century, although it was not specific to Africa and certainly not to Afro-Americans. The twenties vogue of primitivism began primarily among those young intellectuals exposed to modern artists like Picasso or to exhibits of African art and artifacts presented in the teens.[21]

Inspired by Sigmund Freud and others who documented the repression presumed endemic to Western civilization, twenties artists and intellectuals invested primitive culture with "uncivilized" virtues—particularly sexual freedom. African plastic arts were one source of knowledge about primitivism; the other, closer to home, was black culture, especially musical performance. "Jazz," wrote one commentator, "is said to be an attempt to reproduce the marvelous syncopation of the African jungle." Another explained its positive effects: "Modern sophistication has inhibited many native instincts, and the mere fact that our conventional dignity forbids us to sway our bodies or tap our feet when we hear effective music has deprived us of unsuspected pleasures."[22] Experiencing jazz could release and rejuvenate buried emotions or instincts, thus liberating an inner, and perhaps more creative, person.

We have already seen that the Harlem Renaissance writers, particularly Langston Hughes and Claude McKay, tried to use the tempos and phrasing of jazz in their poetry and fiction. White writers hoping to capture the wartime experience likewise experimented with time and timing in their choices of metaphor and language.[23] The growing popularity of ragtime and, later, jazz also led white writers to explore Afro-American themes, but they rarely used the music as a source of innovative language. In 1909, when Gertrude Stein published "Melanctha" in *Three Lives,* the short novel represented a positive departure from many stereotypical descriptions of black women. One of Stein's recurring descriptions of Melanctha evoked classic blues singers. Melanctha "always loved too hard and much too often" and "wondered often how it was she did not kill herself when she was so blue." Some critics heard a more literal music in this story, for example James Mellow describes Stein's language as being "drummed out by the insistent rhythms of speech, the simple blunt declarative sentences of style." Mellow reports that black writer Richard Wright reportedly admired them. Stein's revolutionary style, nevertheless, was primarily determined by her own experiments with narrative structure, not by an attempt at the realistic rendering of black speech.[24]

Vachel Lindsay's "The Congo" (1914), which was subtitled "A Study of the Negro Race," used black music more directly. The poem was a popular success, at least in part because the eccentric poet "acted out" or performed the tom-toms of the verse by pounding on the table top. Lindsay's printed instructions in the margins of the poem showed his somewhat mechanical appropriation of musical practice. He wanted the verse on voodoo to be accompanied "with growing speed and sharply marked dance-rhythm," and the section on Christian worship to be illustrated by "a literal imitation of camp-meeting racket, and trance."

In order to create a form of syncopation, Lindsay employed onomatopoeia for drum rolls in this representative stanza:

> The cake-walk royalty then began
> To walk for a cake that was tall as a man
> To the tune of "Boomlay, boomlay, BOOM,"
> While the witch-men laughed, with a sinister air,

> And sang with the scalawags prancing there:—
> Walk with care, walk with care,
> Or Mumbo-Jumbo, God of the Congo.,
> And all of the other
> Gods of the Congo,
> Mumbo-Jumbo will hoo-doo you.
> Beware, beware, walk with care,
> Boomlay, boomlay, boomlay, boom.
> Boomlay, boomlay, boomlay, boom,
> Boomlay, boomlay, boomlay,
> BOOM.

Lindsay's instructions for this section read "with a touch of negro [*sic*] dialect, and as rapidly as possible toward the end," thereby including performance instructions in the margins. The poem also conflates Afro-American experience as represented by the cakewalk and the so-called "scalawags" of the Reconstruction South with African tribal ritual.

Lindsay's poem celebrated the victory of Christianity over "hoo-doo" and purported to show "the death of the very source of savagery, the Voodoo gods and priests, and to picture Africa free of their influence." Lindsay used rhythmic meter in the poem to parody black culture—not to compliment black language or music practice. Lindsay disliked jazz and compared it to a "midnight diet and a sad morning after." Lindsay was interested in black poets, however, and once claimed credit for "discovering" another young poet of syncopation—Langston Hughes.[26]

Stein and Lindsay were but two white writers who experimented with the presumed primitivism or naturalism of black life. E.E. Cummings's *The Enormous Room* (1922) featured Jean Le Negre as a primitive, and Waldo Frank's *Holiday* (1923) contrasted the ignoble savagery of a white lynch mob in the fictional southern town of "Nazareth" with its victim—black Christ figure John Cloud. In 1925, the year of Locke's *The New Negro*, Sherwood Anderson published *Dark Laughter* and Dubose Heywood the popular novel (and play) *Porgy*. Eugene O'Neill's play *The Emperor Jones* (1921) used tom-toms as a chorus symbolizing the destruction of artifice and civilization embodied in Jones; but the playwright demonstrated no inherent concern with the music itself.

Carl Van Vechten's *Nigger Heaven* (1926) was the most controversial depiction of black life written by a white novelist. Although the book was ostensibly the story of a thwarted love affair between Harlem librarian Mary Love and the aspiring writer Byron Kasson, Van Vechten's descriptions of the Harlem cabarets and night life captured the most attention. Van Vechten was famous for his parties and his friendships with black entertainers and writers, so many readers took a voyeuristic interest in the novel and assumed it provided an insider's view of Harlem.

Although some reviewers hailed the novel as a successful attempt by a white writer to understand the black urban world, many black reviewers were offended. DuBois found the same sensationalistic excesses in Van Vechten that he would latter see in Claude McKay's *Home to Harlem*. "I cannot for the life of me see in this work either sincerity or art, deep thought, or truthful industry," DuBois complained. "It seems to me that Mr. Van Vechten tried to do something bizarre and he certainly succeeded." Despite Van Vechten's interest in black music and his patronage of black musicians, he used musical performance primarily to provide environment for the novel's plot. Those settings were sufficient to draw critics' ire, but not to enable him to develop the language or thematic potentials of black music in fiction.[27]

But it was not Van Vechten's "primitive" fiction that was most associated with the Jazz Age. F. Scott Fitzgerald's fiction about the exploits of young and perhaps "lost" white American youth usually garnered that honor. In fact, there is very little accurate depiction of jazz performance in Fitzgerald's fiction. Looking at one example, the 1923 collection *Tales of the Jazz Age*, one finds some descriptions of cabarets and restaurants featuring jazz. In "May Day," for example, Fitzgerald writes of an orchestra arriving at Delmonico's in New York to play. The band members sit down "arrogantly" and "take up the burden of providing music for the Gamma Psi Fraternity." Fitzgerald's jazz band is led by a flute player "distinguished throughout New York for his feat of standing on his head and shimmying with his shoulders while he played the latest jazz on the flute." The flute was not a prominent instrument in most jazz bands, of course; moreover, it's clear that Fitzgerald cannot capture any sense of interaction among band members. He does provide an atmospheric description of the lights, which were " . . . extinguished, except for the spotlight on the flute player and another roving beam that threw flickering shadows and changing kaleidoscope colors over the massed dancers." Fitzgerald's strength as a jazz age scribe rested more in his ability to capture the affection of young white college students for jazz than in his accuracy about musical performance.[28]

Another improbable association was provided in the story "Porcelain in Pink," in which a young woman in a bathtub sings:

> When Caesar did the Chicago
> He was a graceful child,
> Those sacred chickens
> Just raised the dickens
> The Vestal Virgins went wild.
> Whenever the Nervii got nervy
> He gave them an awful razz
> They shook in their shoes
> With the Consular blues
> The Imperial Roman jazz.

Fitzgerald's use of jazz and its performance is perhaps the literary equivalent of "nut jazz." The music is important as a novelty that provides humorous touches or atmosphere. One can imagine Zora Neale Hurston's comments on this appropriation of black musical idioms.[29]

All these writers were noted for their forays into "primitivism," or the Jazz Age, but most displayed more general artistic interests in modernism and super-naturalism rather than a specific commitment to black culture. None of these writers showed an particular interest in developing the fictional potential of black musical performance. These perspectives in white primitivist writing presented a marked contrast to Harlem Renaissance innovators like Langston Hughes and Claude McKay, who believed black culture could be used as both a theme and language representing a modern vision.

White writers like Van Vechten did not often experiment with jazz performance as an alternative language. Most often they used jazz milieus as settings or developed the idea that primitivistic jazz could liberate overcivilized whites. Primitivism was an escape from identity for these writers, not the exploration of personal and racial pride that it had been for black writers in the Harlem Renaissance. Jazz performance remained a central focus of these white artistic experiments with the primitive, nonetheless, because white readers *believed* jazz performance could transmit the values of a simpler past into the furious present. The music emerged once again as a passageway—in this case, into the exotic world of black culture.

White literary artists were not alone in their fascination with black culture. White musicians such as Eddie Condon, Bix Beiderbecke, Benny Goodman, Wingy Manone, Vic and Ralph Berton, and Milton "Mezz"Mezzrow were ecstatic upon discovering jazz. It excited them musically, as percussionist Vic Berton's brother Ralph explained in this typical story about the first time he heard the Original Dixieland Jazz Band's "Livery Stable Blues":

> I was six, living in Milwaukee, Wisconsin, and I can still recall my sensations as I heard for the first time the sardonic, driving horn of Nick LaRocca, the impudent smears and growls of Daddy Edwards, the barnyard crowings and whinnyings of Larry Shields, the slap-happy poundings of Ragas and Sbarbaro. I must have played it a hundred times before I remembered to breathe. It was the first thing I did in the morning when I ran downstairs in my nightie, the last thing at night before being dragged pleading off to bed. I quickly wore out two copies. . . . For better or worse, jazz had entered my life.

Mezz Mezzrow and Eddie Condon also played the record often enough to wear it out.[30]

The most fortunate musicians heard Louis Armstrong, Sidney Bechet, or a comparable talent at first-hand. Because he grew up in New Orleans, Wingy Manone "heard that rocking music on the main stem—when the colored bands in trucks advertising a dance, battled it out."[31] Mezz Mezzrow listened to blues and work songs in prison and jazz on Chicago's South Side. "That was my night," he recalled, "the night I really began to live. On my first visit to the South Side I managed to hit the two spots that were making history in the jazz world and I met some of the musicians who were already legends. I figured I had found something bigger and better than all the chicks and bankrolls in the world." Mezzrow considered jazz "a new language that would make me shout out loud and romp on to glory." Although he concentrated on music to learn the "vocabulary" he needed to speak, Mezzrow easily became as well known for what he said as for what he played.[32]

White as well as black musicians were stigmatized for performing "disrespectful" or unprofessional music. Wingy Manone's trumpet teacher refused to help him learn jazz because it was played by a "bunch of fakers" who "couldn't play by the book." Another teacher warned him that if he played "low down music" he would "never be anything but a second rate musician."[33]

Other performers came from more supportive backgrounds. A musician like Benny Goodman, who came from a working-class immigrant family, sought economic security as well as emotional satisfaction in jazz. Condon, like Vic Berton, came from a household that tolerated entertainers—the Bertons had been vaudeville performers.

Mezz Mezzrow, by contrast, came from a well-to-do family and, like Bix Beiderbecke, saw jazz as a badge of outsider status. Mezzrow consciously tried to identify himself with blacks and black culture. One reason for his affinity was his own Jewish upbringing. He remembered being impressed when a rabbi told him that "Moses, King Solomon, and the Queen of Sheba were all colored, maybe the whole world was once colored." Mezzrow resolved to "spend all my time from then on sticking close to Negroes. They were my kind of people. And I was going to learn their music and play it for the rest of my days." Mezzrow accepted the negative connotations that accompanied jazz and its practitioners. He found in jazz and black culture an alternative identity based on his empathy for the underdog.[34]

John Hammond, although not a musician, believed his love for jazz acted as a "catalyst" that taught him to protest racial injustice. In his autobiography, Hammond emphasized the role that jazz played in helping him sort out his musical, professional, and personal values—often in opposition to the elitist world of his parents.[35]

Mezzrow developed a deep appreciation for the role of participatory performance in maintaining the jazz idiom. He and musicians like him felt their own participation as audience and band members created a positive alternative to "corny" white musicians. "Hell you even feel better physically when you get to a colored cafe," Mezzrow wrote. "The people all seem to be enjoying everything in a real way. The band always has something that keeps you ear cocked all the time. The dancers all feel the music, and the expression on their faces when somebody takes off really gives me a lift."[36] Certainly, Mezzrow's adoption of black life and language paralleled some of the vogue for the primitive; he romanticized black life and could assume a patronizing tone. But musicians like Mezzrow, unlike shallow slummers, found not only an escape but a new identity in jazz. For Mezzrow, jazz was a language that communicated both cohorts and cronies, similarly expressed their respect by adopting the jazz idiom into their musical performance. They scorned symphonic jazz and identified themselves as the rebellious avant-guard of jazz. "Hot" jazz communicated new values and enabled them to experiment with a novel music idiom.

The music that helped white musicians find a new identity proved deeply disturbing to others of their race. Many critics of jazz attacked the music as "noise," and compared it to a plague or disease threatening to destroy the civilized world. Most criticisms clustered around moral, aesthetic, or professional values challenged by jazz. All objections by whites to the music were, of course, based on the premise that blacks were inferior to whites. In the first scholarly treatment of the jazz controversy Morroe

Berger's 1947 "Jazz and the Diffusion of a Culture Pattern," Berger argued that jazz was produced by a "low status group" and played by musicians labeled marginal by those dominating the music profession. Consequently, many whites and some black community leaders condemned the music.[37]

In a later study, *Jazz and the White Americans* (1962), Neil Leonard echoes some of Berger's research and concluded further that Americans accepted or rejected jazz in direct correlation to the acknowledgment of "traditionalist" or "modernist" values. Modernists were most pro-jazz and thus eventually won the argument. "This surprisingly quick change of taste," Leonard declares, "resulted from the breakdown of traditional values, the esthetics needs jazz seemed to fulfill, its increased diffusion by new sound reproducing devices and the modifications that made it increasingly acceptable." Specifically, Leonard showed—and most jazz historians concur—that white audiences embraced the Paul Whiteman style of symphonic jazz at the expense of more improvisational and rhythmically interesting jazz played primarily by blacks. Leonard described this process as a dialectical one, in which the clash between modernists and traditionalists created moderates who mediated tastes for the general public.[38]

As we have seen, however, jazz was a language and an experience that conveyed change—not merely an aspect of culture affected by change. It was not just what the moderates said or how jazz was described by its listeners that determined its dissemination; in the battle between the so-called traditionalists and modernists, jazz performance also influenced the outcome. On this issue, it is important to note what early critics thought they heard in jazz performance.

For some, the form of jazz was a crucial issue. Ernest Newman wrote in the *New York Times Magazine* that "Jazz is not a 'form' like let us say the waltz of the fugue, that leaves the composer's imagination free within the form: it is a bundle of tricks—of syncopation and so on." Another music critic felt jazz was not distinctive enough because it "is possible to take any conventional piece of music and jazz it." Most critics assumed art should express beauty and idealism through symmetrical patterns, represented in music by the relationship of melody, harmony, and rhythm. Jazz, to them, had simplistic melodies and syncopated rhythms character-istic of popular, and therefore inferior, music. They did not con-ceive of it as an alternative aesthetic.[39]

American composer and critic Virgil Thomson took jazz seri-ously enough to analyze its formal qualities. But he also saw it invading American preserves of decency and decorum. Accord-ing to Thomson, the spread of jazz took place largely because of the popularity of dancing. He singled out the fox trot as a sym-bol of the "disturbance that shook all of polite society when the lid of segregation was taken off of vice and the bordello irrupted into the drawing room."[40]

According to Thomson, jazz passed into orchestra sensibili-ties because of "union musicians who play one night at the movie, and the next night with the local symphony orchestra," and thereby get the styles confused. Thomson's contemporary, Daniel Gregory Mason, was less polite and characterized jazz as the "doggerel of music" that attracts the attention of listeners with unrefined musical tastes: "If I am so dull that I cannot recognize a rhythm unless it kicks me in the solar plexus at every other beat my favorite music will be jazz. . . . " Using George Gershwin as his example of jazz, Mason declared that the music of Igor Stravinsky and Gershwin were alike—esthetically they are tweedledum and tweedledee."[41]

Another critic who used Gershwin as a major point of refer-ence was Critical Theorist Theodor Adorno. Providing one of the most serious and yet unflattering treatments of jazz, Ador-no's analysis of the development of mass culture within ad-vanced capitalist societies included an attack on jazz because it created the *illusion* rather than the reality of free creation, and thus revealed its location in mass culture. Adorno complained that: "The authority of the written music is still apparent behind the liberty of the performed music." Adorno was not informed nor was he sensitive to the origins of jazz in black music and he regarded the use of popular songs in some jazz compositions as evidence indicating its commercialization.[42]

Most critics in the 1920s did not attempt a political critique like Adorno's and they attacked jazz on aesthetic grounds that often presumed the music should communicate moral absolutes. They exhorted listeners to resist the evil or wicked powers that jazz could exert over human behavior, especially of the young. Along these lines of criticism, most complainants believed the music reduced moral restraints and encouraged sexual permissiveness, interracial mixing, lewd and lascivious behavior, and a state of mind similar to alcoholic intoxication. John Philip Sousa, whose marching band music was itself an influence on some jazz musicians, objected to the music on the grounds that it "excited the baser instincts." Dr. E. Elliot Rawlings diagnosed jazz as causing "drunkenness . . . [by sending] . . . a continuous whirl of impressionable stimulations to the brain, producing thought and imaginations which overpower the will. Reason and reflection are lost and the actions of the persons are directed by the stronger animal passions." Given this assessment, it is not surprising that some twenties reformers hoped to pass legislation similar to the prohibition of alcohol in order to control or stop the flow of jazz.[43]

A *New York Times* editorial captured well this style of objection, while demonstrating some understanding of the popular Freudian underpinnings of the cult of primitivism. "Our energetic jazz bands seem to have made themselves the vanguard of the movement to do away with repression in America, " the editor exclaimed:

> A dose of jazz band music has an especially good chance to be effective because the listener seldom fully realizes what is being done. He is caught at a dance, perhaps, while his attention is ransacking his mind for darts of wit to direct to his charming partner, or at a vaudeville show or revue when the stage is crowded with distractions. Then while he is half conscious of the main melody, a subtle bombardment is carried on by all the other overtones, the curlicues, the rasps, the blares, the moans.[44]

Listeners could not control themselves, according to the *Times,* when exposed to the siren strains of jazz. The *Times* writer, of course, did not examine the question of why audiences *chose* to alter their consciousness through experiencing jazz, or consider that there might be some substance to the desire to "do away with repression."

Prominent women's magazines decried jazz because it encouraged dancing and other licentious behavior, an accusation that in an ironic way demonstrated a sensitivity (although a disapproving one) to the importance of performance and participation in jazz. Mrs. Max Obendorfer, president of the General Federation of Women's Clubs, explained the origins of the music to readers of *Ladies' Home Journal*. "Jazz," she pontificated, "originally was the accompaniment of the voodoo dancer, stimulating the half-crazed barbarian to the vilest of deeds."[45] Another author combined aesthetic and moral criticism, concluding that jazz led to mindlessness:

> If Beethoven should return to earth and witness the doings of a jazz orchestra, he would thank heaven for his deafness. . . . All this music has a droning, jerky, incoherence interrupted with the spasmodic "blah, blah" that reminds me of the way live sheep are turned into mutton.[46]

Critics of the aesthetic and moral qualities of jazz referred not only to the music itself, but also to the places in which it was played and the activities it accompanied. The entertainment traditions in which black music was rooted were poorly understood and utterly unappreciated by these opponents. The skill of a great improviser or the creative aspects of audience response and participation were irrelevant for Mrs. Obendorfer and her ilk.

Additional complaints about jazz came from white music educators and professional musicians who believed jazz spoiled the appetite of young people for "classical" music—a line of attack that rather directly recognized the degree to which the conflict was one between very different cultural values. Dr. Walter Damrosch told a convention of public school music supervisors in 1928 that jazz "stifles the true musical instinct by turning away many of our talented young people from the persistent and continued study and execution of good music."[47] A concert pianist allowed that jazz was acceptable in the cabaret or bar, "But it should not be permitted to invade the sacred precincts of our concert halls." (A nice acknowledgment of the point that each type of music had its appropriate performance setting.) Occasionally, jazz was deemed acceptable if it helped young people learn an instrument or become exposed to classical music. Dr. John French, a professor of English at Johns Hopkins University, reported that student interest in jazz helped get a symphonic orchestra established, and he concluded that consequently it was of some value.[48]

A concern with the self-control is common to all of these speculations about jazz. That theme, of course, was hardly new in the twenties—it permeated much nineteenth-century cultural criticism and often recurs in America during times of great social change. What gave it force in the twenties, however, was not just the fluid social contest of the decade but also the kinds of behavior the participatory nature of jazz called forth. The most strident critics feared that jazz would led to a degeneration of "civilized" refinements to "primitive" instincts. In these estimations, primitive meant regressive. To illustrate this point, the sounds of jazz were compared, unfavorably, to animal noises in order to emphasize some presumed bestiality in the music. "The noble trombone is made to bray like an ass," one English musician complained, "guffaw like a village idiot, and moan like cow in distress. The silver-tongued trumpet, associated in poetry with seraphim, is made to screech and produce sounds like drawing a nail on a slate, tearing calico, or the wailing of a tomcat." The writer concluded that jazz "would lower the prestige of the white classes."[49]

This animal motif—most likely inspired by the Original Dixieland Jazz Band's "Livery Stable Blues—was also used by J.W. Henderson, music critic for the *New York Herald-Tribune* in 1924 to explain the "real" jazz:

Jazz was originally the introduction of portamento effects on the trombone. Afterward the ingenious players of the popular music found out how to produce these wailing, sliding tones on other instruments and now at last we have such a wizard as Ross Gorman, who can evoke the laugh of a hyena from a clarinet and the bark of a dog from a hecklephone. The shrieking of cats, the baying of hounds and the crowing of roosters are not essential to jazz music. They have been made part of it because such instrumental antics amuse the crowd. . . . Portamento effects on wind instruments are the real jazz.[50]

Henderson stressed portamento in order to distinguish jazz from ragtime, which depended on the "syncopated music that rested on the basis of the old-time Negro jig." Henderson, who disdained the role of the audience in the performance of the music, reported with relief that Paul Whiteman's Aeolian Hall concert pointed the way to freedom from the animalistic—and obviously Afro-American—aberration of jazz.[51]

Henderson was typical of the "traditionalist" critic, described by Leonard, who welcomed the development of commercial and symphonic jazz. Whiteman, who became the "King of Jazz," saw his role as that of dignifying and legitimating jazz. He, too, explained away certain characteristics and performance practices original to the music. Whiteman warned musicians against using syncopation, which "gives a sense to the ignorant of participation in the world's scientific knowledge." But, Whiteman continued, with a sense of relief, "Syncopation no longer rules American music. . . . as we use it in the United States [it] is an African inheritance . . . but to-day it is no longer a necessary thing. It has been retained much as an ornament."[52] Whiteman's popular music became so closely identified with jazz that many Americans had no knowledge of its Afro-American origins. Whiteman himself, who disliked the association with jazz and dance music, titled his Aeolian Hall concert an "Experiment in Modern Music."

Many of the white music critics who tried to analyze jazz sympathetically found that their opponents had shaped the terms of the debate. The issues raised by moralists and other opponents of jazz informed early attempts to treat jazz as a new and praiseworthy music. When writing about jazz in his 1924 study *The Seven Lively Arts,* Gilbert Seldes challenged its detractors by declaring: "If—before we have produced something better—we give up jazz we shall be sacrificing nearly all the gaiety and liveliness and rhythmic power in our lives." Seldes conceded, however, that "something better" in American music would need to measure up to the symphonic standards of George Gershwin and Paul Whiteman.[53]

Most white critics writing in the twenties assumed Whiteman should serve as the musical norm for jazz orchestras, The few who dissented, like Olin Downes of the *New York Times,* stand out in clear contrast. Downes gave Whiteman's Aeolian Hall concert one of the few negative reviews it received from a jazz-lover because of Whiteman's condescending treatment of "Livery Stable Blues":

> The concert was referred to as "educational," to show the development of this type of music. Thus the "Livery Stable Blues" was introduced apologetically as an example of the depraved past from which modern jazz has risen. The apology is herewith indignantly rejected, for this is a glorious piece of impudence, much better in its unbuttoned jocosity and Rabelaisian laughter than other and more polite compositions that came later.[54]

Downes found the spontaneity represented by "Livery Stable Blues" preferable to the pomposity of Whiteman's band. But even Downes did not understand the importance of improvisation to the continued development of jazz. Like most twenties music critics, Downes believed that George Gershwin's composed orchestral music like "Rhapsody in Blue" pointed to the future of jazz.

In a sense, Whiteman and others like him were trying to have it both ways. They wanted to disassociate jazz from its Afro-American traditions, but preserve the excitement of the music. They did not entirely want to abandon participation—their emphasis on dancing belies that notion—but they wanted to stylize and formalize it, virtually to codify it. The audience would dance and the musicians would play (even with some bursts of carefully controlled improvisation), but there would be little of the spontaneity and none of the challenge to conventional morality that cabaret and rent party jazz posed.

What is so interesting about many of the white critics of jazz—and about a practitioner of sanitized jazz like Whiteman— is the degree to which their attacks acknowledged the importance of participation in jazz (which produced the behavior they disliked). They understood the degree to which both jazz and its milieu assaulted old entertainment.

Naturally, there were other intellectual postures whites could take toward jazz. We have already seen the attitudes of white intellectuals who accepted the stereotype of black culture as "primitive" and who saw the "primitivism" of jazz as a positive counterpoise to the discontents of civilization. Yet another response was that of the white jazzmen or critics who rejected Paul Whiteman and sought some kind of affiliation with black cultural traditions.

One final possibility for understanding would have been a "pluralist" approach of appreciating jazz on its own terms while enjoying other cultural forms, such as classical music, on theirs— a position rarely taken in the twenties. That was a difficult feat in those years, when men and women were far closer to the moral absolutes of Victorian culture. It was, nonetheless, the way modern American culture would resolve the debate in the decades after it flourished in the twenties.

Conclusion: Performance Crossroads

> There is in the Southern Syncopated Orchestra an extraordinary clarinet virtuoso who is, so it seems, the first of his race to have composed perfectly formed blues on the clarinet. I've heard two of them which he had elaborated at great length [and] they are equally admirable for their richness of invention, force of accent, and daring in novelty and the unexpected. Already, they gave the idea of style, and their form was gripping, abrupt, harsh, with a brusque and pitiless ending like that of Bach's second "Brandenburg Concerto." I wish to set down the name of this artist of genius—it is Sidney Bechet . . . what a moving thing it is to meet this very black, fat boy with white teeth and that narrow forehead, who is very glad one likes what he does, but who can say nothing of his art, save that he follows his "own way." . . . His "own way" is perhaps the highway the whole world will swing down tomorrow.[1]

Ernest Ansermet, the Swiss conductor who introduced Igor Stravinsky's "L'Histoire du Soldat" to the world, penned this tribute to Sidney Bechet in 1919. In spite of Ansermet's demeaning physical description of Bechet, the conductor's enthusiasm for the jazzman's talents was genuine. Ten years later, a whole generation of Americans echoed Ansermet's praise of jazz. Widespread public acceptance of jazz suggested that the defenders of genteel values had lost yet another round to modernists. In fact, some aspects of the jazz controversy, in particular the fate of participatory performance traditions in American entertainment, remained unresolved long after the world did indeed swing down the jazz road.

Much of the public outcry against jazz had dissipated by the early 1930s. One reason was that social critics and reformers were preoccupied with graver economic and social changes than nightclub behavior and jazz bands. Equally important, syncopation and a strong beat became the rhythmic base of most popular music. The sounds of working-class black culture crossed some class and racial divisions, although participatory performance traditions usually did not. Greater familiarity with the music inured critics to "ragged" jazz tones.

In addition, much of the lewd and antisocial behavior moralists once blamed on jazz was not typical of the polite audiences who patronized large jazz bands and orchestras in hotel ballrooms. Most Americans could stay home and listen to jazz on the radio or phonograph. The growth of recordings and radio broadcasts made jazz performance a household commodity rather than an adventurous foray into an exotic world. Censorship boards and regulatory agencies further sanitized the offerings available in electrically reproduced jazz.

The rise of professional jazz critics signaled greater appreciation of jazz as an art form. In the early 1930s, Charles Edward Smith, Hughes Panassie, John Hammond, and Winthrop Sargeant published analyses of jazz that commented favorably on its Afro-American origins rather than pointing to its possibilities for symphonic orchestration. All of them noted the importance of improvisation and rhythmic complexities as definitive features of the music. Panassie emphasized the importance of preserving jazz on records rather than notated scores, since only records could capture performance style in jazz.[2]

Even though the public debate quieted and critics moved to legitimate jazz, the struggle to define the music and maintain participatory performance traditions continued. Issues left over from the jazz controversy continued to influence jazz performers and their audiences.

Performers who did not or could not conform to the expectations of the commercial music industry faced exclusion from the most lucrative job opportunities. Musicians who wanted to perform in small combos that encouraged improvisation and participation played in small clubs, dives, and on the road. Racial segregation at all levels of the music industry continued to restrict black musicians. These economic, social, and artistic restraints prompted disgruntled performers to experiment with new jazz

styles—in particular bop and cool jazz—which maintained improvisation even as they retreated into a more private style with less
audience participation.

The waning of the jazz controversy did not break the association of jazz and jazzmen with non-conformity. In fact, psycholo-
gists and sociologists documented a subculture of jazz performance that may have intensified the public's perception of
jazzmen as deviants. Psychoanalysts in the 1950s, to take just one
example, declared that jazz was " 'produced' by a 'primitive'
group in an area where a less repressive morality flourished"
and which "was by its very nature associated with vital libidinal
impulses—sex, drink, sensual dancing—precisely the id drives
that the superego of the bourgeois culture sought to repress."[3]
In a similar article, Dr. Norman Margolis concluded that jazz
had always been a "protest music" that appealed to "perpetual
adolescents." A group of dance musicians studied by Howard
Becker in the same decade conformed exactly to Margolis's assessment. The jazzmen in Becker's sample group disdained the
adult world of "square" audiences and "commercial" musicians.[4]

These legacies of the jazz controversy do not suggest that
twenties arguments over jazz were futile, but rather that participatory performance traditions continued to symbolize changes
under way in the 1920s. The rise of a "jazz age" did signal the
demise, however, of the genteel cultural values typical of the late
nineteenth century. Jazz sounded modern because its lively and
improvisational characteristics clearly differed from older formal and sentimental music. Furthermore, listening and dancing
to jazz also enabled many whites to break with a tradition of
more restrictive public behavior.

At the same time, jazz also served a social and cultural purpose
for blacks. It communicated the migration of Afro-Americans
from the agricultural South to cities and industrial life. From rent
parties to Harlem Renaissance salons, jazz performance enabled
black Americans to affirm—not reject—their individual and collective pasts.

One of the most important changes symbolized by jazz, however, transcended racial differences. Given the intense clash of

cultures expressed in the jazz controversy, it is surprising to find some people—both black and white—who could move between the two. Many musicians, artists, and intellectuals who wanted to understand jazz adopted cultural relativist attitudes. Their numbers were not great and their understanding of one or the other culture was frequently limited, but their disdain for absolutes and appreciation of diversity set them apart from the genteel tradition with its commitment to moral absolutes. They were men and women of modern sensibilities.

Jazz performance made it possible for many Americans to saunter down the roads paved by Sidney Bechet and other jazz performers. But as Bechet understood so well, improvisational music promises no sure passages; rather it captures the inevitability of mobility and change. The jazz controversy signified the attempts of Americans to analyze the difficult and contested routes they had followed in the past, and their willingness to chart a more flexible, "modern" future.

Notes

Introduction

1. One of the standard histories of the 1920s that conveys some of the typical stereotypes of the decade is Frederick Lewis Allen's *Only Yesterday: An Informal History of the Nineteen-Twenties* (New York: Harper and Row, 1931). Historians have recently suggested that conventional portraits of the "Jazz Age" are overdrawn. Paul Carter, for example, in his study *Another Part of the Twenties* (New York: Columbia University Press, 1977), tries to move beyond stereotypes to what he sees as the middle ground between the "period's various polar opposites—bond salesman and Bohemian, prude and rebel, snob and sweated worker, all the liberated women and all the sad young men" (p.x). Similarly, Paula Fass examined the behavior of young people in *The Damned and the Beautiful: American Youth in the Twenties* (New York: Oxford University Press, 1977), 7. She concluded their rebelliousness was balanced by adaptation to institutions such as family and school. Fass concluded that portrayals of youth as either "beautiful or damned" were projections of adult observers rather than realistic descriptions of "flaming youth."

2. A standard interpretation of pre- and post-World War I changes in sensibility is Henry May, *The End of American Innocence: A Study of the First Years of Our Own Time, 1912–1917* (Chicago: Quadrangle Books, 1959). May is interested in establishing the context in the prewar years for postwar changes. His model of a battle between traditionalists and moderns also characterized Neil Leonard's fine study of the jazz controversy: *Jazz and the White Americans: The Acceptance of an Art Form* (Chicago: University of Chicago Press, 1962). Leonard's new

study, *Jazz: Myth and Religion* (New York: Oxford University Press, 1987), puts his earlier work in a larger and different context that sees jazz as part of a spiritual quest. Macdonald Smith Moore's study of the arguments over turn-of-the-century music, *Yankee Blues: Musical Culture and American Identity* (Bloomington: University of Indiana Press, 1985), likewise studies discussions by composers seeking to redeem American culture through genteel aesthetic standards. Entertainment histories by Lewis A. Erenberg, *Steppin' Out: New York Nightlife and the Transformation of American Culture* (Chicago: University of Chicago Press, 1981) and John Kasson, *Amusing the Million: Coney Island at the Turn of the Century* (New York: Hill and Wang, 1978), both describe changes in leisure time activities that encouraged the relaxation of genteel Victorian moral codes prior to World War I. In jazz itself, many of the musical characteristics that made it sound novel were present in its precursors: ragtime and blues.

3. The best study on postwar racial violence is William M. Tuttle, Jr., *Race Riot: Chicago in the Red Summer of 1919* (New York: Atheneum, 1982).

4. See William E. Leuchtenburg, *The Perils of Prosperity, 1914–1932* (Chicago: University of Chicago Press, 1958), 96, 188, and 178–203, on the postwar economic boom.

5. Ibid., 204–24, on the decade generally; and Neil Leonard, *Jazz and the White Americans,* on jazz specifically.

6. See Malcolm Cowley, *Exile's Return* (New York: Viking, 1956), on the lost generation.

7. Leopold Stokowski is quoted in J.A. Rogers, "Jazz at Home," in *The New Negro,* ed. Alain Locke (New York: Atheneum, 1975), 221–22. See also "Stokowski Declares in Favor of Jazz," *Musical Leader* 47 (April 24, 1924).

8. It is essential that jazz be analyzed in its performance context. Jazz historian Charles Nanry points out that jazz " . . . is a music where creation (formally, musical composition) usually occurs during performance. One of the key elements of jazz—improvisation—demands that new melodic, harmonic, and rhythmic patterns emerge in the context of performance. But limits have to be imposed both by audiences and by performers. Performing jazz is not a random process. The narrow line between authenticity and creativity must be perceived and manipulated by the good jazz player." Charles Nanry with Edward Berger, *The Jazz Test* (New York: Transaction Books, 1979), 20.

Victor Turner used social drama analysis to explain the structure, function, and process of various rituals—including theatre—in society. He identified common focal points in each social drama: breach, crisis, redressive action, and reintegration. Although the scale of the jazz controversy does not fit Turner's model, the identification of jazz with cultural crisis suggests some applicability. See Victor Turner, "Frame, Flow, and Reflection: Ritual and Drama as Public Liminality," in Michael Benamou and Charles Caramello (eds.), *Performers in Post-Modern Culture* (Madison, Wisc.: Coda Press, 1977), 33–35.

9. Houston Baker, *Blues, Ideology, and Afro-American Literature* (Chicago: University of Chicago Press, 1984), 2.

10. Oral histories provide crucial information, but are of course, problematic sources. Many of the subjects interviewed were elderly and their memories possibly unreliable. Consequently, I have avoided those comments that seem implausible. Some interviewees give stock answers, in part because they have been interviewed many times over the course of their musical careers. I have chosen not to analyze these somewhat formulaic responses here, although I think that these oral performances can profitably be studied alongside the informant's musical performances. The questions and attitudes of interviewers can give cues to the respondent that shape the answers, too. Still, I find the oral histories in the Tulane Oral History of New Orleans Jazz Collection at the William Ransom Hogan Jazz Archive at Tulane University (*TOHNOJC*), and the Institute for Jazz Studies at Rutgers University, Newark (*RIOJS*), valuable, and I have used them in conjunction with other primary sources. For further comments on oral history and jazz, see the Bibliographic Essay and Selected Readings.

11. Sidney Bechet, *Treat It Gentle* (New York: Hill and Wang, 1980), 5.

Chapter One

1. Good general histories of early jazz are Gunther Schuller, *Early Jazz: Its Roots and Musical Development* (New York: Oxford University Press, 1968) and Marshall Stearns, *The Story of Jazz* (New York: Oxford University Press, 1956. 1979). For discussions of the African influence on black music, see John F. Szwed's "Afro-American Musical Adaptation," in *Afro-American Anthropology*, eds. Norman E. Whitten, Jr., and John F. Szwed (New York: Free Press, 1970), 219–31; LeRoi Jones, *Blues People: Negro Music in White America* (New York: Morrow, 1963). (In the text and in subsequent notes, LeRoi Jones is referred to by his current name Amiri Baraka.) On women and jazz, see Linda Dahl, *Stormy Weather: The Music and Lives of a Century of Jazz Women* (New York: Pantheon, 1984) and Sally Plackstin, *American Women in Jazz: 1900 to the Present, Their Words, Lives and Music* (New York: Putnam Publishing Group, 1982); and Marian McPartland, *All in Good Time*

(New York: Oxford University Press, 1987). A brief overview of ideas about the history of jazz is provided in Irving Louis Horowitz and Charles Nanry, "Ideologies and Theories about American Jazz," *Journal of Jazz Studies* 2 (1975): 24–41.

My discussion of the jazz language is loosely based on the scheme provided by Charles Nanry and Edward Berger in *The Jazz Text* (New York: Van Nostrand, 1979), 7–10. On jazz as language, see also Ben Sidran, *Black Talk* (New York: DaCapo Press, 1971) and Baraka, *Blues People*.

2. Charles Nanry describes the development of improvisation out of the heterophonic ensemble style band in *Jazz Text*, 78–79 and 97–99.

3. James Lincoln Collier, *Louis Armstrong: An American Genius* (New York: Oxford University Press, 1983), 47.

4. See Richard Allen Waterman, "African Influences on the Music of the Americas," in Sol Tax (ed.), *Acculturation in the Americas* (Chicago: University of Chicago Press, 1949), 207–18.

5. Performance style as well as specific features of black speech show the similarities between distinctive black-speaking and music. Roger Abrahams describes how "rapping and capping," which are "spontaneous clever conversation" and "an attempt to fully display verbal ability in contest," are both kinds of performance "art" typical of many black communities. Participants in these contests, like jazz musicians, are judged on the basis of their command of traditional materials, effective delivery, and improvisation. See Roger D. Abrahams, "Rapping and Capping, Black Talk as Art," in John Szwed (ed.), *Black America* (New York: Basic Books, 1970), and in his own study: Roger D. Abrahams, *Positively Black* (Englewood Cliffs, N.J.: Prentice-Hall, 1970), 132–42.

6. Eileen Southern, *The Music of Black Americans: A History* (New York: W.W.Norton, 1971), 49. See Edward A. Berlin, *Ragtime: A Musical and Cultural History* (Berkeley: University of California Press, 1980), 5–17, on the origins of ragtime.

7. Rudi Blesh and Harriet Janis, *They All Played Ragtime: The True Story of an American Music* (New York: Oak Publications, 1966), 17–19, describes the regional background of ragtime players. See Berlin, *Ragtime*, 9, on ensemble playing.

8. Stearns, *Story of Jazz*, 142.

9. Gilbert Seldes, *The Seven Lively Arts* (New York: Sagamore Press, 1924), 70.

10. Blesh and Janis, *They All Played*, 8.

11. Ibid., 7. Berlin, *Ragtime*, 32–60, describes the "ragtime debate."

12. Berlin, *Ragtime*, 32–60.

13. Ibid., 46–47.

14. Nanry, *The Jazz Text*, 76–77; Danny Barker said boogie-woogie

was called "the horses" in New Orleans (Danny Barker, *TOHNOJC*, interview 6–18–1959).

15. Willie "the Lion" Smith and George Hoefer, *Music on My Mind: The Memoirs of an American Pianist* (New York: Doubleday, 1964), 85.

16. Southern, *Music of Black Americans*, 333. On blues see, Nanry, *The Jazz Text*, 62–74; and Giles Oakley, *The Devil's Music: A History of the Blues* (New York: Taplinger, 1976); Charles Keil, *Urban Blues* (Chicago: University of Chicago Press, 1966); Jeff Todd Titon, *Early Downhome Blues: A Musical and Cultural Analysis* (Urbana: University of Illinois Press, 1979); Paul Oliver, *Conversation with the Blues* (London: Cassell, 1965); and Baraka, *Blues People*.

17. Baraka, *Blues People*, 62. David Evans describes the kind of improvisation typical in blues performance in his study *Big Road Blues: Tradition and Creativity in the Folk Blues* (Berkeley: University of California Press, 1982), especially chap. 5.

18. See Stearns, *The Story of Jazz*, 104, and Nanry, *The Jazz Text*, 18, on the combining of West African and American scales.

19. Baraka, *Blues People*, xii. The meaning of blues lyrics has been addressed by many writers, including Gregory R. Staats, "Sexual Imagery in Blues Music: A Basis for Black Stereotypes," *Journal of Jazz Studies* 5 (1970): 40–60. Staats's article is interesting for this study since he contrasts the reception of blues and that of jazz in the 1920s. On the role of women blues singers in the decade, see Chapter Four.

20. Anthropologists and folklorists point out that the musical traditions of blacks have been discussed regularly, if not always adequately, since the seventeenth century. Roger Abrahams and John Szwed point out that each generation of observers passed judgment about what black music meant. The earliest observers wanted to prove that African rituals made slaves more animalistic than whites; missionaries and abolitionists often pointed to musical practices as evidence of pagans in need of redemption; and social scientists of the early twentieth century sought pathological evidence in the music subcultures they observed. See John F. Szwed, "Afro-American Musical Adaptation," and Sidney Mintz, "Foreword," in *Afro-American Anthropology*, eds. Whitten and Szwed, 1–16 and 219–27.

21. John W. Blassingame, *The Slave Community* (New York: Oxford University Press, 1979), 23–39; Lawrence Levine, *Black Culture and Black Consciousness: Afro-American Folk Thought from Slavery to Freedom* (New York: Oxford University Press, 1978) provides a description of the role of participant black entertainment in the twentieth century (p. 203).

22. Southern, *Music of Black Americans*, 27.

23. Frederick Douglass, *My Bondage, My Freedom* (Salem, N.H.: Ayer, 1968), 253.

24. Whitten and Szwed (eds.), *Afro-American Anthropology*, 5. Nanry, *Jazz Text*, 4–12.

25. Stearns, *Story of Jazz*, 33. As in other southern cities, society in New Orleans was racist. Its reputation for tolerance was established by comparison with other cities and was largely an outgrowth of its multi-cultural and Catholic past.

26. Jelly Roll Morton and Alan Lomax, *Mr. Jelly Roll: The Fortunes of Jelly Roll Morton, New Orleans Creole and "Inventor of Jazz"* (New York: Duell, Sloan, & Pearce, 1950), 11; Bechet, *Treat It Gentle*, 61; see also Danny Barker, *A Life in Jazz*, ed. Alyn Shipton (London: Macmillan, 1986), 50–51.

27. Barker, *A Life in Jazz*, 7. See also Barker in Nat Shapiro and Nat Hentoff, *Hear Me Talkin' to Ya* (New York: Dover Publications, 1955), 38; and Danny Barker, *TOHNOJC* interview, 6–18–1959 and 6–30–1959.

28. Paul Barbarin, *TOHNOJC*, interview 3–27–1957.

29. See Donald M.Marquis, *In Search of Buddy Bolden, First Man of Jazz* (Baton Rouge: Louisiana State University Press, 1978) for a thorough study of the legend of Buddy Bolden. His musical style is described on pp. 99–111. Harrison Barnes's comments are from a *TOHNOJC* interview, (1–25–1959). Paul Barbarin, *TOHNOJC*, interview, 3–27–1957. Danny Barker comments from, Shapiro and Hentoff, *Hear Me*, 25. William Schafer," Buddy Bolden Blues," 1–13, discusses the source of confusion and mythology about Buddy Bolden in oral histories; Michael Ondaatje's novel *Coming Through Slaughter* (New York: W.W. Norton, 1977) puts the mythologies to creative use.

30. Harrison Barnes, *TOHNOJC,* interview 1–25–59. Punch Miller, *TOHNOJC,* interview 5–24–1958.

31. Wingy Manone in Shapiro and Hentoff, *Hear Me*, 38. On cutting contests and advertisements see also Dave Bailey, *TOHNOJC,*interview 10–25–1959; Kid Ory, *TOHNOJC*, interview 4–20–1957; Harrison Barnes, *TOHNOJC*, interview 1–25–1959; and Barker, *A Life in Jazz*, chap. 10.

32. Manual Manetta, *TOHNOJC*, interview 3–21–1957. George "Pops" Foster, *TOHNOJC*, interview 4–21–1957.

33. Kid Ory, *TOHNOJC*, interview 4–20–1957.

34. Tom Bethell, *George Lewis: A Jazzman from New Orleans,* (Berkeley: University of California Press, 1977), 56.

35. Manuel Manetta, *TOHNOJC*, interview 3–21–1957. Louis Armstrong, *Swing That Music* (London: Longmans, Green, 1936), 36. Armstrong's biographer James Lincoln Collier disputes this memory of Armstrong's by pointing out that Marable said, "I first heard Louis in the Cooperative Hall with Kid Ory's band playing Chris Smith's 'Honky

Tonk Town'." Collier, *Louis Armstrong*, 78. My thanks to Curt Jerde for pointing out that these performances should be seen as taking place on a continuum of street and saloon.

36. John Handy, *TOHNOJC*, interview 12–4–1958. Paul Barbarin, *TOHNOJC*, interview 12–23–1959. Punch Miller, *TOHNOJC*, interview 5–24–1958. George "Pops" Foster, *The Autobiography of George "Pops" Foster* as told to Tom Stoddard (Berkeley: University of California Press, 1971), 16.

37. Frank Adams, *TOHNOJC*, interview 1–20–1959. Kid Ory claimed he got his nickname "Kid" from female admirers in Lincoln Park, *TOHNOJC*, interview 4–20–1957. Peter Bocage described the battles between the park bands in a *TOHNOJC* interview (1–29–1959).

38. See Paul Barbarin, *TOHNOJC*, interview 3–27–1957, on the social club second liners. Barney Bigard, *RIOJS*, interview July 1976.

39. Tom Bethell, *George Lewis*, 23; John Handy, *TOHNOJC*, interview 12-4-1958. Morton, *Mr. Jelly Roll*, 12.

40. Barker, *A Life in Jazz*, 62–63.

41. Barnes, *TOHNOJC*, interview 1–25–1959.

42. Ory, *TOHNOJC*, interview 4–20–1957.

43. Barker, *A Life in Music*, 35.

44. Ibid. Chap. 7 concerns the Boozan Kings.

45. A list of all the musicians I studied who credited their families with helping them get started in music includes: Adolphe Alexander, Alvin Alcorn, Isidore, Louis, and Paul Barbarin, Eddie Barefield, Lawrence Brown, Ted Brown, Danny Barker, John Casimir, Buck Clayton, Eddie Durham, Manuel Manetta, Bill Matthews, Punch Miller, Red Norvo, Nathan Robinson, Johnny St. Cyr, Zutty Singleton, Willie "the Lion" Smith, George "Pops" Foster, John Handy, Monk Hazel, Horace Henderson, Milt Hinton, John Joseph, Nick LaRocca, Johnny Lala, and Jimmy McPartland.

Collier, *Louis Armstrong*, 27 and 34–55. A nice case study of a popular orphanage band that toured both nationally in Europe is provided by John Chilton, *A Jazz Nursery: The Story of the Jenkins' Orphanage Jazz Bands* (Chicago: Chicago Public Library, 1980).

46. Sonny Greer, *RIOJS*, interview 1–15–1979. Dicky Wells, *The Night People: Reminiscences of a Jazzman* as Told to Stanley Dance (Boston: Crescendo Press, 1971), 4–5.

47. Jimmy McPartland, *RIOJS*, interview no date. On the Austin High Gang, see also Bud Freeman in Travis Dempsey, *An Autobiography of Black Jazz* (Chicago: Urban Research Institute, 1983), 323–24. Milt Hinton, *RIOJS*, interview 4–19–1976. Hinton said he'd never heard of the Austin High Gang while he was in high school himself.

48. Lawrence Brown, *RIOJS*, interview 6–12–1976.

49. Reb Spikes, *RIOJS*, interview 1980. Handy, *TOHNOJC*, interview 12-4-1958. Nick LaRocca, *TOHNOJC*, interview 5-21-1958.

50. Barney Bigard, *RIOJS*, interview July 1976. John Casimir, *TOHNOJC*, interview 1-17-1959.

51. Johnny Lala, *TOHNOJC*, interview 10-24-1958. Barnes, *TOHNOJC*, interview 1-25-1959. See also Art Hodes, "The Rainbow Cafe," in *Selections from the Gutter: Portraits from the Jazz Record*, eds. Art Hodes and Chadwick Hansen (Berkeley: University of California Press, 1977), 10.

52. Albert Glenny, *TOHNOJC*, interview 3-27-1957. Ed Allen, *TOHNOJC*, interview 1-14-1961. Bocage, *TOHNOJC*, interview 1-29-1959. I have read dozens of examples of the "note as big as this room" or "this house" in jazz autobiographies and oral histories. For further examples, see Horace Henderson, *RIOJS*, interview 4- to 9-12-1975.

53. Foster, *The Autobiography of Pops Foster*, 44.

54. Curt Jerde's work on New Orleans suggests that black Creole and black performers may have begun playing together as early as Reconstruction. On the history of the collaboration between black Creole and other black musicians, see Gilbert Ostransky, *Understanding Jazz* (Englewood Cliffs, N.J.: Prentice-Hall, 1977), 121; Collier, *Louis Armstrong*, 13-14; and Martin Williams, *Jazz Masters of New Orleans* (New York: Macmillan, 1967), 4-10.

55. On Storyville, see Al Rose, *Storyville: New Orleans, Being an Authentic, Illustrated Account of the Notorious Red Light District* (Tuscaloosa: University of Alabama Press, 1974); Collier, *Louis Armstrong*, 14–17; and Ronald Morris, *Wait Until Dark* (Bowling Green: Bowling Green University Popular Press, 1980), 93.

56. Shapiro and Hentoff, *Hear Me*, 8.

57. Morris suggested that the criminal activities of club owners—gambling and prostitution—enabled them to pay entertainment taxes more easily than more legitimate entrepreneurs. By 1870 New Orleans levied "$100 for saloons featuring music, $200 if singing was allowed, and $300 for stage shows and other pernicious divertisements" (*Wait Until Dark*,89). I think patronage is a misleading concept when applied by Morris since musicians continued to depend on (and most of their job opportunities were determined by) the entertainment market.

Many Italian-American jazz performers clearly did want to imitate the black and black "Creole" musicians' styles, but I have seen few references to the presence of Italian-Americans as audiences. Of all the primary sources I used, Danny Barker gives the most attention to Italians in New Orleans (*A Life in Jazz*) and Travis Dempsey discusses the same subject in *An Autobiography of Black Jazz*, 49.

58. Specifically, Collier explains the change from ragtime to jazz

as: " . . . if the standard two beat ragtime is undergirded with a four beat ground beat, the character of the music changes . . . If every third beat is given added weight, you have three-beat clusters, or measures, to use the standard term, of 3/4 time, the first and third beats are strong, the second and fourth weak; but because these four-beat clusters divide into subsets of two beats each, the first note is slightly stronger than the third and the second a lttle less weak than the fourth . . . In the very first years of the twentieth century, some person or persons in the black and black Creole subculture tried the epochal experiment of making the double speed secondary pulse in ragtime explicit—that is to say, putting a four beat tap under a two-beat rag." *Louis Armstrong*, 51–52.

59. Sigmund Spaeth, *A History of Popular Music in America* (New York: Random House, 1948), 369.

60. Laurance James is quoted in Marshall and Jean Stearns, *Jazz Dance: The Story of American Dance* (New York: Schirmer Books, Macmillan, 1964), 98.

61. Berlin, *Ragtime*, 13.

62. Stearns and Stearns, *Jazz Dance*, 99.

63. Ibid., 104.

64. Ibid., 106.

65. Johnson quoted in Southern, *Music of Black Americans*, 348.

66. Europe died an untimely death in 1919 at the hands of one of his bandsmen. Many scholars would agree with jazz historian Gunther Schuller, who called Europe "the most important transitional figure in the pre-history of jazz on the East Coast" in *Early Jazz*, 249. See also, Samuel B. Charters and Leonard Kunstadt, *Jazz: A History of the New York Scene*, (New York: DaCapo, 1962), 24–41 and 63–72;; and Tony Scherman, "When Europe Took Europe by Storm," *American Visions: A Magazine of Afro-American Life and Culture* 2 (1987): 28–31.

67. Stearns and Stearns, *Jazz Dance*, 97. Kathy Peiss points out that many of these dances were presumed to have originated in whorehouses in San Francisco's Barbary Coast, and many reformers hoped to clean up the "tough dances" of the dive and the levee. See Kathy Peiss, *Cheap Amusements: Working Women and Leisure in Turn-of-the-Century New York* (Philadelphia: Temple University Press, 1986), 100–104. The evolution of dancing and jazz will be discussed further in Chapter Two.

68. Willie "the Lion" Smith, *Music on My Mind*, 66–67. See also Lynn Fauley Emery, *Black Dance in the United States from 1619 to 1970* (Salem, N.H.: Ayer, 1972), chap. 6.

69. James P. Johnson,"Conversation with James P. Johnson," by Tom Davin in *Jazz Panorama: From the Pages of the Jazz Review*, ed. Martin Williams (New York: DaCapo, 1979), 49–50.

70. Barker, *A Life in Jazz*, 87. Similarly, George "Pops" Foster complained that "about 1935 or 1936 we started playing for audiences that just sat there. I never liked this, I always liked to play for an audience that danced." *The Autobiography of Pops Foster*, 166.

71. For a useful discussion of the relationship between professional black entertainers and their white and black audiences, see Collier, *Louis Armstrong*, 87–90; "The Faking of Jazz: How Politics Distorted the History of the Hip," *New Republic* 193 (Nov. 18, 1985): 33–40; and "The Politics of Jazz," *New Republic* 193 (Dec. 16, 1985): 6. Collier argues that many early histories of jazz distorted its dissemination by suggesting that it was rarely heard or appreciated by white audiences, when in fact white entrepreneurs and club owners promoted jazz, and while I agree with Collier's general point, the participatory qualities of the music were frequently affected by the racial composition of the audiences.

72. Stearns and Stearns, *Jazz Dance*, 78.

73. W.C. Handy, *Father of the Blues* (London: Macmillan, 1957), 33.

74. Jack "Papa" Laine, *TOHNOJC*, interview 4-21-1951; Eddie Durham, *RIOJS*, interview 1978.

75. Southern, *Music of Black Americans*, 271–72; Stearns and Stearns, *Jazz Dance*, 58; and Kasson, *Amusing the Million*, 24; Blesh and Janis, *They All Played Ragtime*, 149–51.

76. Eileen Southern describes the process that created a separate black music tradition as one in which "the black music maker developed a distinctive style of entertainment music, fitted to his own personal needs and expressive of his own individuality. It was not intended to be understood by whites. Rag music was one of the earliest manifestations of this distinctive music. The other was the blues." *Music of Black Americans*, 312.

77. Smith, *Music on My Mind*, 23–26; Buck Clayton, *RIOJS*, interview 1975; Eubie Blake interviewed in *Voices from the Harlem Renaissance*, ed. Nathan Huggins (New York: Oxford University Press, 1976), 337.

78. Norvo, *RIOJS*, interview 5-22-1977; Spikes, *RIOJS*, interview 1980.

79. Spikes, *RIOJS*, interview 1982.

80. Foster, *TOHNOJC*, interview 4-21-1957, and *The Autobiography of Pops Foster*, 116–17.

81. Mary Lou Williams, *RIOJS*, interview 6-26-73; also see Dahl, *Stormy Weather*, 61.

82. Southern, *Music of Black Americans*, 370.

83. Chicago, as Richard Wright pointed out in the introduction to St. Clair Drake and Horace B. Clayton's *Black Metropolis: A Study of Negro Life in a Northern City*, is a "known city" because it has been extensively studied by sociologists and historians for decades. Several of these

studies provide a good background for understanding the Chicago of the early twentieth century. In addition to *Black Metropolis* (New York: Harcourt Brace Jovanovich, 1945), there is Allen Spear's *Black Chicago: The Making of a Ghetto, 1890–1920* (Chicago: University of Chicago Press, 1969) and Thomas Lee Philpott's, *The Slum and the Ghetto: Neighborhood Deterioration and Middle-Class Reform, Chicago 1880-1920* (New York: Oxford University Press, 1978). William Tuttle's excellent study *Race Riot: Chicago and the Red Summer of 1919* (New York: Atheneum, 1982) remains indispensable on the riot and provides (chap. 3) a valuable survey on the migration experiences of southern blacks.

84. Bill Matthews, *TOHNOJC*, interview 3-10-1959.

85. Frederick Ramsey and Charles Smith, *Jazzmen* (New York: Harcourt Brace Jovanovich, 1939), 95.

86. On riverboat excursions see Collier, *Louis Armstrong*, 76; Williams, *Jazz Masters of New Orleans*, 183–84; Earl Wiley, "Drummer from Chicago," in *Selections from the Gutter*, eds. Hodes and Hansen, 135–37.

87. Zutty Singleton quoted in Shapiro and Hentoff, *Hear Me*, 76; Handy, *TOHNOJC*, interview 12-4-1958; Foster, *TOHNOJC*, interview 4-21-1957.

88. Collier, *Louis Armstrong*, 79–81.

89. Barker, *TOHNOJC*, interview 6-18-1959.

90. Foster, *TOHNOJC*, interview 4-21-1957; Allen, *TOHNOJC*, interview 1-14-1961.

91. Handy quoted in Southern, *Music of Black Americans*, 336–37; Barker, *TOHNOJC*, interview 6-18-1957.

92. Houston Baker, *Blues, Ideology, and American Literature*, 7.

93. Cow-Cow Davenport, "Cow-Cow and the Boogie-Woogie," in *Selections from the Gutter*, eds. Hodes and Hansen, 40–41.

94. See Whitney Balliett, *Jelly Roll, Jabbo, and Fats: Nineteen Portraits in Jazz* (New York: Oxford University Press, 1983), 16–30, on Morton's migration.

95. Thomas H. Hennessey, "Black Chicago Establishment, 1919–1930," *Journal of Jazz Studies*, Dec. 1974, p. 21.

96. John Lax, "Chicago's Black Jazz Musicians in the Twenties: Portrait of an Era," *Journal of Jazz Studies* 1 (June 1974): 106–27.

97. Hinton, *RIOJS*, interview 4-19-1976. Hinton's positive memories of Chicago in the twenties are all the more striking since he witnessed the Chicago race riot of 1919.

98. Morris, *Wait Until Dark*, chap. 5.

99. Quoted in Shapiro and Hentoff, *Hear Me*, 129.

100. Quoted in ibid., 110–11.

101. Garvin Bushell, "Jazz in the Twenties," in Martin Williams, (ed.), *Jazz Panorama*, 82.

102. Sonny Greer, *RIOJS*, interview 4-19-1976; Barker, *A Life in Jazz*, 113 and chap. 15.
    103. Quoted in Shapiro and Hentoff, *Hear Me*, 116.
    104. Quoted in ibid., 93.

Chapter Two

1. Malcolm Cowley, *Exile's Return*, 308.
    2. I use the concept marginal zone to mean an area where normative rules of public social behavior are not well enforced, and where the boundaries between polite and risqué or legal and illegal behavior are likewise ill-defined. In some cases, as we shall see, legal restrictions or zoning laws prescribe a marginal area. In other cases, marginality results from the perception of urbanites. I mean no pejorative connotation.
    3. The most complete description and history of Storyville to date is Al Rose, *Storyville, New Orleans, Being an Authentic, Illustrated Account of the Notorious Red-Light District* (Tuscaloosa: University of Alabama Press, 1974). The introduction, and chaps. 4 and 10 give the best overview of the establishment and subsequent closing of Storyville and the "uptown district." Marquis, *In Search of Buddy Bolden*, chap. 5, provides a detailed description of this area between 1900 and 1906. Storyville was named for Alderman Sidney Story, who drafted the ordinance.
    4. Rose, *Storyville*, 42–47.
    5. Morton quoted in Shapiro and Hentoff, *Hear Me*, 6.
It is important not to romanticize the quality of vice districts. Many musicians did remember them affectionately, but an alternate (and extreme) view can be found in Ronald Morris, *Wait Until Dark*, chap. 3.
    6. Rose, *Storyville*, 106, 204, 123–24.
    7. Glenny, *TOHNOJC*, interview 3-27-1957; Morton quoted in Rose, *Storyville*, 50–52; and Foster, *The Autobiography of George "Pops" Foster*, 26–37.
    8. For information on the Progressives crusade to stop vice, see Paul Boyer, *Urban Masses and Moral Order, 1820–1920* (Cambridge: Harvard University Press, 1978), chaps. 13 and 14; and Howard Chudacoff, *The Evolution of American Urban Society* (Englewood Cliifs, N.J.: Prentice-Hall, 1975), chaps. 4–7. Ruth Rosen's *The Lost Sisterhood: Prostitution in America, 1900–1918* (Baltimore: Johns Hopkins University Press, 1982), chaps. 1–3, is an insightful study of turn-of-the-century prostitution and its reformers. See Douglas Henry Daniels, *Pioneer Urbanites: A Social and Cultural History of Black San Francisco* (Philadelphia: Temple University Press, 1980), 152–53, on San Francisco reformers. Lewis A. Erenberg,

"From New York to Middletown: Repeal and the Legitimization of Night-life in the Great Depression," *American Quarterly* 38 (1986): 763.

9. Smith, *Music on My Mind*, 127; Collier, *Louis Armstrong*, 85-86; see also Travis Dempsey, *Autobiography of Black Jazz*, 11–49.

10. Dempsey, *Autobiography of Black Jazz*, 39. Eddie Condon quoted in Morris, *Wait Until Dark*, 26.

11. See Walter Reckless, *Vice in Chicago* (Chicago: University of Chicago Press, 1933), 103; and Tuttle, *Race Riot*, 192–93, on the role of black and tans in the riot.

12. James Weldon Johnson. *The Auto-biography of an Ex-Coloured Man* (New York: Garden City Publishers, 1912), 103–4.

13. Ross Russell, *Jazz Style in Kansas City and the Southwest* (Berkeley: University of California Press, 1971), 18, chap. 2. On the importance of Kansas City to jazz see also Martin Williams, "What Happened in Kansas City?," *Jazz Heritage* (New York: Oxford University Press, 1985), 17–28

14. Morton, *Mr. Jelly Roll*, 161–63; Driggs and Lewine, *Black Beauty, White Heat*, 182–83; Williams, *Jazz Masters of New Orleans*, 52–54.

15. Leonard Feather, "L.A.: A Jazz Hotbed for Seven Decades," *Los Angeles Times*, Special Supplement, Feb. 21, 1987, pp. 10–11. Brown, *RIOJS*, interview 6-12-1976; see also Driggs and Lewine, *Black Beauty, White Heat*, 180–85. One study reports that a large number of black musicians worked in the twenties in Los Angeles: Emory J. Tolbert, *The UNIA amd Black Los Angeles: Ideology and Community in the American Garvey Movement* (Los Angeles: Center for Afro-American Studies at the University of California at Los Angeles, 1980), 37.

On "rounders and slummers" in San Francisco and Oakland, see Douglas Henry Daniels, *Pioneer Urbanites*, chap. 9. Purcell's is described on pp. 145–48.

16. Smith, *Music on My Mind*, 39. Smith might have been thinking about the landmark Coney Island Elephant Hotel. Historian John Kasson explains its importance: "A trip to the Elephant Hotel quickly became an essential part of the Coney Island visitor's itinerary, and the phrase 'seeing the elephant,' often accompanied by a broad wink, became a euphemism for ilicit pleasures." Kasson, *Coney Island*, 33.

17. See Nathan Huggins, *The Harlem Renaissance* (New York: Oxford University Press, 1971), 244–54.

18. Langston Hughes and Milton Meltzer, *Black Magic: Pictorial History of the Negro in Entertainment* (Englewood Cliffs, N.J.: Prentice-Hall, 1967), 48. See also, Southern, *Music of Black Americans*, chap. 10 and pp. 438–41. Blake discussed this phenomenon in an interview with Huggins, *Voices from the Harlem Renaissance*, 336–40.

19. Albert F. McClean, Jr., *American Vaudeville as Ritual* (Lexington: University of Kentucky Press, 1965), 196–205.

20. Ibid., chap. 1 and 2,

21. Chapter 24, "Some Like It Hot," in Kyra Markham, *Burleycue: An Underground History of Burlesque Days* (New York: B. Franklin, 1975), 317–37, provides an overview of New York nightlife. Lewis A. Erenberg's *Steppin' Out* is a superb study of changing middle-class values and entertainment practices in New York City. Chapters 3–6, in particular, concern the development of cabarets and nightclubs. Erenberg's article "The Legitimization of Nightlife in the Great Depression," *American Quarterly* 38 (1986): 761–78, further develops his case. On a similar process in films, see Robert Sklar, *Movie-Made America: A Cultural History of American Movies* (New York: Vintage Books, 1976). See also Stanley Walker, *The Night Club Era* (New York: Blue Ribbon Books, 1953).

22. Erenberg, *Steppin' Out*, 21 and 132–33. Erenberg applies sociologist Erving Goffman's definition of an "action" to the institutions that evolved in New York: "Commercialized action, Goffman asserts, develops when everyday life—business, home and community—has become too routine and organized and people turn to amusement to find new kinds of fateful activities, new forms of heightened meaning."

23. Ibid., 122–27.

24. Ibid., 129.

25. Hunter quoted in Shapiro and Hentoff, *Hear Me*, 88; Garvin Bushell, "Jazz in the Twenties," in Martin Williams, *Jazz Panorama*, 74; Lawrence Brown, *RIOJS*, interview 6-12-1976.

26. Erenberg, *Steppin' Out*, 207–18.

27. Reckless, *Vice in Chicago*, 101; Stephen Kern, *The Culture of Time and Space, 1890–1918* (Cambridge: Harvard University Press, 1983), documents the emergence of the cabaret in New York as at the same time as innovations in German and Austrian theatre (pp. 197–99). German cabaret does not seem to have influenced American entrepreneurs directly, although there are some interesting parallels. Peter Jelavich describes the appeal of the cabaret to the German and Austrian bourgeoisie in terms similar to Erenberg's. See "Die Eif Scharfrichter: The Political and Sociocultural Dimensions of Cabaret in Wilhelmine Germany," in Gerald Chapple and Hans H. Shulte, *The Turn of the Century: German Literature and Art, 1890–1915* (Bonn: Bouvier Verlag Herbert Grundmann, 1983), 507–25. Erenberg indicates that it was the Parisian cafes and cabarets associated with bohemian life-styles that most influenced American cabaret design.

28. On jazz and organized crime, see Dempsey, *Autobiography of Black Jazz*, 39–49.

29. Charters and Kunstadt, *Jazz: The New York Scene*, 52.

30. Armstrong quoted in Shapiro and Hentoff, *Hear Me*, 65.

31. *Selections from the Gutter,* eds. Hodes and Hansen, 10; Kid Ory, *TOHNOJC,* interview 4-21-1957.

32. Jimmy McPartland quoted in Shapiro and Hentoff, *Hear Me,* 133; Rugg quoted in Harvey Lebow, "Modest George," *Selections from the Gutter,* eds. Hodes and Hansen, 163. Sebastian's Cotton Club advertisement from the George P. Johnson Negro Film Collection, Reel 11, Special Collections, University of California Library, University of California at Los Angeles.

33. Russell, *Jazz Style in Kansas City,* 19–22.

34. Erenberg, *Steppin' Out,* 253–54.

David Levering Lewis, *When Harlem Was in Vogue* (New York: Viking, 1979), 206–77; Jervis Anderson, *This Was Harlem* (New York: Farrar, Straus & Giroux, 1981), 161–80; and Charters and Kunstadt, *Jazz: The New York Scene,* chap. 16. Many Harlemites could not enter the famous bars and clubs because of racial bans or expensive cover charges. As many histories of twenties Halem emphasize, the community was not best characterized by the visits of "slummers," but rather by a struggle to survive against increasing poverty, unemployment, and housing shortages." See Gilbert Osofsky, *Harlem: The Making of a Ghetto, 1890–1930* (New York: Harper & Row, 1966).

35. Smith, *Music on My Mind,* 46.

36. Johnson, "Conversation with James P. Johnson," by Tom Garvin in *Jazz Panorama,* 48–49; Willie "the Lion" Smith provided a similar description in *Music on My Mind,* 65.

37. Smith, *Music on My Mind,* 87–88; Driggs and Lewine, *Black Beauty, White Heat,* 133. Despite the exclusiveness of Barron's, James Lincoln Collier argues that it was an important Harlem institution, where musicians like Duke Ellington made important contacts. James Lincoln Collier, *Duke Ellington* (New York: Oxford University Press, 1987), 39–40.

38. Smith, *Music on My Mind,* 87: Dicky Wells, *Reminiscences,* 18.

39. John Hammond, *John Hammond on Record: An Autobiography* (New York: Summit Books, 1977), 55; see also Driggs and Lewine, *Black Beauty, White Heat,* 133; Charters and Kunstadt, *Jazz: The New York Scene,* 194.

40. Quoted in Charters and Kunstadt, *Jazz: The New York Scene,* 194.

41. Barker, *A Life in Jazz,* 134; Morris, *Wait Until Dark,* 31.

42. Huggins, *Harlem Renaissance,* chap. 6.

43. Jim Haskins, *The Cotton Club* (New York: Random House, 1977), 33; Driggs and Lewine, *Black Beauty, White Heat,* 111. See also Collier, *Duke Ellington,* pp. 75–91, on the Cotton Club.

44. Haskins, *Cotton Club,* 53; Dempsey, *Autobiography of Black Jazz,* 41.

45. Durante quoted in Haskins, *The Cotton Club,* 37.

46. Greer, *TOHNOJC,* interview 1-15-1979; Collier, *Duke Ellington,* 31; Wells, *Reminiscences,* 19. Wells said: "I know sometimes we nearly melted away, it was so hot in there."

47. Hunter quoted in Shapiro and Hentoff, *Hear Me,* 87.

48. Eddie Condon and Thomas Sugrue, *We Called It Music: A Generation of Jazz* (New York: Henry Holt, 1947), 111. James Lincoln Collier points out that Lincoln Gardens was not a black and tan and he says that white musicians were uncomfortable at the club. See Collier, *Louis Armstrong,* 94. Dempsey, *Autobiography of Black Jazz,* 65–66, describes the importance of Lincoln Gardens to black Chicago nightlife.

49. George Wettling quoted in Shapiro and Hentoff, *Hear Me,* 99.

50. Russel B. Nye, "Saturday Night at the Paradise Ballroom: Or Dance Halls in the Twenties," *Journal of Popular Culture* 7 (1973): 14–15. New Orleans musicians described their frequent dance hall gigs in: Barker, *A Life in Jazz,* 18; Foster, *The Autobiography,* 64; Slow Drag Pavageau, *TOHNOJC,* interview 12-10-1958; Barney Bigard, *RIOJS,* interview July 1976.

51. Reckless, *Vice in Chicago,* 99; Buck Clayton, *RIOJS,* interview 1975; see also Hodes and Hansen (eds.), *Selections from the Gutter,* 25–26. James Lincoln Collier believes the specification of bands by the dancing public helped build the careers of Duke Ellington and other "name" bands. Collier, *Duke Ellington,* 34.

52. Charters and Kunstadt, *Jazz: The New York Scene,* chap. 2.

53. Armstrong quoted in Shapiro and Hentoff, *Hear Me,* 111. Collier points out that "Jazz had a comic tradition and Armstrong a comic bent . . . ," *Louis Armstrong,* 166.

54. Charters and Kunstadt, *Jazz: The New York Scene,* 178; Barefield, *RIOJS,* interview 1978; on working-class women and the dance halls, see Peiss, *Cheap Amusements,* chap. 4.

55. Charters and Kunstadt, *Jazz: The New York Scene,* 186. See also Lewis, *When Harlem Was in Vogue,* 170–71, and Erenberg, "The Legitimation of Nightlife," 772. Cab Calloway's description of a battle he was in at the New York Savoy is in Dempsey, *Autobiography of Black Jazz,* 224; and Dempsey himself describes the Savoy in Chicago (pp. 77–90).

56. Stearns and Stearns, *Jazz Dance,* 322.

57. Ibid., 316.

58. Ibid., 325.

59. Ellington quoted in Shapiro and Hentoff, *Hear Me,* 168; Wells, *Reminiscences,* 20.

60. Langston Hughes, *The Big Sea* (New York: Knopf, 1940), 229.

61. Willie "the Lion" Smith, *Music on My Mind,* 153–55; and James P. Johnson, "Conversation," 46.

62. Barefield, *RIOJS,* interview November 1978.

63. Smith, *Music on My Mind,* 154.
64. Morris, *Wait Until Dark,* 20.
65. Durante quoted in ibid., 4.
66. Erenberg, *Steppin' Out,* 237.
67. Art Hodes insists that the basement is probably the best place to play jazz: "Well, the smarter the setting, the less chance you had of hearing jazz played there." Hodes and Hansen (eds.), *Selections from the Gutter,* 233.

Chapter Three

1. For example, see Leonard, *Jazz and the White Americans,* chap. 5; Baraka, *Blues People,* chaps. 10 and 11; and Nanry (with Berger), *The Jazz Text,* 120.
2. Leonard, *Jazz and the White Americans;* and Leonard, "The Impact of Mechanization," in Charles Nanry (ed.), *American Music: From Storyville to Woodstock* (New Brunswick, N.J.: Transaction Bks., 1972), 44–64.
3. Cyril Ehrlich, *The Piano: A History* (Totowa, N.J.: Rowman and Littlefield, 1976), chap. 7.
4. Ehrlich, *The Piano;* and Arthur Loesser, *Men, Women, and Pianos: A Social History* (New York: Simon and Schuster, 1954), 600–602.
5. Cynthia A. Hoover, *Music Machines—American Style: A Catalog of the Exhibition* (Washington, D.C.: Smithsonian Institution Press, 1971), 62.
6. Cow-Cow Davenport, "Mama Don't Low No Music," in Hodes and Hansen (eds.), *Selections from the Gutter,* 43; see George "Pops" Foster for a description of James P. Johnson making piano rolls, *Autobiography of Pops Foster,* 151.
7. Leonard, "The Impact," 45.
8. Ibid., Manufacturing data based on U.S. Department of Commerce, *Biennial Consensus of Manufactures from 1909–1932* support the conclusions about sales of piano rolls versus those of phonograph recordings.
9. Hoover, *Music Machines,* 54; and Roland Gelatt, *That Fabulous Phonograph: 1877–1977* (New York: Macmillan, 1977), 69 and 191.
10. Harrison Barnes, *TOHNOJC,* interview 1–25–1959.
11. Perry Bradford, *Born with the Blues: Perry Bradford's Own Story, the True Story of Pioneering Blues Singers and Musicians in the Early Days of Jazz* (New York: Oak Publications, 1956), 14; and Robert Dixon, *Recording the Blues* (New York: Stein and Day, 1970).
12. Stearns, *Story of Jazz,* 168.

13. Titon, *Downhome Blues*, 205.

14. Clarence Williams quoted in Stearns, *Story of Jazz*, 168; Reb Spikes, *RIOJS*, interview 1980. The influence of classic woman blues singers on black entertainment and culture has received much serious attention and analysis. Biographies such as Sandra Leib, *Mother of the Blues: A Study of Ma Rainey* (Boston: University of Massachusetts Press, 1981); and Chris Albertson, *Bessie* (New York: Stein and Day, 1972) provide thorough discussions of leading performers' lives. Derrick Stewart-Baxter, *Ma Rainey and the Classic Blues Singers* (New York: Stein and Day, 1970) is a general overview of major careers. For an analysis of women's blues and 1920s black culture, see Hazel B. Carby. "It Jus Be's Dat Way Sometime: The Sexual Politics of Women's Blues," *Radical America* 20 (June–July 1986): 9–22.

15. Foreman, "Jazz and Race Records," 92. Foreman argued that the Harlem Renaissance and race pride helped give a positive connotation to race records among blacks. James Lincoln Collier makes a similar point in *Louis Armstrong* (pp. 96–97). Collier's ideas about the race catalogs represent a break with the conventional view of race records as a marketing strategy that endorsed segregation. See Collier, *Louis Armstrong*, 96–97.

But black critics were also anxious to see "refined" music produced that was pleasing to European classical standards. Foreman analyzed the contradictions presented by these two positions. For a comparable discussion of this ambivalence in the black press, see Ronald G. Walters, "The Negro Press and the Image of Success: 1920–1939," *Midcontinental American Studies Journal* 11 (1970): 39.

16. Charters and Kunstadt, *Jazz: The New York Scene*, 97.

17. Eddie Edwards, "Once Upon a Time," Hodes and Hansen (eds.), *Selections from the Gutter*, 109–10.

18. Edwards, "Once Upon A Time," 109–10; Leonard, *Jazz and the White Americans*, 12–13; Williams, *Jazz Masters of New Orleans*, 26–37. For a full-length discussion of the Original Dixieland Jazz Band (ODJB), see H.O. Brunn, *The Story of the Original Dixieland Jazz Band* (Baton Rouge: Louisiana State University Press, 1960), 63–107.

19. There is some question as to whether or not this story about Keppard is true. In any case, it has been repeated so often that it is a staple of jazz histories and has passed into the folklore of early jazz. Certainly many musicains considered it worth repeating. See Ramsey and Smith, *Jazzmen*, 22; Bechet, *Treat It Gentle*, 113; Smith, *Music on My Mind*, 218.

20. Collier on the Creole Jazz Band, in *Louis Armstrong*, 109, 123; Martin Williams, *The Jazz Tradition* (New York: Oxford University Press, 1983), 10.

21. Ory quoted in Shapiro and Hentoff, *Hear Me,* 109; Collier on Armstrong and the Hot Five recordings, *Louis Armstrong,* chap. 14, p. 178.

22. Hoover, *Music Machines,* 72; Foster, *Autobiography,* 126; Wingy Manone and Paul Vanderoot, *Trumpet on the Wing* (New York: Doubleday, 1948), 52–53.

23. Manone, *Trumpet on the Wing,* 52–53; Lawrence Brown, *RIOJS,* interview 6–12–1976.

24. The Armstrong story is repeated many places. This quotation from Lorraine Lion's transcription of a radio broadcast entitled, "Mr. Armstrong and Mr. Robbins," in *Selections from the Gutter,* eds. Hodes and Hansen, 81. See also Dempsey, *Autobiography of Black Jazz,* 372. Collier says the accuracy of the story is questionable, but that scat singing did become a popular new novelty effect on jazz recordings (*Louis Armstrong,* 172–73). Ellington was reputed to put some studio compositions together at the last minute in order to meet a deadline. Collier, *Duke Ellington,* 69.

25. Collier, *Louis Armstrong,* 170.

26. Gaines quoted in Shapiro and Hentoff, *Hear Me,* 177.

27. Collier describes Williams's influence in *Louis Armstrong* (pp. 96, 140). Several musicians commented on Williams's business acumen. George "Pops" Foster, for example, claimed that Williams was nicknamed "Spool Head" because he was always sharp witted in the recording business and "always cut himself in" on the records he made. "After he got through," Foster claimed, "he had more of your number than you did." Foster, *Autobiography,* 100. On Williams, see also, Ed Allen, *TOHNOJC,* interview 1–14–1961. Ory, *TOHNOJC,* interview 4–20–1957; also see Alma Hubner, "Kid Ory," in Hodes and Hansen (eds.), *Selections from the Gutter,* 113.

28. Walker quoted in Shapiro and Hentoff, *Hear Me,* 177–78; Eddie Barefield, *RIOJS,* interview 11–1978; Ory, *TOHNOJC,* interview 4–20–1957.

29. Foreman, "Jazz and Blues Records," 65.

30. Gelatt, *Phonograph,* 188–89.

31. Foreman, "Jazz and Blues Records," 234.

32. Ibid., 66.

33. Ibid., 78.

34. Ibid., 78.

35. Singleton quoted in "I Remember the Queen," in Hodes and Hansen (eds.), *Selections from the Gutter,* 65.

36. Gelatt, *Phonograph,* 255. Philip K. Eberly, *Music in the Air: America's Changing Tastes in Popular Music 1920–1980* (New York: Hastings, 1982), 13; Roland Marchand, *Advertising the American Dream: Making*

Way for Modernity, 1920–1940 (Berkeley: University of California Press, 1985), 92, provides the figures on radio audiences. Marchand's study suggests that advertising executives debated the influence of jazz on consumers.

37. Foster R. Dulles, *America Learns to Play* (New York: Appleton-Century, 1940), 325; Collier on the kind of music performed on radio, *Louis Armstrong*, 90.

38. Eberly, *Music in the Air*, 5; and Harrison B. Summers, *A Thirty-Year History of Programs Carried on National Radio Networks, 1926–1956* (Salem, N.H.: Ayer, 1971); Leonard, "Impact of Mechanization," 46.

39. Marchand, *Advertising the American Dream*, 90–91; Meyer quoted in the *New York Times,* Oct. 12, 1924.

40. Shapiro and Hentoff, *Hear Me,* 301.

41. Count Basie quoted, ibid.

42. Bigard, *RIOJS,* interview July 1976; Hinton, *RIOJS,* interview 4–19–1976.

43. Leonard, "Impact of Mechanization," 52–53.

44. Ibid., 57–59. In *Jazz and the White Americans,* Leonard analyzed the content of songs to measure the effectiveness of regulation.

45. The most thorough analysis of blacks and films is Thomas Cripps's *Slow Fade to Black: The Negro in American Film, 1900–1941* (New York: Oxford University Press, 1977), especially chaps. 4–10. This quotation is from p. 207. Other good studies include: Daniel J. Leab, *From Sambo to Superspade: The Black Experience in Motion Pictures* (Boston: Houghton Mifflin, 1973); and Donald Bogle, *Toms, Coons, Mulattoes, Mammies, and Bucks* (New York: Viking 1973). Driggs and Lewine, *Black Beauty, White Heat,* 248–74, provides many film stills. George P. Johnson, interview 10–29–1985, University of California at Los Angeles Oral History Collection, in Special Collections, University of California Library.

46. Singleton, *RIOJS,* interview 1975; Mary Lou Williams, *RIOJS,* interview 6–26–1973. Maurice Waller describes Fats's introduction to the Lafayette Theatre, in Maurice Waller and Anthony Calabrese, *Fats Waller* (New York: Schirmer Books, 1977), 18–19.

47. Hennessey, "The Chicago Establishment," 19.

48. See Cripps, *Slow Fade to Black,* 229; and Driggs and Lewine, *Black Beauty, White Heat,* 250–52. Jane Freuer, in *The Hollywood Musical* (Bloomington: University of Indiana Press, 1982), 58–59, sees the growth of jazz in the movies as a victory of popular art over elitist conventions.

49. Plot synopsis based on Cripps, *Slow Fade to Black,* 207, and Driggs and Lewine, *Black Beauty, White Heat,* 252.

50. Huggins, *The Harlem Renaissance,* 91.

51. Howard Odum, "Folk Song and Folk Poetry as Found in the Secular Songs of the Southern Negroes,"*Journal of American Folklore* 24 (1911): 255–94. Paul Oliver, *Songsters and Saints* (London: Cambridge University Press, 1984), 68.

52. Barker, *A Life in Music,* 42; Wells, *Reminiscences,* 33; Clayton, *RIOJS,* interview 1975; Mose Allison, in Kitty Grime, *Jazz Voices* (London: Quarter Books, 1983), 33; Frazier, *TOHNOJC,* interview 1–19–1972.

53. See Leonard, *Jazz and the White Americans,* 95–96, on musicians learning from recordings. McPartland, quoted in Shapiro and Hentoff, *Hear Me,* 118–20.

Chapter Four

1. Lawrence Levine describes the importance of musical expression in what he calls the "sacred world" of slaves, *Black Culture and Black Consciousness,* chaps. 1 and 2. See also Southern, *Music of Black Americans,* 175, and John Blassingame, *The Slave Community,* 50–76.

2. John Szwed, "Afro-American Musical Adaptation," Whitten and Szwed (eds.), *Afro-American Anthropology,* chap. 11, pp. 219–24. Szwed provides a succinct overview of various ways to interpret the roles of bluesmen and preachers in this essay. See also, Charles Keil, *Urban Blues* (Chicago: University of Chicago Press, 1966), introduction and pp. 143–63. On blues and community sanctions, see Baraka, *Blues People,* for a discussion of class and migration (pp. 122–41 and 176); and Titon, *Downhome Blues,* 200–202.

3. W.C. Handy, *Father of the Blues: An Autobiography* (London: Macmillan, 1957), 10. Johnson, *Conversation,* 46. Collier makes a similar point about Duke Ellington's musical background and stresses that middle-class homes were most likely to have pianos. Collier, *Duke Ellington,* 19.

4. Jelly Roll Morton, *Mr. Jelly Roll,* 26; Al Rose, *Eubie Blake* (New York: Schirmer Books, 1979), 10–15 and 19–21; Lawrence Brown, *RIOJS,* interview 6–12–1976; Smith, *Music on My Mind,* 26.

5. Rose, *Blake,* 22.

6. Ory, *TOHNOJC,* interview 4–20–1957; Matthews, *TOHNOJC,* interview 3–10–1959; Smith, *Music on My Mind,* 1–2.

7. The anecdote about the sheep and goats is based on Carrie Smith's recollections, in Grime, *Jazz Voices,* 32.

8. Smith, *Music on My Mind,* 100–101.

9. Nancy J. Weiss, *The National Urban League 1910–1940* (New York: Oxford University Press, 1974), 117.

10. Hinton, *RIOJS,* interview 4–19–1976.

11. Weiss, *Urban League,* 110 and 117. Douglas Henry Daniels describes some of the same attempts by the YMCA and YWCA in San Francisco, in, *Pioneer Urbanites,* 152–53.

12. Hennessey, "Black Chicago Establishment," 119. In addition to this article by Hennessey, the role of the establishment musicians on musical style and black musical taste has also been described in two key articles: Chadwick Hansen, "Social Influences on Jazz Style: Chicago, 1920–30," *American Quarterly* 12 (Winter 1960): 493–507; and John Lax, "Chicago's Black Musician in the 1920s—Portrait of an Era," *Journal of Jazz Studies* 1 (June 1974): 106–27. All focus on Dave Peyton's *Defender* articles.

13. Hennessey, "Black Chicago Establishment," 21.

14. Ibid., 22.

15. James Lincoln Collier points out that Duke Ellington, for example, though "not an intellectual" still "appears to have soaked up a good deal of [the] zeitgeist of the Harlem Renaissance" when its leading writers and artists patronized the clubs where he worked (*Duke Ellington,* p. 40).

16. I have restricted my discussion to Harlem, although similar literary and artistic experimentation took place elsewhere. In Los Angeles, for example, Eric Walrond helped edit a literary journal called *The Outlet,* which included commentary on jazz.

17. See Michael B. Stoff on primitivism, in "Claude McKay and the Cult of Primitivism," *The Harlem Renaissance Remembered,* ed. Arna Bontemps (New York: Dodd, Mead, 1972), 126–46.

18. Just as black and white intellectuals debated jazz and blues in the 1920s, so too, do contemporary scholars of the Harlem Renaissance disagree about the role of these music forms in the Renaissance. Nathan Huggins, as indicated in the quotation from the *Harlem Renaissance* (pp. 9–11), argues that the indifference to jazz resulted from "self-consciousness" about white judgments and from provincialism about black culture which "crippled" their appreciation of an art form like jazz. David Levering Lewis feels that Fletcher Henderson's popularity marked a turning point, at which time "upper-crust Afro-Americans" found someone suitably dignified to win them over to the sufferance if not the approval of jazz." Lewis, *When Harlem Was in Vogue,* 173. Most recently, literary critic Houston Baker suggests we should apply a new problematic to the study of the Harlem Renaissance that assumes it *succeeded* as a discursive strategy out of which "Afro-American modernism's defining moment is signalled by *The New Negro*'s confidently voiced plays within a field of form and the deformation of mastery." Baker sees musical forms (particularly the

blues and spirituals and to a lesser degree jazz) as a significant part of Renaissance discourse. See Houston Baker, "Modernism and the Harlem Renaissance," *American Quarterly* 39 (1987): 84–97 (quotation from pp. 95–96); and Baker's book *Modernism and the Harlem Renaissance* (Chicago: University of Chicago Press, 1987).

19. David Levering Lewis, "Parallels and Divergences: Assimilationist Strategies of Afro-American and Jewish Elites from 1910 to the Early 1930s," *Journal of American History* 70 (1984): 560–61.

20. Arnold Rampersad, *The Art and Imagination of W.E.B. DuBois* (Cambridge: Harvard University Press, 1976), 191.

22. Ibid., chap. 2.

22. W.E.B. DuBois, *The Souls of Black Folk* (New York: Signet Classics. 1969 orig. pub., 1903); James Weldon Johnson, *Along This Way* (New York: Viking, 1968), 203. Houston Baker sees DuBois's rejection of the popular sounds of minstrelsy in favor of spirituals as an example of the "deformation of mastery," important to Harlem Renaissance discourse; Baker, "Modernism and the Harlem Renaissance," 94.

23. James Weldon Johnson, *The Book of American Negro Poetry* (New York: Harcourt Brace Jovanovich, 1922), 16.

24. James Weldon Johnson, *Along This Way*, 378. Aaron Douglas's illustrations in the original version of *God's Trombones* represent typical Renaissance uses of music in the visual arts.

25. J.A. Rogers, "Jazz at Home," in *The New Negro,* ed. Alain Locke (New York: Boni, 1925). The collection was based on the special edition of *Survey Graphic* that Locke was asked to edit (Vol. 6, No. 6, March 1925).

26. J.A. Rogers, "Jazz at Home," 218. Many musicians described inventing instruments out of cardboard boxes and cigar crates. Others practiced percussion with table legs.

27. J.A. Rogers, "Jazz at Home," 219. The Jasbo Brown story is based on the experiences of Tom Brown's Dixieland Jass Band. See Chapter Five.

28. Jazz dance historians Marshall and Jean Stearns describe a process of development for these vernacular dances very similar to Rogers's: see Stearns and Stearns, *Jazz Dance,* 78. The most comprehensive treatment of black dance generally is Lynn Fauley Emery's *Black Dance.*

29. Rogers did not object to commercialization on Broadway, in fact, he considered the use of jazz on Broadway a high form of compliment.

30, Locke, "The Negro Spirituals," in *The New Negro,* 199–210. Alain Locke's changing views on art, culture, and race relations were masterfully outlined in Jeffrey Stewart's edited collection, *The Critical Temper of Alain Locke: A Selection of His Essays on Art and Culture* (New York: Garland Press, 1983). On music specifically, Stewart explains, "Locke valued the spirituals as folk music, and welcomed research into their African origins in his review 'The Technical Study of the Spirituals' (1925). But Locke also saw the spirituals as part of an evolutionary process of internal development in Afro-American culture. Thus " 'the spirituals, ragtime, and jazz' constituted 'one continuous sequence of Negro music' " (p. 105). An additional perspective was provided by Paul Joseph Burgett, who sees Locke's contributions as part of an evolving black aesthetic in his paper "Vindication As a Thematic Principle in the Writings of Alain Locke on the Music of Black Americans," unpublished, presented to *Heritage: A Reappraisal of the Harlem Renaissance Conference,* Hofstra University, May 1985.

31. Alain Locke, in Huggins: *Voices from the Harlem Renaissance,* 312.

32. W.H. Handy and Abbe Niles, *Blues: An Anthology* (New York: A. &. C. Boni, 1926).

33. Locke, *The Negro and His Music* (New York: Associates in Negro Folk Education, 1936), 78. Locke clearly challenges the claims made by jazz detractors that jazz was formless and required little skill to perform.

34. Locke, *The Negro and His Music,* 223.

35. Rogers, "Jazz at Home," in Locke (ed.), *The New Negro,* 223.

36. See James Weldon Johnson, *Book of American Negro Poetry,* 23. Contemporary novelist Ishmael Reed used Johnson's "jes grew" analogy as one theme in his novel *Mumbo Jumbo* (New York: Avon Books, 1971).

37. Locke (ed.), *The Negro and His Music,* 82–83.

38. Ibid., 87.

39. Ibid., 89–90.

40. Many Harlem Renaissance authors used jazz and blues for language, subjects, and environments in their literature. I have selected these authors because their descriptions of jazz performance were among the most influential of the Renaissance generation. For the influence of music on visual artists, see the essays and illustrations in a volume produced by the Studio Museum in Harlem, New York, *Harlem Renaissance Art of Black America* (New York: Harry N. Abrams, 1987).

41. Claude McKay, *Home to Harlem* (New York: Harper and Row, 1928), 8. Michael B. Stoff offered a good description of McKay's primitivism: "For McKay, this meant the conscious and studied illumination of a black folk-art tradition and whose central themes would be the indestructible vitality of the primitive black man and the inextricable dilemma of the educated Negro," in "Claude McKay and the Cult of Primitivism," *The Harlem Renaissance Remembered,* ed. Arna Bontemps, 132. On McKay's life and art generally, see Wayne F. Cooper, *Claude McKay: Rebel Sojourner in the Harlem Renaissance* (Baton Rouge: Louisiana State University Press, 1987).

42. McKay, *Home to Harlem,* 15–21. For descriptions of Harlem caba-

rets, see Jervis Anderson, *This Was Harlem* (New York: Farrar, Straus, & Giroux, 1981), 161–80; and David Levering Lewis, *When Harlem Was in Vogue,* 206–11.

43. McKay, *Home to Harlem,* 155.

44. W.E.B. DuBois reviewed the book in *The Crisis* (June 1928) and gave it a scathing dismissal: "*Home to Harlem* for the most part nauseates me, and after the dirtier parts of its filth, I feel distinctly like taking a bath . . . It looks as though McKay has set out to cater to that prurient demand on the part of white folks for a portrayal in Negros of that utter licentiousness which convention holds white folks back from enjoying— if enjoyment it can be labelled."

45. Claude McKay, *A Long Way from Home* (New York: Harcourt Brace Jovanovich, 1970), 321.

46. "Jazzonia," in Langston Hughes, *Weary Blues* (New York: Knopf, 1926), 25. See Onwuchekwa Jemie, *Langston Hughes: An Introduction to the Poetry* (New York: Columbia University Press, 1976), 35.

47. "Jazzonia," in Langston Hughes, *Weary Blues,* p. 25. On Hughes's poetry, see Jemie, *Langston Hughes;* and Arnold Rampersad, *The Life of Langston Hughes,* Volume I, *1902–1941, I, Too, Sing America* (New York: Oxford University Press, 1986), 110–13.

48. Langston Hughes, *The Big Sea,* 208; Langston Hughes, *Fine Clothes to the Jew* (New York: Knopf, 1927). On Hughes's life on Seventh Street, see Rampersad, *The Life of Langston Hughes,* vol. I, pp. 102–3.

49. Langston Hughes, *Weary Blues,* 27. The title "Cat and the Saxophone" may be a reference to the nightclub with a similar name—Cat on a Saxophone—patronized by Hughes and other Harlem Renaissance writers.

50. In his biography of Hughes, Arnold Rampersad points out that the degree of praise for *Weary Blues* was often determined by the "attitude of the critic to blues and jazz," *Life of Langston Hughes,* vol. I., p. 129. For Rampersad's discussion of the critical response to *Fine Clothes to the Jew,* see pp. 141–46. Rampersad asserts that the volume is more "deliberately within the range of authentic blues emotion and blues culture" than *Weary Blues.*

51. For reviews on Hughes see: Jessie Fauset, "One Book Shelf," *Crisis* (March 1926): 30–31; Alain Locke, "Weary Blues," *Palms* 1 (1926): 25–27; and Countee Cullen, "Poet on Poet," *Opportunity* 4 (March 4, 1926): 662–63 and 692–94.

52. George Schuyler, "The Negro Art-Hokum," *Nation* (June 16, 1926): 662–63.

53. Langston Hughes, "The Negro Artist and the Racial Mountain," *Nation* (June 23, 1926): 692–93. Rampersad, *The Life of Langston Hughes,* vol. I, pp. 130–31.

54. Hughes, "Negro Artist," 693.

55. See Robert Hemenway, *Zora Neale Hurston: A Literary Biography* (Urbana: University of Illinois Press,1977); Mary Helen Washington, "Zora Neale Hurston: A Woman Half in Shadow," in Walker (ed.), *I Love Myself When I Am Laughing . . . and Then Again When I Am Looking Mean and Impressive: A Zora Neale Hurston Reader* (Old Westbury, N. Y.: Feminist Press,1979), 7–23; Alice Walker, "Zora Neale Hurston: A Cautionary Tale and a Partisan View" and "Searching for Zora," *In Search of Our Mother's Gardens: Womanist Prose by Alice Walker* (New York: Harcourt Brace Jovanovich, 1983), 83–116.

56. Hurston wrote a great deal more on music than I have suggested here. She, like Locke, was concerned that radio and phonograph recordings would commercialize folk music. She also hoped to bring authentic folk music performance into the theatre (in *The Great Day*). See Hemenway, *Zora Neale Hurston,* 178–85. Hemenway describes Hurston's aesthetic as one that recognized "no distinctions between the lore inherited by successive generations of folk and the imagination with which each generation adapted the tradition and made the lore its own" (p. 80). On Hurston's interpretation of the spirituals, a good place to start is Zora Neale Hurston, "Spirituals and Neo-Spirituals," in Huggins, *Voices from the Harlem Renaissance,* 344–47.

57. Zora Neale Hurston, "Characteristics of Negro Expression," in *Negro Anthology,* ed. Nancy Cunard (New York: Ungar, 1934), 43.

58. Ibid., 44–46.

59. Ibid.

60. Ibid.

61. Walker (ed.), *I Love Myself,* 154.

62. For a comparison of Zora Neale Hurston and twenties classic blues artists, see Lorraine Bethel, " 'This Infinity of Conscious Pain': Zora Neale Hurston and the Black Literary Tradition," *All the Women Are White, All the Blacks Are Men: But Some of Us Are Brave,* eds. Gloria T. Hull, Patricia Bell Scott, and Barbara Smith (Old Westbury, N. Y.: Feminist Press, 1982), 176–88. On the blues singers themselves, see Carby, "It Jus Be's Dat Way Sometime: The Sexual Politics of Women's Blues," *Radical America* 20 (June/July 1986): 9–22.

Chapter Five

1. For useful jazz bibliographies, consult Alan P. Merriam, *A Bibliography of Jazz* (Philadelphia: American Folklore Society, 1954) and Donald Kennington and Danny Read, *The Literature of Jazz: A Critical Guide* (Chicago American Library Association, 1980). These headlines are

from the *New York Times:* March 11, 1928, Jan. 7, 1934, March 7, 1926, and Nov. 11, 1928, respectively. A fascinating debate about jazz took place in the Soviet Union in the twenties, see Frederick Starr, *Red and Hot: The Fate of Jazz in the Soviet Union* (New York: Oxford University Press, 1983).

2. "Delving Into the Genealogy of Jazz," *Current Opinion* 67 (Aug. 1919): 97. See also Henry Osbourne Osgood, *So This Is Jazz!* (Boston: Little, Brown, 1926), 22. Edward Berlin notes that a similar etymological debate over ragtime took place, see *Ragtime*, 27–29.

3. Osgood, *Jazz*, 9.

4. Ibid., 10–11.

5. Ibid., 11.

6. Ibid., 28–29; see also *Literary Digest*, March 26, 1927, pp. 26–27.

7. "Why Jazz Sends Us Back to the Jungle," *Current Opinion* 65 (Sept. 1918): 165; "Delving Into the Genealogy of Jazz," *Current Opinion* 67 (Aug. 1919): 97–98.

8. "A Negro Explains Jazz," *Literary Digest*, April 26, 1919, p. 28.

9. See Williams, *Jazz Masters of New Orleans*, 28, for one version of the Brown story. No one knows for sure the origin of the word "jazz."

10. Historian Warren Susman described the twenties as a "period dedicated to knowledge and experience and the effective use of both." The many articles citing anthropologists, sociologists, and other "experts" on jazz indicated that the music was one of the aspects of American life that readers most wanted explained. See Warren Susman, "Culture and Civilization in the Nineteen Twenties," in his book *Culture As History: The Transformation of American Society in the Twentieth Century* (New York: Pantheon, 1985), 105–21.

11. Bushell, *Jazz in the Twenties*, 69; Wells, *Reminiscences*, 7–8; Smith, *Music on My Mind*, xiii.

12. Spikes, *RIOJS*, interview 1980.

13. "Delving Into the Genealogy of Jazz," *Current Opinion* (Aug. 1919): 97.

14. Osgood, *Jazz*, 11.

15. *Literary Digest*, April 26, 1924, pp. 29–30.

16. "Jazz Comes To Stay," *Current Opinion* 77 (Sept. 1924): 337.

17. Kern, *The Culture of Time and Space*, 123.

18. *Literary Digest*, Sept. 3, 1927, p. 29.

19. Malcolm Cowley, *Exile's Return*, 9.

20. The importance of primitivism for the twenties intellectual and artistic community has been the subject of a lively debate provoked by New York's Museum of Modern Art's 1984 exhibit: "Primitivism in 20th Century Art: Affinity of the Tribal and Modern." Several reviews deserve mention here because they offer interesting readings of the primi-

tivism vogue and are applicable to jazz. See for instance, "Modernist Primitivism: An Introduction," in *Primitivism in 20th Century Art: Affinity of the Tribal and Modern,* ed. William Rubin (New York: Museum of Modern Art, 1984), 1–78. James Clifford, "Histories of the Tribal and the Modern," and Yves-Alain Bois, "La Pensee Sauvage," in *Art in America* 73 (1984): 164–89. See also Dore Ashton, "On an Epoch of Paradox: 'Primitivism' at the Museum of Modern Art," and Gail Levin, " 'Primitivism' in American Art: Some Literary Parallels of the 1910s and 1920s," in *Arts Magazine* (Nov. 1984): 76–80 and 101–5 respectively.

21. Rubin (ed.), *Affinity of the Tribal and the Modern,* " 1–78.

22. "Why Jazz Sends Us Back to the Jungle," *Current Opinion,* Sept. 1918, p. 165.

23. European soldiers felt a clear break in their conception of time, as Paul Fussell masterfully documents in *The Great War and Modern Memory* (New York: Oxford University Press, 1975). "The image of strict division clearly dominates the Great War conception of the Time Before and Time After," Fussell wrote, "especially when the mind dwells on the contrast between the prewar idyll and the wartime nastiness" (p. 80). Fussell attributed at least some of this sensibility to the experience of trench warfare. Stephen Kern similarly saw the war as a culmination of "sweeping changes in technology and culture that created distinctive new modes of thinking about and experiencing time and space." One change was the sense that the world "sped up" after the war—and that jazz kept drumming the rapid tempo that ragtime had begun. Kern, *Culture of Time and Space,* 1.

24. Gertrude Stein, *Three Lives* (New York: Vintage Books, Random House, 1933: orig. pub. 1909), 89. See Michael J. Hoffman, *Gertrude Stein* (Boston: Twayne Publishers, 1976), 32–37, on her use of dialect and other black cultural forms. James Mellow commented on Stein's primitivism in *Charmed Circle: Gertrude Stein and Company* (New York: Praeger, 1974), 71. The information on Richard Wright is from John Malcolm, *The Third Rose: Gertrude Stein and Her World* (Boston: Little, Brown, 1959), 120–21. Gail Levin points out that Stein's "creation of Melanctha . . . coincides with her initial acquaintance with Matisse and his growing interest in African sculpture," in Levin, "Primitivism in American Art," 103.

25. Vachel Lindsay, *The Congo and Other Poems* (New York: Macmillan, 1920), 8.

26. Excerpts from the poems are based on the edition cited above, pp. 3–11. John R. Cooley's *Savages and Naturals: Black Portraits by White Writers in Modern Literature* (Newark: University of Delaware Press, 1982) provided a useful overview of white writers and primitivism in the teens and twenties. On Vachel Lindsay, see Ann Massa, *Vachel Lind-*

say: Fieldworker for the American Dream (Bloomington: Indiana University Press, 1970), 195–201. Hughes (*The Big Sea,* 210–13) described meeting Lindsay when Hughes was working as a busboy at a Washington, D.C., hotel. Lindsay publicized Hughes as a "Negro busboy poet," and Hughes considered it his first "publicity break."

27. Huggins, *Harlem Renaissance,* provides a thorough and sound reading of *Nigger Heaven,* the quotation is from pp. 103–13. See also Edward J. Lueders, *Carl Van Vechten and the Twenties* (Albuquerque: University of New Mexico, 1955), 86–90, regarding the novel. Langston Hughes, *The Big Sea,* 268–72, provides a sympathetic account of Van Vechten's efforts.

28. F.Scott Fitzgerald, *Tales of the Jazz Age* (London: Collins, 1923), 97. For a discussion of the role of jazz in the 1920s college youth culture, see Helen Lefkowitz Horowitz, *Campus Life: Undergraduate Cultures from the End of the Eighteenth Century to the Present* (New York: Knopf, 1987), 128–29.

29. Fitzgerald, *Tales from the Jazz Age,* 127.

30. For more information, see these biographies and autobiographies: Eddie Condon, *We Called It Music: A Generation of Jazz* (New York: Henry Holt, 1947); Wingy Manone with Paul Vanderoot, *Trumpet on a Wing* (New York: Doubleday, 1948); Milton "Mezz" Mezzrow, *Really the Blues* (New York: Random House, 1946); Benny Goodman and Irving Kolodin, *The Kingdom of Swing* (New York: Stackpole, 1939); and Ralph Berton, *Remembering Bix: A Memoir of the Jazz Age* (New York: Harper and Row, 1947). The Berton quotation is from p. 27.

31. Manone, *Trumpet,* 27.

32. Mezzrow, *Blues,* 27. See Collier, *Louis Armstrong,* on Mezzrow's determination to "turn himself black"; and Al Rose, *I Remember Jazz: Six Decades Among the Great Jazzmen* (Baton Rouge: Louisiana State University Press, 1987), 17–19.

33. Manone, *Trumpet,* 13–14.

34. Mezzrow, *Blues,* 18.

35. Hammond, *On Record,* 43–44 and 67–69.

36. Mezzrow, *Blues,* 83.

37. Morroe Berger, "Jazz: Resistance to the Diffusion of a Culture Pattern," *Journal of Negro History* 32 (1947): 461–94.

38. Leonard, *Jazz and the White Americans,* 133.

39. Ernest Newman, "Summing Up Music's Case Against Jazz," *New York Times,* March 6, 1927, Section IV, pp. 3, 22; Sigmund Spaeth, "Jazz Is Not Music," *Forum* 80 (Aug. 1928): 267–71.

40. Virgil Thomson, "Jazz," in *American Mercury* 2 (Aug. 1924): 465–67.

41. Daniel Gregory Mason, "Stravinsky As a Symptom," *American*

Mercury 4 (April 1925): 465–66. See Moore, *Yankee Blues,* for an extended discussion of Mason's aesthetics.

42. Although I have only given brief attention to Adorno, I am indebted to the extensive discussion of Adorno and jazz in Bob Bernotas's dissertation, "Critical Theory, Jazz, and Politics: A Critique of the Frankfurt School," Johns Hopkins University, Baltimore, 1987, for my understanding of Adorno's analysis of jazz. Bernotas makes it clear that Adorno's lack of appreciation for the performance history and context of jazz resulted in serious misunderstandings.

43. Leonard, *Jazz and the White Americans,* 33.

44. "Jazz and Its Victims, *New York Times,* Oct. 7, 1928

45. Ann Shaw Faulkner, "Does Jazz Put the Sin in Syncopation? " *Ladies' Home Journal* 38 (Aug. 1921): 16, 34.

46. John R. McMahon, "Back to Pre-War Morals," *Ladies' Home Journal* 38 (Nov. 1921): 13.

47. *New York Times,* April 17, 1928.

48. "Laud Jazz in High Places," *New York Times,* Aug. 16, 1921.

49. *New York Times,* Sept. 20, 1927.

50. "Jazz Comes to Stay," *Current Opinion* 77 (Sept. 1924): 337.

51. *Ibid.* See also *Scribner's* (Feb. 1925): 200–203.

52. *Scribner's* (Feb. 1925): 202.

53. Gilbert Seldes, *The Seven Lively Arts,* 84.

54. Charters and Kunstadt, *Jazz: The New York Scene,* 139.

Conclusion

1. Ernest Ansermet, quoted in Whitney Balliett, *Jelly Roll, Jabbo, and Fats: 19 Portraits in Jazz,* 32.

2. See Roger Pryor Dodge, "Consider the Critics," in Ramsey and Smith, *Jazzmen,* 301–42, for an early survey of jazz criticism. See Collier, "The Faking of Jazz," on the possible political implications of these critical approaches.

3. Aaron H. Esman, "Jazz—a Study in Cultural Conflict," *The American Imago: A Psychoanalytic Journal for the Arts and Sciences* 8 (Sept. 1951): 219–25.

4. Norman Margolis, "A Theory on the Psychology of Jazz," *The American Imago: A Psychoanalytic Journal for the Arts and Sciences* 11 (Fall 1954): 263–91; Howard S. Becker, "Careers in a Deviant Occupational Group: The Dance Musician," in *Outsiders: Studies in the Sociology of Deviance* (New York: Free Press, 1973), 101–19.

Bibliographic Essay and Suggested Readings

This study is based on primary and secondary material collected from several sources that best capture and explain jazz performance and its meaning. Readers should also consult discographies in the general jazz histories and biographies described below. Two comprehensive bibliographies of jazz are Alan P. Merriam, *A Bibliography of Jazz* (Philadelphia: American Folklore Society, 1954) and Donald Kennington and Danny Read (eds.), *The Literature of Jazz: A Critical Guide* (Chicago: American Library Association, 1980).

Many of the debates over jazz raged in newspapers and magazines. The *New York Times, Baltimore Sun,* and *Baltimore Afro-American* chronicled the rise of jazz as a popular music advertised in the entertainment section, as well as a subject debated on the opinion and music review pages. The magazines and journals that provided a representative sampling of the jazz debate are *American Mercury, American Musician, Atlantic Monthly, Collier's, Crisis, Current Opinion, Etude, Forum, Ladies' Home Journal, Living Age, Literary Digest, Melody, Metronome, Musical America, Musical Courier, Musical Leader, Musical Observer, New Republic, Opportunity, Saturday Evening Post,* and *Scribner's.*

Two oral history collections proved invaluable as sources of performance history. The Tulane Oral History of New Orleans Jazz Collection of the William Ransom Hogan Jazz Archive at the Tulane University in New Orleans, Louisiana (TOHNOJC), and the Jazz Oral History Project of the Rutgers Institute of Jazz Studies, Newark, New Jersey

(RIOJS), provided me with many more. I also surveyed materials from the George P. Johnson Negro Film Collection, Special Collections, University of California Library, University of California at Los Angeles.

At Tulane, I gathered information from the interviews of Frank Adams, Adolphe Alexander, Jr., Don Albert (Albert Dominique), Alvin Alcorn, Ed Allen, Dave Bailey, Adolphe Paul Barbarin, Isidore Barbarin, Louis Barbarin, Danny Barker, Emile Barnes, Harrison Barnes, Stuart Bergen, Peter Bocage, Ted Brown, John Casimir, Anatie "Natty" Dominique, Eddie "Daddy" Edwards, George "Pops" Foster, Josiah "Cie" Frazier, Albert Glenny, George Gueson, John Handy, Arthur "Monk" Hazel, John Joseph, George Justin, Jack "Papa" Laine, Alfred Laine, Dominique J. "Nick" LaRocca, Johnny Lala, Charlie Love, George Lewis, Joe Loyacano, Manuel Manetta, William Matthews, Ernest "Kid Punch" Miller, Roger Mitchell, Eddie Morris, Stella Oliver, Edward "Kid" Ory, Willie Parker, Slow Drag Pavageau, Nathan Robinson, Johnny St. Cyr, and Verne Streckfus.

For the Rutgers collection, I chose to review interviews with Eddie Barefield, Charlie Barnet, Barney Bigard, Andrew Blakeney, Lawrence Brown, Buck Clayton, Eddie Durham, Sonny Greer, Horace Henderson, Milt Hinton, Jimmy McPartland, Red Norvo, Zutty Singleton, Reb Spikes, and Mary Lou Williams.

Both archives further aided my efforts with their libraries and photo files. I did not conduct any oral histories with living performers. Furthermore, time constraints prevented me from listening to taped oral histories in most cases, consequently, I read transcripts in order to survey as broad a sample as possible. On the strengths and weaknesses of oral histories for jazz research, see Douglas H. Daniels, "Oral History, Masks, and Protocol in the Jazz Community," *Oral History Review* 15 (1987):143–64; and Ronald J. Grele, "On Using Oral History Collections: An Introduction," *Journal of American History* 74 (1987): 570–78.

One way to measure the accuracy of interviews is to use them in conjunction with other relevant primary materials. Oral histories can be profitably compared with the growing autobiographical literature written by jazz musicians or told to an editor-amanuensis. Beginning with the wind, string, and percussion musicians most closely identified with New Orleans, one should consult Louis Armstrong's *Swing That Music* (New York: Longmans, Green, 1936) and *Satchmo: My Life in New Orleans* (New York: Prentice-Hall, 1954). Sidney Bechet, *Treat It Gentle* (New York: Hill and Wang, 1960) is a literary performance of equal virtuosity to Bechet's musical ones. George "Pops" Foster, *The Autobiog-*

raphy of George "Pops" Foster as Told to Tom Stoddard (Berkeley: University of California Press, 1971) is a detailed memoir.

Danny Barker, *A Life in Jazz*, ed. Alyn Shipton (London: Macmillan, 1986) is full of valuable insights; and Barney Bigard, *With Louis and the Duke: The Autobiography of a Jazz Clarinetist*, ed. Barry Martyn (New York: Oxford University Press, 1986) recounts a long life in the music business in and out of New Orleans. Wingy Manone with Paul Vandervoot, *Trumpet on the Wing* (New York: Doubleday, 1948) gives a white musician's perspective on New Orleans. Al Rose, *I Remember Jazz: Six Decades Among the Great Jazzmen* (Baton Rouge: Louisiana State University Press, 1987) contains valuable vignettes about jazz and its practitioners.

Alan Lomax, *Mr. Jelly Roll: The Fortunes of Jelly Roll Morton, New Orleans Creole and 'Inventor' of Jazz* (New York: Duell, Sloane and Pearce, 1950) and Willie "the Lion" Smith, with George Hoefer, *Music on My Mind: The Memoirs of an American Pianist* (New York: Doubleday, 1964) profile two legendary pianists who provided a wealth of information on performance. Bandleaders Duke Ellington and Cab Calloway told their stories in Edward "Duke" Ellington, *Music Is My Mistress* (New York: Doubleday, 1973) and Cab Calloway, with Bryant Rollings, *Of Minnie the Moocher and Me* (New York: Crowell, 1976).

Eddie Condon and Thomas Sugrue, *We Called It Music: A Generation of Jazz* (New York: Henry Holt, 1947) and Benny Goodman with Irving Kolodin, *Kingdom of Swing* (New York: Stackpole, 1939) capture well the experiences of musicians who started their careers in and around Chicago. Max Kaminsky with V.E. Hughes, *My Life in Jazz* (New York: Harper and Row, 1963) discusses the twenties and thirties. Milton Mezzrow with Bernard Wolfe, *Really the Blues* (New York: Random House, 1946) presents the persona of a white American who found the jazz life a viable alternative to the dominant culture.

Hoagy Carmichael with Stephen Longstreet, *Sometimes I Wonder: The Story of Hoagy Carmichael* (New York: Farrar, Straus & Giroux, 1965) describes the experiences of jazzmen on college campuses. Dicky Wells with Stanley Dance, *The Night People: Reminiscences of a Jazzman* (Boston: Crescendo, 1971) is valuable on New York and the trials and tribulations of the road. W.C. Handy, *Father of the Blues: An Autobiography* (New York: Macmillan, 1941) describes rural as well as urban performance settings and Handy's early attempts to publish blues lyrics.

A number of biographies and collections of musicians' reminiscences also provide good information on jazz in the 1920s. On Louis Armstrong and Duke Ellington, one needs to begin with James Lincoln

Collier's thorough studies, *Louis Armstrong: An American Genius* (New York: Oxford University Press, 1983) and *Duke Ellington* (New York: Oxford University Press, 1987). Pianist Eubie Blake is well profiled by Al Rose in *Eubie Blake: A Biography* (New York: Schirmer Books, 1979). Walter C. Allen, *Hendersonia: The Music of Fletcher Henderson and His Musicians. A Bio-discography* (Highland Park: N.J.: Walter C. Allen, 1973) provides important information on one of the most popular and influential of twenties bandleaders. Ralph Berton, *Remembering Bix: A Memoir of the Jazz Age* (New York: Harper and Row, 1974) captures the ambience of young aspiring musicians in the 1920s.

Several biographies and autobiographies of blues musicians provide useful information on the jazz controversy and jazz performance. Perry Bradford, *Born with the Blues: Perry Bradford's Own Story. The True Story of the Pioneering Blues Singers and Musicians in the Early Days of Jazz* (New York: Oak Publications, 1965) contains Bradford's history of early blues and jazz recordings. Chris Albertson, *Bessie* (New York: Stein and Day, 1972) is the standard source on Bessie Smith and particularly revealing about the Harlem soirées thrown by Carl Van Vechten. Sandra Leib, *Mother of the Blues: A Study of Ma Rainey* (Boston: University of Massachusetts Press, 1981) places Rainey and other blues women in the social history of the 1920s and 1930s. Hazel Carby analyzes the cultural significance of blues women for black culture in "It Jus Be's Dat Way Sometime: The Sexual Politics of Women's Blues," *Radical America* 20 (1986): 9–24. Dexter Stewart Baxter surveys the careers of all the classic blues singers in *Ma Rainey and the Classic Blues Singers* (New York: Stein and Day, 1970).

H.O. Brunn's *The Story of the Original Dixieland Jazz Band* (Baton Rouge: Louisiana State University Press, 1960) remains the most detailed treatment of this famous group. Donald M. Marquis, *In Search of Buddy Bolden: First Man of Jazz* (Baton Rouge: Louisiana State University Press, 1978) effectively distinguishes the man from his legend. Michael Ondaatje's fictional *Coming Through Slaughter* (New York: W.W. Norton, 1977) accomplishes the opposite—Ondaatje creatively combines Bolden and his myths. Jack Buerkle and Danny Barker, *Bourbon Street Black: The New Orleans Black Jazzmen* (New York: Oxford University Press, 1974) places the twenties musicians in a continuum to the present. Raymond Joseph Martinez captures some of the ambience of New Orleans in his *Portraits of New Orleans Jazz* (New Orleans: Hope, 1971). Al Rose and Edmond Souchon, *New Orleans: A Family Album* (Baton Rouge: Louisiana State University Press, 1984) is an indispensable reference.

Art Hodes and Chadwick Hansen (eds.), *Selections from the Gutter: Portraits from the Jazz Record* (Berkeley: University of California Press, 1977) collects a wide variety of materials about jazz performance by and about performers. Travis Dempsey, *An Autobiography of Black Jazz* (Chicago: Urban Research Institute, 1983) contains the perspectives of both a performer and an observer of jazz. Nat Shapiro and Nat Hentoff, *Hear Me Talkin' to Ya: The Story of Jazz as Told by the Men Who Made It* (New York: Dover Publications, 1955) excerpts interviews with musicians active primarily in the 1920s through the 1940s. Kitty Grimes, *Jazz Voices* (London: Quarter Books, 1983) also brings together the observations of performers. The most comprehensive visual compilation of performers and performance locations is Frank Driggs and Harris Lewine, *Black Beauty, White Heat: A Pictorial History of Classic Jazz, 1920–1950* (New York: Morrow, 1982). Several fascinating accounts of early jazz are collected in Martin Williams (ed.), *Jazz Panorama: From the Pages of the Jazz Review* (New York: Da Capo, 1979).

Several studies of musical and verbal performance offer insights into the cultural and historical role of musical performance. Alan P. Merriam, *The Anthropology of Music* (Evanston: Northwestern University Press, 1964) is an excellent overview of the functions and meanings of music in society. Paul Stoller's "Sound in Songhay Cultural Experience," *American Ethnologist* 2 (1984):559–70, provides a useful comparison for students of the jazz controversy because Stoller analyzes how sound itself is presumed by many cultures to have transforming powers. The symbolic meaning of performance is addressed in many studies, and Victor Turner's *Drama, Fields, and Metaphors* (Ithaca: Cornell University Press, 1974) is a good starting point. I found Turner's essay "Frame, Flow, and Reflection: Ritual Drama as Public Liminality," in Michael Benamou and Charles Ceramello (eds.), *Performance in Post-Modern Culture* (Madison, Wisc.: Coda Press, 1977), 33–35, especially useful

Richard Schechner applies Turner's ideas to the performing arts in *Essays on Performance Theory, 1970–1976* (New York: Drama Books, 1977). Richard Bauman's *Verbal Art As Performance* (Austin: University of Texas Press, 1977) further suggests the importance of performance as a transmitter of "emergent culture" that can bridge traditions and new cultural forms. Bauman's collection builds on the concepts of "emergent culture" forms delineated by Raymond Williams in *The Sociology of Culture* (New York: Schocken Books, 1982). A similar approach to understanding music specifically is offered in Jacques Attali, *Noise: The*

Political Economy of Music (Minneapolis: University of Minnesota Press, 1985), which argues that music can anticipate certain social and historical changes.

Judith Lynne Hanna analyzes symbolic exchanges that take place in performance in *The Performer-Audience Connection: Emotion to Metaphor in Dance and Society* (Austin: University of Texas Press, 1983). The introduction to Jack B. Kammerman and Rosanne Martorella's edited collection *Performers and Performances: The Social Organization of Work* (New York: Praeger, 1983) discusses how the performing arts industry reflects the social milieu.

The importance of oral performance in black culture has received extensive attention. The studies most useful to understanding the development of participatory music traditions include Roger Abraham's *Deep Down in the Jungle: Negro Narrative Folklore from the Streets of Philadelphia* (Hawthorne, N.Y.: Aldine Publishers, 1970); *Positively Black* (Englewood Cliffs, N.J.: Prentice-Hall, 1970); and Abraham's collection edited with John Szwed, *Discovering Afro-America* (Leiden, The Netherlands: E.J. Brill, 1975). Szwed's edited collection *Black America* (New York: Basic Books, 1970) contains several articles on the links between musical and oral performance in black culture. LeRoi Jones(now Amiri Baraka), *Blues People: Negro Music in White America* (New York: William Morrow, 1963) studies the relationship between political power, music, and black cultural traditions. It is complemented nicely by Ben Sidran, *Black Talk* (New York: Da Capo, 1971).

Norman E. White and John F. Szwed (eds.), *Afro-American Anthropology: Contemporary Perspectives* (New York: Free Press, 1970) contains several useful articles on the role of the African Diaspora in American black music. Sol Tax, *Acculturation in the Americas* (Chicago: University of Chicago Press, 1952) collects important research on cross-cultural musical relationships between Africa, the Caribbean, and the United States.

Lawrence Levine analyzed participatory performance traditions during slavery in Lawrence Levine, *Black Culture and Black Consciousness: Afro-American Folk Thought from Slavery to Freedom* (New York: Oxford University Press, 1978). John Blassingame, *The Slave Community: Plantation Life in the Ante-bellum South* (New York: Oxford University Press, 1979) also documents the significance of performance in slave communities. Frederick Douglass's autobiography *My Bondage and My Freedom* (Salem, N.H.: Ayer, 1968) gives examples of performance on the plantation.

The social and cultural context for the jazz controversy can be found in Frederick Lewis Allen, *Only Yesterday: An Informal History of the 1920s* (New York: Harper and Row, 1931); Henry May, *The End of American Innocence: A Study of the First Years of Our Own Time, 1912–1917* (Chicago: Quadrangle Books, 1959); and William Leuchtenburg, *The Perils of Prosperity: 1914–1932* (Chicago: University of Chicago Press, 1958). Warren Susman's chapter "Culture and Civilization: The Nineteen Twenties" in *Culture As History: The Transformation of American Society in the Twentieth Century* (New York: Pantheon, 1985), 105–29, describes the importance of communication—including music—as a defining feature of the twenties. Paul Carter's *Another Part of the Twenties* (New York: Columbia University Press, 1977) dispelled some of the roaring twenties myths.

Paula Fass's *The Damned and the Beautiful: American Youth in the Twenties* (New York: Oxford University Press, 1977) and Helen Lefkowitz Horowitz, *Campus Life: Undergraduate Cultures from the End of the 18th Century to the Present* (New York: Knopf, 1987) both give serious attention to the development of a youth culture and the differences in taste betweeen young Americans, their parents, and other adult authorities.

Stephen Kern's *The Culture of Time and Space, 1880–1918* (Cambridge: Harvard University Press, 1983) is a provocative study of America and Europe, which gives a broad and challenging reading of the changes of time and meter associated with jazz and World War I. Similarly, Paul Fussell, *The Great War and Modern Memory* (New York: Oxford University Press, 1975) analyzes changing literary conventions that followed World War I.

The jazz controversy itself is addressed in many jazz histories, but four studies specifically concern debate over the new music. The first was Morroe Berger's article, "Jazz: Resistance to the Diffusion of a Culture Pattern," *Journal of Negro History* 32 (1974): 461–94, followed by Neil Leonard's *Jazz and the White Americans: The Acceptance of a New Art Form* (Chicago: University of Chicago Press, 1962). Leonard also analyzes jazz as a social ritual in *Jazz: Myth and Religion* (New York: Oxford University Press, 1987). Macdonald Smith Moore, *Yankee Blues: Musical Culture and American Identity* (Bloomington: Indiana University Press, 1985) sees the 1920s battle over music values ending when Jewish composers resolved the primitive and mechanical tensions Yankee composers found in jazz. Ishmael Reed's *Mumbo Jumbo* (New York: Avon Books, 1971) is a contemporary novel that provides a unique treatment of the arguments about jazz and black culture in the early twentieth century.

The musical histories that provide the best background for understanding the changes brought by ragtime, blues, and jazz are Sigmund
Spaeth, *A History of Popular Music in America* (New York: Random
House, 1948); Gilbert Chase, *America's Music* (New York: McGraw-Hill,
1955); and David Ewen, *All the Years of American Popular Music* (Englewood Cliffs, N.J.: Prentice-Hall, 1977). Charles Nanry provides a useful
collection of interpretive essays on popular music in *American Music:
From Storyville to Woodstock* (New Brunswick, N.J.: Transaction Books,
1972). Henry Kmen, *Music in New Orleans: The Formative Years 1791–
1841*(Baton Rouge: Louisiana State University Press, 1966) describes
early New Orleans music.

Afro-American music is thoroughly surveyed and analyzed in Eileen
Southern, *The Music of Black Americans: A History* (New York. W.W.
Norton, 1971). Hildred Roach, *Black Music: Past and Present* (New York:
Taplinger, 1973) is another valuable general study. Dana J. Epstein,
Sinful Tunes and Spirituals: Black Folk Music to the Civil War (Urbana:
University of Illinois Press, 1977) established background materials on
folk music practice. It complements Harold Courlander's classic *Negro
Folk Music U.S.A.* (New York: Columbia University Press, 1963). See
also Howard Odum, "Folk Song and Folk Poetry As Found in the Secu-
lar Songs of the Southern Negro," *Journal of American Folklore* 24,
(1911): 255–94, 351–96.

A comprehensive history of black entertainment that combines the
social and economic organization of theatre, black vaudeville, and circus
with black performance history has yet to be written. Langston Hughes
and Milton Meltzer wrote *Black Magic: A Pictorial History of the Negro in
Entertainment* (Englewood Cliffs, N.J.: Prentice-Hall, 1967), which surveys entertainment trends and is beautifully illustrated. Robert Toll,
Blacking Up: The Minstrel Show in Nineteenth-Century America (New York:
Oxford University Press, 1977) is a good starting place for understanding minstrelsy history. A collection of essays that provides insights into a
wide range of Afro-American music and politics is Dominique-René De
Larma, *Reflections on Afro-American Music* (Kent State: Kent State University Press, 1973).

On jazz and dance traditions, see Marshall and Jean Stearns, *Jazz
Dance: The Story of American Vernacular Dance* (New York: Schirmer
Books, Macmillan, 1968) and Lynne Fauley Emery, *Black Dance in the
United States: 1619–1970* (Salem, N.H.: Ayer, 1972).

Two thoughtful studies of ragtime are the standard work by Rudi
Blesh and Harriet Janis, *They All Played Ragtime* (New York: Oak Publica-

tions, 1966) and the newer study by Edward Berlin, *Ragtime: A Musical and Cultural History* (Berkeley: University of California Press, 1980).

Gunther Schuller, *Early Jazz: Its Roots and Musical Development* (New York: Oxford University Press, 1968); and Marshall W. Stearns, *The Story of Jazz* (New York: Oxford University Press, 1956) introduce readers to early jazz history. Frederick Ramsey, Jr., and Charles Smith published an early and enthusiastic study of jazz in their 1939 *Jazzmen* (New York: Harcourt Brace Jovanovich). It remains a useful example of early jazz criticism. Hughes Panassie, *The Real Jazz* (New York: Smith and Durrell, 1942) and Sidney Finkelstein, *Jazz: A People's Music* (New York: Da Capo, 1975 reprint of 1948 edition) are two other early historical and critical studies of jazz. H.O. Osgood, *So This Is Jazz* (Boston: Little, Brown, 1926) gives a representative 1920s history of jazz.

James Lincoln Collier analyzes early jazz history and criticism in "The Faking of Jazz: How Politics Distorted the History of the Hip," *New Republic* 193 (1985): 33–40. Frederick Starr, *Red and Hot: The Fate of Jazz in the Soviet Union* (New York: Oxford University Press, 1983) helps explain the larger political context for the discussion of jazz by the American left during the 1920s and 1930s.

Useful general histories of jazz include Winthrop Sargeant, *Jazz: A History* (New York: McGraw-Hill, 1964); and Rudi Blesh, *Shining Trumpets: A History of Jazz* (New York: Knopf, 1958); and André Hodier, *Jazz: Its Evolution and Essence* (New York: Grove Press, 1956). Jazz histories that take a more sociological approach include Francis Newton, *The Jazz Scene* (New York: Da Capo Press, 1959); and Charles Nanry and Edward Berger (eds.), *The Jazz Text* (New York: Van Nostrand, 1979). Frank Kofsky analyzes black nationalism and jazz in *Black Nationalism and the Revolution in Music* (New York: Pathfinder Press, 1970).

Martin Williams, one of the most prolific of jazz historians and critics, discusses twenties jazz in several texts, particularly *Jazz Masters of New Orleans* (New York: Macmillan, 1967) and *The Jazz Tradition* (New York: Oxford University Press, 1983). Dan Morgenstern's *Jazz People* (Englewood Cliffs, N.J.: Prentice-Hall, 1976) and his "Jazz as an Urban Music," in George McCue (ed.), *Music in American Society, 1776–1976* (New Brunswick, N.J.: Transaction Books, 1977), 133–43, analyze practitioners and the urban setting for jazz. Robert W. Bernotas, "Critical Theory, Jazz, and Politics: A Critique of the Frankfurt School" (Ph.D. dissertation, Johns Hopkins University, 1987) looks at Theodor Adorno and other critical theorists who also debated jazz and popular culture in the early twentieth century.

Chicago musicians are extensively described in the articles by Chadwick Hansen, "Social Influences in Jazz Style, Chicago, 1920–30," *American Quarterly* 12 (Winter 1960):493–506; Thomas J. Hennessey, "The Black Chicago Establishment, 1919–30," *Journal of Jazz Studies* 1 (December 1974):15–45; and John Lax, "Chicago Black Musicians in the 1920s—Portrait of an Era," *Journal of Jazz Studies* 1 (June 1974):106–27.

Martin Williams, "What Happened in Kansas City,?" *Jazz Heritage* (New York: Oxford University Press, 1985), 17–28, should be read in conjunction with Ross Russell's meticulous study, *Jazz Style in Kansas City and the Southwest* (Berkeley: University of California Press, 1971). Similarly, Samuel Charters and Leonard Kunstadt, *Jazz: A History of the New York Scene* (New York: Doubleday, 1962) is a thorough treatment of early New York jazz.

Secondary information on locations for jazz performance comes from several studies of entertainment and leisure. On urban history and the social control of vice, see Al Rose, *Storyville, New Orleans: Being an Authentic Illustrated Account of the Notorious Red Light District* (Tuscaloosa: University of Alabama Press, 1974); and Ruth Rosen, *The Lost Sisterhood: Prostitution in America, 1900–1918* (Baltimore: Johns Hopkins University Press, 1982); and Paul Boyer, *Urban Masses and Moral Order, 1820–1920* (Cambridge: Harvard University Press, 1978). Kathy Peiss, *Cheap Amusements: Working Women and Leisure in Turn-of-the-Century New York* (Philadelphia: Temple University Press, 1986) describes the attempts of urban working women to preserve autonomous space and time for leisure.

Lewis A. Erenberg's *Steppin' Out: New York Nightlife and the Transformation of American Culture, 1890–1930* (Chicago: University of Chicago Press, 1981) analyzes changing tastes in and locations for middle-class leisure. Erenberg's "From New York to Middletown: Repeal and the Legitimization of Nightlife in the Great Depression," *American Quarterly* 38 (1986): 761–78, develops further Erenberg's observations about entertainment patterns. Russel B. Nye, "Saturday Night at the Paradise Ballroom: Or Dance Halls in the Twenties," *Journal of Popular Culture* 7 (1973):14–32, surveys the growth of ballroom dancing. Alfred F. McLean, Jr.'s study *American Vaudeville as Ritual* (Lexington: University of Kentucky Press, 1965) describes theatre decor and ambience. Jim Haskins provides a detailed history of the most famous New York jazz club, in *The Cotton Club* (New York: Random House, 1977).

Descriptive studies of nightlife are provided by Lloyd Morris, *Incredible New York: High Life and Low Life of the Last 100 Years* (New York:.

Random House, 1951); Stanley Walker, *The Night Club Era* (New York: Blue Ribbon Books, 1953); and Robert Sylvester, *No Cover Charge: A Backward Look at the Nightclubs* (New York: Dial Press, 1956). Ronald Morris, *Wait Until Dark: Jazz and the Underworld, 1880–1940* (Bowling Green: Bowling Green University Popular Press, 1980) analyzes the role of gangster patronage in the development of nightclubs and jazz.

Foster Rhea Dulles, *America Learns to Play: A History of Popular Recreation* (New York: Appleton-Century, 1940) establishes a background for analyzing musical entertainment as one of many leisure-time choices. John F. Kasson, *Amusing the Million: Coney Island at the Turn of the Century* (New York: Hill and Wang, 1978) addresses the broad changes in leisure represented by the amusement park. Twenties moral arguments about leisure as a form of consumption are described in Daniel Horowitz, *The Morality of Spending: Attitudes Toward the Consumer Society in America, 1875–1940* (Baltimore: Johns Hopkins University Press, 1985).

Piano histories that provide some background for understanding the social and musical developments relevant to ragtime and Harlem stride piano can be found in Cyril Ehrlich, *The Piano: A History* (Totowa, N.J.: Rowman and Littlefield, 1976) and Arthur Loesser, *Men, Women, and Pianos: A Social History* (New York: Simon and Schuster, 1964). Radio programming is chronicled in Harrison B. Summers, *A Thirty-Year History of Programs Carried on National Radio Networks in the United States* (Salem, N.H.: Ayer, 1971) and Fred J. Macdonald, *Don't Touch That Dial: Radio Programming in American Life* (Chicago: Nelson-Hall, 1979). Philip K. Eberly, *Music in the Air: America's Changing Tastes in Music, 1920–1980* (New York: Hastings, 1982) describes the kind of jazz played on radio. Roland Marchand, *Advertising the American Dream: Making Way for Modernity* (Berkeley: University of California Press, 1985) suggests that radio jazz was used with other programming to promote modernity in American Life.

Cynthia Hoover, *Music-Machines—American Style: A Catalog of the Exhibition* (Washington, D.C.: Smithsonian Institution Press, 1971) surveys the relevant technological developments necessary for phonograph and radio dissemination of jazz. Roland Gelatt, *The Fabulous Phonograph: 1877–1977* (New York: Macmillan, 1977) is the standard general technological and industrial history of phonograph recording. Serge Denisoff, *Solid Gold: The Popular Record Industry* (New Brunswick, N.J.: Transaction Books, 1975) analyzes the development of the record industry as an example of American mass culture. Ronald Clifton Jr.'s dissertation "Jazz and Race Records, 1920–1932: Their Origin and the Significance for the Recording Industry and Society" (University of Illinois, 1968), is the best starting place for the study of race records and race record advertisting.

David Meeker surveys jazz musicians on film in *Jazz in the Movies: A Guide to Jazz Musicians, 1917–1977* (New Rochelle, N.Y.: Arlington House, 1977). Thomas Cripps, *Slow Fade to Black: The Negro in American Film, 1900–1942* (New York: Oxford University Press, 1977) is an excellent and detailed analysis of the changing images of and opportunities available to blacks in film. Donald Bogle, *Toms, Coons, Mulattoes, Mammies, and Bucks: An Interpretive History of Blacks in American Films* (New York: Viking, 1973) and Daniel Leab, *From Sambo to Superspade: The Black Experience in Motion Pictures* (Boston: Houghton Mifflin, 1975) are well-illustrated film histories that discuss some jazz motion pictures. Jane Freuer, *The Hollywood Musical* (Bloomington: University of Indiana Press, 1982) sees jazz as a powerful symbol in this emerging film genre.

Several social histories of black communities provide the necessary background for understanding the great migration and the Afro-American urban culture of the 1920s. James Alan McPherson and Miller Williams provide various perspectives on the role of railroads as a source of transportation and an important employment opportunity for black Americans in *Railroad: Trains and Train People in American Culture* (New York: Random House, 1976). On Chicago, see St. Clair Drake and Horace Clayton, *Black Metropolis: A Study of Negro Life in a Northern City* (New York: Harcourt, Brace, 1945) and Allen Spear, *Black Chicago: The Making of a Ghetto, 1890–1920* (Chicago: University of Chicago Press, 1969). Thomas Lee Philpott, *The Slum and the Ghetto: Neighborhood Deterioration and Middle-Class Reform, Chicago, 1880–1920* (New York: Oxford Unversity Press, 1978) explains reform sentiments in Chicago.

Nancy Weiss, *The National Urban League, 1910–1940* (New York: Oxford University Press, 1974) focuses specifically on the aims of black reformers. Elliott J. Rudwick, *Race Riot at East St. Louis* (New York: Atheneum, 1972) and William J. Tuttle, *Race Riot: Chicago and the Red Summer of 1919* (New York: Atheneum, 1970) are exemplary studies of two of the most important World War I race riots. On the San Francisco area, see Douglas H. Daniels, *Pioneer Urbanites: A Social and Cultural History of Black San Francisco* (Philadelphia: Temple University Press, 1980).

On New York, Gilbert Osofsky, *Harlem: The Making of a Ghetto, 1890–1930* New York: Harper and Row, 1966) describes the economic and social conditions left relatively untouched by the Renaissance and the Jazz Age. Jervis Anderson, *This Was Harlem: A Cultural Portrait, 1900–1950* (New York: Farrar, Straus & Giroux, 1981) provides descriptive information on musicians and nightclubs. Anderson's book is thoughtfully reviewed by Gregory "Ironman" Tate in "Harlem When It Sizzled," *Village Voice Literary Supplement,* Dec. 1982, pp. 11–15, in which Tate discusses the relevance of the Harlem Renaissance to average Harlemites.

Participants in the Harlem Renaissance describe the community, in James Weldon Johnson's *Black Manhattan* (New York: Atheneum, 1968) and Claude McKay, *Harlem: Negro Metropolis* (New York: Harcourt Brace Jovanovich, 1940).

The primary literature and art of the Harlem Renaissance is rich with references to jazz and blues performance. W.E.B. DuBois, *The Souls of Black Folk* (New York: Signet Classics, 1969 orig. pub., 1903) is a necessary starting point because many writers were influenced by DuBois's treatment of the spirituals. Langston Hughes's *The Weary Blues* (New York: Alfred Knopf, 1926) and *Fine Clothes to the Jew* (New York: Alfred Knopf, 1927) contain many of his 1920s jazz and blues poems.

James Weldon Johnson describes the tribulations of a ragtime pianist in his novel *The Autobiography of an Ex-Coloured Man* (New York: Garden City Publishing Co., 1912) and his own adventures in *Along This Way* (New York: Viking, 1933). Johnson's Introduction to *The Book of American Negro Poetry* (New York: Harcourt, Brace, 1922), which Johnson edited, establishes important links between oral traditions in poetry and music. J.A. Rogers and Alain Locke discuss Afro-American music and especially jazz in their contributions to *The New Negro,* ed. Alain Locke (New York: A. & C. Boni, 1925). Locke fully explored black music in *The Negro and His Music* (Washington, D.C.: Associates in Negro Folk Education, 1936). Claude McKay used jazz performance as a major motif in his novel *Home to Harlem* (New York: Harper and Row, 1928).

Some of Zora Neale Hurston's observations on performance style are included in Nancy Cunard (ed.), *Negro Anthology* (New York: Ungar, 1934). A more complete collection of Hurston's writing on performance and Afro-American oral traditions is provided in *The Sanctified Church* (Berkeley: Turtle Island Foundation, 1983) and Alice Walker (ed.), *I Love Myself When I Am Laughing . . . And Then Again When I Am Looking Mean and Impressive,* which is described below. Nathan Huggins, *Voices from the Harlem Renaissance* (New York: Oxford University Press, 1976) has many other examples of twenties literature characterized by musical performance themes.

Secondary sources on the Harlem Renaissance and black literature that proved most useful to understanding jazz performance and the jazz controversy in the Harlem Renaissance begin with Nathan Huggins, *The Harlem Renaissance* (New York: Oxford University Press, 1971). Arna Bontemps, *The Harlem Renaissance Remembered* (New York: Dodd, Mead, 1972) contains several interpretive articles. David Levering Lewis, *When Harlem Was in Vogue* (New York: Vintage Books, 1979) provides useful information about the entertainment tastes of Harlem Renaissance participants as well as a detailed social history of the community. Lewis analyzed the political issues that motivated some of the aesthetic judgments of the Harlem Renaissance in "Parallels and Divergences: Assimilationist Strategies of Afro-American and Jewish Elites from 1910 to the Early 1930's," *Journal of American History* 71 (1984):543–64.

Houston Baker, *Blues, Ideology, and Afro-American Literature: A Vernacular Theory* (Chicago: University of Chicago Press, 1984) discusses the role of blues as a central mode of expression in Afro-American culture. Baker has specifically addressed the significance of the Harlem Renaissance to our understanding of modernism in "Modernism and the Harlem Renaissance," *American Quarterly* 39 (1987):84–97, and *Modernism and the Harlem Renaissance* (Chicago: University of Chicago Press, 1987).

Biographies of major Harlem Renaissance writers are also quite valuable for understanding the attitudes of major writers towards music. Arnold Rampersad, *The Art and Imagination of W.E.B. DuBois* (Cambridge: Harvard University Press, 1968) explains DuBois's cultural philosophy and taste. Rampersad has also detailed Langston Hughes's views in *The Life of Langston Hughes*, Volume I. *I, Too, Sing America* (New York: Oxford University Press, 1986). Onwuchekwa Jemie, *Langston Hughes: Introduction to the Poetry* (New York: Columbia University Press, 1973) has an excellent chapter on jazz and blues themes in Hughes's poems.

Jeffrey Stewart, *The Critical Temper of Alain Locke: A Selection of His Essays on Art and Culture* (New York: Garland, 1983) offers a sound background for Locke's views. Alain Locke's general philosophical writings are explicated by Jonny Washington, *Alain Locke: A Quest for Cultural Pluralism* (Westport, CT.: Greenwood Press, 1986).

Wayne F. Cooper, *The Passion of Claude McKay: Selected Prose and Poetry* (New York: Schocken Books, 1973) is the most comprehensive single source for McKay's aesthetic views. Cooper's biography of Mc-Kay, *Claude McKay: Rebel Sojourner in the Harlem Renaissance* (Baton Rouge: Louisiana State University Press, 1987), provides a detailed account of McKay's life and travels in the 1920s and 1930s. Robert Hemenway's *Zora Neale Hurston: A Literary Biography* (Chicago: University of Illinois Press, 1977) describes Hurston's personal and intellectual struggles. Alice Walker and Mary Helen Washington interpret Hurston's artistic legacy in Alice Walker (ed.), *I Love Myself When I Am Laughing. . .And Then Again When I Am Looking Mean and Impressive* (Old Westbury, N.Y.: Feminist Press, 1979). Lorraine Bell compares Hurston's style with that of classic blues singers in " 'This Infinity of Conscious Pain': Zora Neale Hurston and the Black Female Literary Tradition," in Gloria Hull (ed.), *All the Women Are White, All the Blacks Are Men: (But Some of Us Are Brave): Black Women's Studies* (Old Westbury, N.Y.: Feminist Press, 1981), 176–88.

Carl Van Vechten, *Nigger Heaven* (New York: Octagon (reprint of the 1926 edition), 1973) was the most controversial Harlem novel by a white writer. Van Vechten's career and influence are evaluated in Bruce Kellner, *Carl Van Vechten and the Irreverent Decades* (Norman: University of Oklahoma Press, 1968) and Edward G. Lueders, *Carl Van Vechten and the Twenties* (Albuquerque: University of New Mexico, 1955). Representative primitivist novels, plays, and poems by white writers include: Gertrude Stein, *Three Lives* (New York: Vintage Books, Random House, 1933, orig. pub. 1909); F. Scott Fitzgerald, *Tales of the Jazz Age* (London: Collins, 1923); Vachel Lindsay, *The Congo and Other Poems* (New York: Macmillan, 1920); Sherwood Anderson, *Dark Laughter* (New York: Liveright, 1925); Eugene O'Neill, *Emperor Jones* (Englewood Cliffs, N.J.: Prentice-Hall, 1960; orig. pub. 1920).

Nineteen-twenties commentators on the Jazz Age include: Malcolm Cowley, *Exile's Return* (New York: Viking, 1956); and Gilbert Seldes, *The Seven Lively Arts* (New York: Sagamore Press, 1924). John R. Cooley, *Savages and Naturals: Black Portraits by White Writers in Modern American Literature* (Newark: University of Delaware Press, 1982) offers a contemporary reading of literary primitivism.

Primitive styles in art are collected in William Rubin (ed.), *Primitivism in 20th Century Art: Affinity of the Tribal and Modern* (New York: Museum of Modern Art, 1984). The exhibit on which Rubin's book is based is thoughtfully critiqued by James Clifford, "Histories of the Tribal and Modern," *Art in America* 73: (1984), 164–76, and Yves-Alain Bois, "La Pensee Sauvage," *Art in America* 73 (1984):178–89. Gail Levin analyzes the relationship between primitivism and American art and literature in " 'Primitivism' in American Art: Some Literary Parallels of the 1910s and 1920s," *Art Magazine* (Nov. 1984):101–5. The primitivism debate can be profitably compared with the artistic assessment of Harlem Renaissance artists in, Studio Museum in Harlem, *Harlem Renaissance: Art of Black America* (New York: Harry N. Abrams, 1987).

Charles Nanry, "Jazz and Modernism: Twin Born Children of the Age of Invention," *Annual Review of Jazz Studies* 1 (1982): 146–54, studies the primitivism debate from a sociological perspective. Howard S. Becker, *Outsiders: Studies in the Sociology of Deviance* (New York: Free Press, 1973) critiques the use of labeling theory in the sociology of musicians. Irving Louis Horowitz, "Style and Stewardship: Sociological Considerations on the Professionalization of Music" analyzes the role of jazz in the development of twentieth-century musical eclecticism. Frederick W. Turner III contrasts the jazz artist with traditional American success values in "Black Jazz Artists: The Darker Side of Horatio Alger," *The Massachusetts Review* 10 (1969): 341–53.

Index